Family Plots

Family Plots

Balzac's Narrative Generations

JANET L. BEIZER

YALE UNIVERSITY PRESS
New Haven and London

A much abridged form of chapter 1 earlier appeared in *Novel: A Form in Fiction,* vol. 16 (Fall 1983), copyright © Novel, Corp. 1983. Lines from Emily Dickinson's poem #1129 are reprinted by permission of the publishers and the Trustees of Amherst College from *The Poems of Emily Dickinson,* edited by Thomas H. Johnson, Cambridge, Mass.: The Belknap Press of Harvard University Press, copyright 1951, © 1955, 1979, 1983 by the President and Fellows of Harvard College. Lines from W. B. Yeats's "The Second Coming," *The Collected Poems of W. B. Yeats,* are reprinted with permission of Macmillan Publishing Company, copyright 1924 by Macmillan Publishing Company, renewed 1952 by Bertha Georgie Yeats, and of Macmillan, London Ltd. and Michael B. Yeats.

Designed by James J. Johnson

and set in Sabon and Fournier Roman type by Graphic Composition, Inc. Printed in the United States of America by The Alpine Press, Inc., Stoughton, Mass.

Library of Congress Cataloging-in-Publication Data

Beizer, Janet L., 1952–
   Family plots.

   Bibliography: p.
   Includes index.
   1. Balzac, Honoré de, 1799–1850—Criticism and interpretation. 2. Family in literature. 3. Fathers in literature. 4. Narration (Rhetoric) I. Title.
PQ2184.F34B45 1986   843'.7   86–4121
ISBN 0–300–03586–1 (alk. paper).

The paper in this book meets the guidelines for permanence and durability of the Committee on Production Guidelines for Book Longevity of the Council on Library Resources.

10   9   8   7   6   5   4   3   2   1

To the memory of my grandfather

Contents

Acknowledgments ix

Introduction 1

PART I VISIONS 13

CHAPTER 1 Victor Marchand:
The Narrator as Story Seller
El Verdugo 15

CHAPTER 2 Thrice-Told Tale
Une Passion dans le désert 48

PART II REVISIONS 101

CHAPTER 3 Mirrors and Fatherhood
Le Père Goriot 103

CHAPTER 4 Madmen and Visions, Sages and Codes
*Illusions perdues, Splendeurs et misères
des courtisanes* 140

Afterword 180

Notes 187

Index 209

Acknowledgments

Over the years during which this study took form, it benefited from the wisdom and encouragement of friends and colleagues. It is a pleasure to express my deepest gratitude to Peter Brooks, who advised and inspired the project in its original version, as a dissertation at Yale University; he has never ceased to provide critical insight, counsel, and an intellectual influence too pervasive to be detailed. I am profoundly grateful to Jessica Feldman and David Miller, whose invaluable close readings of the manuscript at different stages shaped my revisions. I wish also to thank Robert Denommé, Mary McKinley, Laura Rivkin-Goldin, and David Rubin, each of whom read parts of the manuscript and offered perceptive criticism, and Holly Laird, whose discerning responses to many unwritten ideas helped me to work them through into writing. Thanks to conversations with Karen and Michael Chase Levenson, this book at last found a title; more significantly, their friendship sustained and stimulated the project at a critical point. And my family deserves a special note of gratitude for their unfailing confidence and interest.

Preliminary stages of my research were facilitated by fellowships from the Georges Lurcy Foundation in 1978–79, and the Mark and Viva Kanzer Fund for Psychoanalytic Studies in the

Humanities in 1979–80. Their support is most gratefully ac-
knowledged.

The jacket illustration was made available to me through
the courtesy of Stanford University Libraries; I am particularly
indebted to Bernard J. Denham for his gracious cooperation.

I wish to express my appreciation to Gail Moore and her
staff, Nora Lane, Benjamin McAmoss, and Wolfgang Woerner,
for their assistance in preparing the manuscript. Ellen Graham,
of Yale University Press, was a consistently helpful editor, and
Nancy Woodington, a most sympathetic manuscript editor.

Finally, a formal but no less heartfelt thanks to a fellow
traveler, Rob Grainger, for his company and faith on what
turned out to be a more adventurous journey than either of us
had imagined.

Introduction

Il peut être significatif que ce soit au même moment (vers l'âge de trois ans) que le petit de l'homme "invente" à la fois la phrase, le récit et l'Oedipe.

ROLAND BARTHES,
"Introduction à l'analyse structurale des récits"

 HERE is a well-known passage in the *Avant-propos de La Comédie humaine** which at once offers social commentary and a program for reading Balzac. Having just proclaimed the writer's moral duty to the public, Balzac presents the following in explanation of the principles basic to the "heart and soul" of his work:

Le christianisme . . .étant . . . un système complet de répression des tendances dépravées de l'homme, est le plus grand élément de l'Ordre Social. . . . J'écris à la lueur de deux Vérités éternelles: la Religion, la Monarchie, deux nécessités que les événements contemporains proclament. . . . Aussi regardé-je la Famille . . . comme le véritable élément social.[1]

[Christianity . . . being . . . a comprehensive system for the repression of man's depraved tendencies, is the greatest element of Social Order. . . . I write by the light of two eternal Truths: Religion and Monarchy, two necessities made evident by contemporary events. . . . I regard the Family . . . as the real social unit.]

---

*I have italicized the titles of all Balzac's texts, regardless of length, to avoid imposing an arbitrary distinction on a continuum ranging from short story to novel. All translations, unless otherwise noted, are my own, although I have consulted various existing editions.

Family, monarchy, and religion (in Balzac's sense) are of course all patriarchal institutions, hierarchic structures which order society. Since Balzac is speaking here about both society and his written record of it, we may infer that the organizing elements of society organize his narrative as well. If such elements serve to repress man's depraved tendencies, as Balzac claims, they can also work to repress narrative's more "depraved" or dissolute tendencies, that is, its inclinations toward formlessness and incoherence.

Balzac's *Avant-propos* becomes useful to my own because his invocation of the family and other like hierarchies or regulatory models implicitly embraces narrative orderings, or plot, and suggests a correlation between family and narrative imperatives. This book is about the ways in which plot, or the narrative patterning of fiction, in Balzac uses family motifs to express, mime, and even shape its constitutive ordering principles. It is also about how this enterprise falters. The *Avant-propos* tells a story which is elsewhere contradicted. In his remarks preceding *L'Elixir de longue vie,* an early tale of parricide, Balzac asks his reader:

Ne venez-vous pas de reconnaître au sein de la société une foule d'êtres amenés par nos lois, par nos moeurs, par les usages, à penser sans cesse à la mort des leurs, à la convoiter?[2]

[Have you not just admitted that there are great masses of people within our society who are led by our laws, our mores, and our customs, to think constantly about—to long for—the death of their loved ones?]

Balzac's query here again is crucial to my inquiry because the negative charge it affixes to the concept of family emphasizes the ambiguities of my title and, more fundamentally, of my subject. Balzac's plots about the family are inextricably engaged with schemings against the family and with burial sites for the family. Plot, in its Balzacian narrative context, persistently reminds us of its alternative lexical affinities with subversion on the one hand and death on the other. These plots are grounded in semantic overlap; they are narrative constructs which can never be purged of connotations of destruction.

My book is located in the thick of this semantic conflict. Since Balzac's plots about the family depend upon literal or figurative death or death-dealing, and since there comes a point at which death *in* the family can no longer be distinguished from death *of* the family, the notion of family plots as ordering devices is impaired from within.

The instability of Balzac's family plotting suggests the need to reappraise some of our most basic assumptions about nineteenth-century narrative as an institution. Our experience as readers links traditional or classical narrative (rubrics I use interchangeably with "nineteenth-century narrative") to themes of the father and the family line and to related issues of authority, subordination and insubordination, legitimacy, genealogy, heredity, and transmission. A chain of associations further attaches this tradition to formal principles of mimesis, order, coherence, linearity, unity, closure, and totalization.

But it is important to remember that the nineteenth-century narrative tradition is retrospectively instated; it is informed by its subsequent development into the modernist and postmodernist traditions. Narrative typology is often dichotomous in this respect and conceptualizes the nineteenth century as prelapsarian foil to the twentieth. Modernist and postmodernist narrative is then defined as a negation of the father principle and its formal manifestations. Twentieth-century fictions are said to represent the father's subversion, genealogical confusion or disruption, and tangled or overlaid family lines; they use themes of incest, adultery, family murder, celibacy, and other such crimes against the family. Their concomitant formal attributes are given as auto-referentiality, disorder, fragmentation, discontinuity, and the suspension or pluralization of meaning.

So Patricia Tobin speaks of the nineteenth century's "unshaken faith in the structural reliability of the genealogical imperative," while Edward Said claims that twentieth-century writing replaces such structures (which he calls "dynastic, bound to sources and origins, mimetic") with relationships of "complementarity and adjacency." And Roland Barthes can evoke an entire genre theory in a terse but plaintive cry: "S'il n'y a plus de Père, à quoi bon raconter des histoires?"[3] (If there is no more Father, why bother telling stories?)

My own argument both depends upon and departs from the reasoning developed by these critics. Overarching historical distinctions have typological value, and nineteenth and twentieth-century narrative can usefully be contrasted following the thematic and formal principles discussed by Tobin, Said, and Barthes. However, such contrastive descriptions erect two contiguous forests of symbols that obscure our perception of the constituent trees. I am not proposing that we deconstruct the distinction between a Balzac and a Robbe-Grillet, nor that we make of Balzac a precursor of modernism. But I am suggesting that when we perceive the nineteenth century as "the century of the paternal prerogative,"[4] we are thinking teleologically, reconstructing a coherent paternal order to set off and explain twentieth-century disorder.

Nineteenth-century fictions do display the father. But they ultimately undermine his status, his authority, and his power as lawgiver and regulator of family, social and narrative codes.[5] The nineteenth-century text, divided against itself, repeatedly undercuts the proffered images of its own authority. The two narrative principles which we usually locate successively were in fact already in place in the nineteenth-century text, which was already rehearsing, on a subtler scale, the split we use to separate modernist from classical narrative.

These are vast issues which lie outside the direct scope of this study of a single author. But the only way to begin to understand the ambiguities inherent in these more general problems is through extremely close textual analysis. Since Balzac is an exemplary representative of the traditional novelist, the questions we raise about the father principle in his works will have larger implications for the status of nineteenth-century textual paternity.

Before returning to Balzac, a word of explanation is in order concerning a discourse that will oscillate between family and paternity. The sociopolitical structures of the ancien régime which laid so heavy a claim to the nostalgia of Balzac and many of his contemporaries were notably patriarchal; father, king, and God exercised an analogous power in their respective (but continuous) domains.[6] What Balzac laments in postrevolutionary society is the fall from hierarchic authority to a decentered (or multicentered) individualism. Because symbolic systems are inevitably culture-bound, this lack of a center is conceptualized as the loss of a father. To shift, then, from a discourse of the family to a discourse of paternity is to look more closely at the source of narrative regulation as it is represented in the symbolic idiom Balzac speaks.

The problem of paternity is tightly knotted into the Balzacian text, appearing in varying patterns of heredity, succession, paternal tyranny, orphaned and illegitimate children, filial transgression, and parricide. These patterns can be appropriated by a variety of discourses, and have most notably provoked historical analogies or psycho-mythical appraisal.[7] Historical discourse tends to subsume the textual configurations to a sociohistorical dynamic of authority and its subversion. I am thinking specifically of the ancien régime and its fall, the Revolution with its concomitant leveling of social stratifications, the advent of Napoleon as prototypical usurper, and the rise of bourgeois capitalism, constitutive of an unregulated exchange of money and social rank. The psycho-mythical perspective treats the theme's pervasiveness as the projection of a personal myth: since the image of prolific literary progenitor quickly becomes one of Promethean upstart, Balzac is figuratively both father and son. Each of these perspectives points out suggestive analogies.[8] Both, however, situate the thematic matter with either the historical referents or personal myth in a play of mirrors that elucidates neither, though it does highlight the problem.

The image of Balzac as impassioned creator, feverishly revising and rewriting, propagating words, yields the familiar metaphor of the writer as demiurge or patriarch engendering a universe of fiction. Because this metaphor has become a commonplace, its figurative value is often forgotten; the narrative and linguistic tenor it originally conveyed have been all but effaced. My purpose here is to reintegrate the paternal vehicle and its narrative-linguistic tenor, to reconstitute a metaphor that is only apparently banal in order to discover the dialogue it articulates between family structures, narrative forms, and patterns of language.

If, taking as cue Roland Barthes's proposition that all narrative is "une mise en scène du Père"[9] (a staging of the Father), we look carefully at how the paternal drama is staged in Balzac, it becomes apparent that the thematic problem also implicates the narrative process and its language, which reveal a similar underlying structure of law and transgression, conflict and contradiction, authority and its subversion. Balzac's discourse (the essays, prefaces, and extradiegetic commentary within the fictions) overtly espouses an ethic based on monarchy, patriarchy, and religion—in short, hierarchy and authority—while his fictions inevitably play out scenes of filial revolt, parricide, and Promethean transgression. This creates a tension which invites one of two easy but misleading resolutions. One can give credence to Balzac's recurrent pretense of moralizing, of revealing the sickness so that it may be cured. This would mean that we privilege his discourse, accept his statements at face value, and give priority to principles of patriarchy. Or, one can adopt Gérard Genette's conception of extradiegetic discourse in Balzacian narrative as a "démon explicatif," an "invasion du récit."[10] In this case we would privilege the fiction, regard the discourse as purely formal, uncharged (thus, disregard it), and grant priority to the fictions of filial revolt. But I think both solutions avoid the essential conflict by denying the text the virulence that is its distinguishing property.

The language in which the thematic and narrative conflicts are respectively rendered and betrayed is itself informed by a dynamic of authority and insubordination. While on the one hand this language claims to "faire concurrence à l'Etat-Civil"[11] (compete with the Census Bureau), to produce a fictional world that duplicates the real, a mimetic copy in which "*all is true*"[12]— thereby affirming its power to recuperate a referent—on the other, it frequently yields to crises of despairing impotence, bewailing the fact that "les mots ne peuvent pas exprimer . . . ," or "le langage ne suffirait pas . . ." (words cannot express . . .; language would be inadequate . . .), flirting with defeat as it challenges the mimetic intent it otherwise asserts.

The quest for an authentic father and the search for the proper narrative version of this quest are, then, juxtaposed in a self-seeking language that continually puts its own authenticity into question. Together the three quests might be defined as an interrogation of origins, a search slated for failure because, like any desire, it rests upon a founding lack. There is no unproblematic father in the Balzacian text, only a series of paternal figures sought and repudiated, as there is no sufficiently totalizing fiction, and no language masterful enough to render "proper" meaning.

One way to approach the paternal metaphor is to read Balzac with Freud. In his essay "Family Romances" Freud suggests that the child's oedipal desires and disappointments are causally related to early narrative activity.[13] As the child begins to realize that the lofty status originally imputed to the parents is not wholly tenable, disillusionment sets in. The child then begins to fabricate fantasies in which the biological parents are portrayed as adoptive, so that more exalted figures can take their place. The fall from idealism is compensated for by a fiction that denies the knowledge motivating it, and the lost ideal is preserved through the playing out of a wishful corrective. In a second, sexualized stage, the boy's identification with his father, his wish to be like or simply to *be* the father, is complicated by feelings of sexual rivalry, since the father's presence bars access to the mother. With the realization that "pater semper incertus est," the fantasies come to concentrate on vacating the paternal position and filling the empty slot with a surrogate father, thereby staging the son's desire for his mother in scenes of illicit love. It may be significant that the father's "absence" (his fall from filial grace, or repudiation) triggers these primitive fictions; Freud's "family romance" here summarizes Balzac's. Each of the texts treated in this book is a similar attempt to rewrite origins, to replace the unsatisfactory fragments of a primordial past by a totalizing fiction answering desire and recuperating loss.

Barthes (as quoted in the epigraph) recasts Freud's formulation in a way that closely approximates my own when he calls attention to the child's contemporaneous acquisition of the sentence, narrative, and the Oedipus complex. His addition of the sentence (the minimal unit of linguistic closure) to Freud's narrative-Oedipus coupling gives emphasis to the fact that all three elements are paradoxically defined by contraries: on the one hand, by a certain limitlessness (the infinite expandability of embedding, of continuing, of desiring); on the other hand, by the laying down of limits (the restraining structures of syntax, closure, and the father's law).

Together Freud and Barthes outline a pattern which is a useful, if skeletal, model for reading Balzac and also, I will suggest, for reading the nineteenth century. It is particularly helpful to recognize that language, narrative, and family structures all oscillate between the poles of order and disorder, or law and desire, and that each pole exerts a pull. This tension is reflected by the ambiguous status of the father in Balzac and more generally in nineteenth-century fiction. I do not want to imply that narrative structures in Balzac can be wholly absorbed by psychoanalytic explanation. My point has more to do with the fact that Freud and Balzac tell overlapping stories. But this relationship should not be evaluated without briefly representing the epistemological climate which nurtured them both.

A schematic overview of the nineteenth century in Europe might characterize it as the zenith of an age which replaced the Scriptures with the writings of Balzac, Darwin, and Freud and which substituted historicizing modes (the novel, evolutionary biology, and ultimately, psychoanalysis) for divine authority and its sociopolitical analogues. I am alluding here to a major shift in the structures of explanation used to carve human experience into meaningful patterns. One of two separate but continuously interacting developments critical to this shift was the dissolution of Christianity, most pertinently, the wearing out of its mythology, which was no longer a force of inspiration and control. Related to this was science's discovery of the past, which ushered in a radically new conception of time incompatible with biblical temporality.[14]

It is difficult and somewhat arbitrary to situate these developments in well-defined time. The French Revolution is a convenient (and certainly crucial) reference point, but it is at least in part only a symbolic dating of a much more prolonged revolution in thought. For Balzac and many of his contemporaries, the Revolution brought about the fall of Church and King, and the correlative leveling of hierarchically organized society. But Church and King were earthly representations of a sacred order which had long since lost its vigor. We might roughly trace the end of this order to the seventeenth century, for as George Steiner has written, the rise of rationalism led to "the splintering of the ancient hierarchic world image" and to the loss of the "nearly tangible awareness of a continuity between the human and the divine order." [15] Until then, at first classical mythology and later Christianity had organized the imagination of Western society; after this point, these "plots" of transcendence gradually degenerated into mere conventions.

It is equally difficult to assign a precise date to the scientific revolution, for the nineteenth-century discoveries which were definitively to historicize science were significantly prepared by the eighteenth century, and were resisted in varying degrees by the nineteenth. We can, however, locate in the nineteenth century the period most immediately and most sharply affected by these changes, which worked to temporalize and thereby to disrupt an essentially spatial, static conception of nature and society.

This claim deserves further emphasis. That the term *prehistory* first came into use in the nineteenth century reflects the fact that only then did the mutability of the earth and its inhabitants begin to enter into the general stream of human consciousness. A catalogue of the natural and social sciences which arose or rose to significance in the nineteenth century would have to include paleontology, modern biology, archaeology, anthropology, etymology, philology, and psychoanalysis. Each of these emerging fields is concerned with retrieving origins and retracing the chronological pathways that link them to endpoints. All share a common focus on the past and on a particular conception of time as successive or passing, to be understood in contradistinction to divine time, which recuperated and redeemed the unrelenting flow of insignificant moments by subordinating them to the more meaningful eternal order.

We might say that the nineteenth century substituted evolution for Genesis, using Darwin emblematically to express the tenor of an age which began to tell a historicized story of origins. If history is what replaced (or perhaps displaced) the shattered sacred order, I think this is so because history, as Frank Kermode so well describes it, is "a fictive substitute for authority and tradition, a maker of concords between past, present and future, a provider of significance to mere chronicity." [16]

The novel, like evolutionary and psychoanalytic theory, exemplifies the temporalizing proclivities of nineteenth-century explanatory structures, which, as Peter Brooks has noted, postulate that we can explain what we are "through the reconstruction of how we got that way."[17] We must understand the nineteenth-century imagination as properly chronological; newly condemned to exist in time, it seeks its logic in temporal designs and its authority in genealogical tracings.

This is the context in which I am reading Balzac. I want to stress that the rise of the literary form which has been defined as a staging of the father is a response to a world wrenched away from traditional sources of authority and unable to fill or to accept the void. This helps to explain why Balzac, like so many of his novelist contemporaries, insistently plots family lines, why his family plots strive to recover the father's place, but tend instead to discover the father's displacement and the resultant disruption of family order. More critically, it emphasizes the fact that the father being sought is an essentially symbolic figure, that is, a regulating power or an authorizing presence.

Where I earlier appeared to be advancing a psychoanalytic argument, grounding Balzac (and the novel) in Freud, I may now seem to be advancing a historical argument that grounds both Balzac and Freud in history. In fact I am arguing both points. The oedipal theme in literature returns eternally and ignores genre boundaries, but the novel which it structures is essentially a nineteenth-century phenomenon. This is less paradoxical than it seems. Although the Oedipus story (of which Freud's version is one of many) is, like most myths, ageless, it is the myth most representative of the nineteenth century. Perhaps each age defines itself by the myth(s) best suited to it; then Freud's theorization and Balzac's thematization of oedipal structures become parallel explanatory undertakings invoked by the times. I would argue further that it was not by chance that psychoanalysis began to wax as the novel began to wane; if the one replaced the other, it is because each, to extend Susan Sontag's designation of psychology, is "a sublimated spiritualism."[18]

Because the novel is inseparable from a post-sacred attempt to secularize—and thus revivify—the spiritual, to refashion divine authority in temporal (generational) ordering, and to relo-

cate lost origins, it is the summa of nineteenth-century civilization and an index of its discontent. The multilevel play of
authority and subversion in the particular form I have begun to
describe is proper to the Balzacian text but indicative of conflict-
ridden issues of authority and succession which more generally
haunt the nineteenth century and define the nineteenth-century
novel. A more comprehensive (but necessarily less detailed) version of this study could include such texts as Dickens's *Great
Expectations,* Dostoevsky's *Brothers Karamazov,* Flaubert's
Saint Julien l'hospitalier, Stendhal's *Le Rouge et le noir,* Tolstoy's
Anna Karenina, and Zola's *Rougon-Macquart* cycle. This book
can do no more than indicate by example the path such a study
might take. Because Balzac is perhaps the most traditional writer
of the traditional novel (Henry James called him "the master of
us all"[19]), and because his family plots exaggeratedly typify the
use of family themes as structuring force in the traditional novel,
there is no better place to begin reading it.

This book is divided into two complementary parts. The
first is an extremely close reading of two early *contes* which are
characteristic of the Balzac often referred to as "visionary."
Chapter 1 centers on *El Verdugo,* the story of a parricide, and
examines the relationship between the father's death, naming,
and narrative beginnings in order to introduce the unstable metaphor of generation. In chapter 2, the emphasis shifts to the
mother in a reading of *Une Passion dans le désert.* The link between sexual disruption and narrative disturbance is explored by
way of this tale of desire played out through a soldier's amorous
adventure with an exceedingly feminine panther. Together these
two chapters delineate the basic interrelationship between family, narrative, and language which recurs throughout Balzac's
works. Part 2 shifts to the Balzac most often considered "realist."
It is a reading of the three novels which constitute the Vautrin
cycle: *Le Père Goriot,* in chapter 3, and the all but continuous
Illusions perdues and *Splendeurs et misères des courtisanes* together in chapter 4. Building upon the patterns disengaged in
part 1, part 2 focuses on their development and elaboration in
the novels, and deals more specifically with derivative problems
of language and representation. It follows the continuing narra-

tive attempt to cling to integrative family forms, but bears witness to the interrelated disintegration of family, narrative, and language paradigms. As the study proceeds from the first to the second part (and, chronologically, from 1829 to 1847), it traces a passage, or a generative relationship between the early ("visionary") and the later ("realist") works, in the course of which an essential continuity emerges from an overlay of change.

PART I

VISIONS

Victor Marchand:
The Narrator as Story Seller
El Verdugo

—La denomination (dist Epistemon à Pantagruel) de ces deux vostres coronelz Riflandouille et Tailleboudin en cestuy conflict nous promect asceurance, heur et victoire, si, par fortune, ces Andouilles nous vouloient oultrager.
—Vous le prenez bien (dist Pantagruel) et me plaist que par les noms de nos coronelz vous praevoiez et prognosticquez la nostre victoire. Telle maniere de prognosticquer par noms n'est moderne. . . . Voyez le *Cratyle* du divin Platon.

RABELAIS, *Quart Livre*

[Félicité exclame:] "Sterne a raison: les noms signifient quelque chose, et le mien est la plus sauvage raillerie."

BALZAC, *Béatrix*

I N the beginning of the *Quart Livre,* Pantagruel, with his father's benediction, embarks on a journey into the Other World. On the home front, this interim will be used to arrange Pantagruel's marriage and to prepare the wedding. The voyage, situated in the threshold zone dividing youth from adulthood, is a voyage of initiation, a rite of passage. Pantagruel's apprenticeship of the world is in fact quite specialized, for as the chapters progress, the succession of adventures reveals it to be nothing short of a linguistic apprenticeship, an exploration of the origin and essence of words.

Roughly two centuries after Rabelais wrote of Pantagruel's odyssey through language, Balzac had his Louis Lambert contemplate a book which would record his own linguistic peregrinations:

"Souvent, me dit-il, en parlant de ses lectures, j'ai accompli de délicieux voyages, embarqué sur un mot dans les abîmes du passé. . . . Quel beau livre ne composerait-on pas en racontant la vie et les aventures d'un mot?"[1]

["Often," he told me, speaking of his readings, "I have taken delightful trips, embarked upon a word in the abysses of the past. . . . What a fine book one could produce by narrating the life and the adventures of a word!"]

This "fine book" dreamed of by Balzac's mad genius is in fact an anachronistic projection, an intertextual reference to a previously completed project, for the author of *Louis Lambert* (written in 1832) had already recounted such a linguistic journey when he wrote *El Verdugo* three years earlier.

El Verdugo juxtaposes a temporal and spatial journey, a quest for origins which traverses geographical lines as it reverts in time. The text operates as a vehicle—a narrative vehicle whose itinerary shuttles the reader between two stories.

The more prominent of the two is the drama of a Spanish nobleman's son who murders his father and thereby earns the eponymous title "El Verdugo," translated by the narrator as *le Bourreau* (the Executioner). The parricide, however, is presented from the point of view of a young French soldier, the son of a Parisian grocer, whose story is alluded to but suppressed in favor of the Spanish drama it introduces. So the Spanish castle is constructed upon the ruins of a Parisian grocery store, and the text, from the beginning, is structured by a series of substitutions: a *transfer* from France to Spain, a *translation* from French to Spanish, a *transference* (that is, a playing-out of the French soldier's story through the Spanish nobleman's), and a *metaphor* (the title "El Verdugo" replaces the young nobleman's proper name, de Léganès). The common etymological source of these terms, which all have to do with conveying, or displacing, affirms the text's vehicular status, and reflects the thematized voyage—or more accurately, perhaps, is reflected by the voyage motif. For the narrative emphasis upon displacement exhibits the means of textual production, points to the rhetoric of displacement as more fundamentally the displacement of rhetoric, rhetoric *as* displacement.

The text which represents a quest for origins is inherently reflexive, since the language of interrogation is doubled by an interrogation of language, a quest for narrative origins in language. As we turn to *El Verdugo,* it will become evident that the course it follows describes a rather particularized journey through language which, like Pantagruel's, might well be subtitled "Voyage en Cratylie."[2]

I

Dans *El Verdugo* c'est l'idée de dynastie mettant une hache dans la main d'un fils, lui faisant commettre tous les crimes en un seul.

FÉLIX DAVIN, Introduction to the *Etudes philosophiques*

The first part of the text opens with the presentation of Victor Marchand, a young French officer in Napoleon's service, who is stationed in the small Spanish town of Menda dominated by the Marquis de Léganès's château. Victor, posted on a terrace overlooking both the sea and the château, is charged with surveying both sites: the sea for a threatened British debarkation, and the château for a suspected indigenous uprising in collaboration with the British. But Victor is absorbed in a contemplation of the land and seascape (and we are told that his revery is perhaps occasioned by a romantic interest in the marquis's daughter, Clara). He therefore notices all too late that the town is resplendent with light (contrary to curfew orders), and that the sea is covered with sails. Then all moves quickly: one of his soldiers, struck by a bullet, falls dead at his feet, and a cannon thunders over the ocean. While Victor is realizing that his soldiers have been attacked, that the British are about to land, and that he is dishonored, Clara approaches him in the night and offers her brother's horse, urging him to flee. So Victor is saved and delivers himself in shame to his general, who immediately sets out with his soldiers to suppress the rebellion and avenge the massacre. Menda is easily surrounded, for the British have been delayed.

The general agrees to spare the population of Menda in exchange for the rebels' death and the château inhabitants' surrender.

The second part of the story is marked by a decelerated rhythm as the narrative closes in on the fate of the marquis's family. Victor Marchand, acting as mediator between the noble family and the French general, requests three favors on the marquis's behalf. First, he asks that the sentence imposed on the nobles be revised to provide for a more aristocratic death by decapitation rather than by hanging. This request is accorded. Then he presents a double plea: the family asks for the privilege of religious succor, and for permission to be released from their fetters, promising in exchange that they will not attempt to escape. This appeal duly complied with, Marchand conveys the third proposal. The marquis offers his entire fortune in exchange for the life of his son. But the general, who comprehends the import of this last request, strikes a harder bargain. He will allow the marquis to *buy* the eternity of his name: he will spare any one of the three sons who will purchase this privilege by serving as executioner of the remaining family members. Propelled by his intransigent dynastic ethic, determined at all cost to preserve his name from extinction, the father first orders, then, falling to his knees, implores his eldest son and namesake to take on the office of executioner. Juanito inevitably concedes, compelled by the supplications of the entire family. At the penultimate moment, Victor procures a pardon for Clara if she will, in exchange, agree to marry him. She refuses; we then proceed to what is literally a blow-by-blow account of Juanito's murder of his two sisters, his two brothers, and his father. The marquise leaps to her death from the terrace in order to spare her son a last impossible blow. The final paragraph, tantamount to an epilogue, is written from an unspecified later point in time, and spoken in an unidentifiable narrative voice. It informs us that the marquis's successor (and executioner) lives a dark and solitary life, forestalling death only to await assurance of his own posterity.

The few critics who have turned their attention to this text share a striking propensity to neglect the first part,[3] to consider it merely preparatory to the essential drama contained in the second part. The critical consensus might be summarized by Diana McCormick's conclusion that "nous avons eu, dans cette première moitié du récit, le fond du tableau, la préparation à *la vraie histoire,* l'introduction qui doit mener au thème du bourreau"[4] (we have had, in this first half of the narrative, the background, the preparation for *the real story,* the introduction which is to lead to the theme of the executioner). But the critical focus on the second half of the text represents a transfer or displacement of interest which should be challenged on several counts. If we dismiss the first part as introductory or as "background," we are in effect suppressing half the text. But if the first part is truly insignificant, how are we to explain the then apparently superfluous inclusion of the character Victor Marchand? Why does Clara cross over the boundary of significance, entering the devalorized first section to introduce romantic implications for Victor? Can this element of the plot be dispensed with as a dramatic ploy, as McCormick suggests[5]—once again a preparatory element—designed to emphasize Clara's ultimate submission to dynastic duty? Accepting for the moment the rather specious hypothesis that the introduction to a text can be subordinated to the "vraie histoire," we might ask what criteria determine the second part of this text as the "real story." What, in fact, is a "real" story?

The process of extracting the theme of the "real story" situated in the second part seems to repeat the technique of selective suppression which gives priority to the second half of the narrative at the expense of the first. Judging from critical reaction to *El Verdugo,* the most gripping aspect of the Léganès family massacre is the murder of the father.

Furthermore, a well-documented source study by Wayne Conner traces *El Verdugo* back to the following kernel phrase cited in the article "Exécuteur de la haute justice" in the *Encyclopédie:* "On voit encore au milieu de la ville de Gand deux statues d'airain d'un père & d'un fils convaincus d'un même crime, où le fils servit d'exécuteur à son père"[6] (Still standing in the middle of the city of Ghent are two bronze statues of a father and of a son convicted of the same crime, for which the son served as his father's executioner). Conner's study is supported by a fragment from one of Balzac's notebooks, which reads: "Dans *El Verdugo* un fils tua son père pour une idée"[7] (In *El Verdugo* a son killed his father for an idea). But despite the manifest emphasis of this story, despite the declared intention of its author, it is a fact that the text vividly describes the execution of an entire family, and pays particular narrative attention to the sister-murder and the mother's suicide; we cannot ignore that the first half of the text exists and develops a separate but connected intrigue which, though unexplored, can hardly be dismissed as insignificant.

Now, if critical attention focuses on the second half of the text, and, specifically, on the act of parricide within it (which would consequently be designated as the "real story"), it is reasonable to assume that the construction of the text invites and even provokes such a perspective, and that critical inattention to the first half of the narrative, and, in particular, to Clara's role, is a reflection of a textual occultation of these elements. Once we recognize that the course of the narrative, like its title, *El Verdugo,* diverts our attention from the first part of the text, it becomes clear that what has been called the "real story" is in fact the manifest story; this story is important, but it should not prevent us from asking where and what is the latent story.

The beginning of an answer to these questions may be glimpsed in a comment on *El Verdugo* written by Félix Davin, commonly recognized as Balzac's spokesman. "*El Verdugo*," says Davin, represents "l'idée de dynastie mettant une hache dans la main d'un fils, lui faisant commettre *tous les crimes en un seul*"[8] (the idea of dynasty placing an axe in a son's hand, and making him commit *every crime in a single one*). Like the modern-day critics of this text, Davin stresses a single crime, the horror of which he expresses by a hyperbole: "tous les crimes en un seul." But I think we need to realize that rhetoric is never empty, and that we have to question this figure of speech, question the text as to exactly what it means to commit every crime, and how it comes to pass that every crime is condensed to a single one. Since the story of Juanito's parricide provides an inadequate answer, we need to reintegrate the two panels of the text. The text in fact offers us a hinge between its two segments in the shape of a forbidden erotic object: Clara.

II

... ne pensant pas aux noms comme à un idéal inaccessible, mais comme à une ambiance réelle dans laquelle j'irais me plonger.

PROUST, *Du côté de chez Swann*

The text opens with a tableau of darkness and light, as if playing a game of hide-and-seek with the reader, retaining the privilege to veil what it simultaneously reveals. It is midnight, yet "le scintillement des étoiles et la douce lumière de la lune éclairaient une vallée"[9] (the shimmering of the stars and the soft moonlight lit a valley) before the contemplative eyes of Victor Marchand. Turning his head, "il apercevait la mer, dont les eaux brillantes encadraient le paysage d'une large lame d'argent. Le château était illuminé" (p. 1133) (he caught sight of the sea, whose shining waters framed the landscape with a broad silver band. The chateau was illuminated).

Similar images of light and vision proliferate in the suite of this first half of the text, up until the moment when Victor realizes his dishonor and flees "avec la rapidité de l'*éclair*" (p. 1136; emphasis added here and below). Between the starlit opening and Victor's lightning-like escape, he glimpses "une assez grande quantité de *lumières*" in the town, despite his orders that "*les feux fussent éteints* à l'heure prescrite"; also, "il vit bien *briller* çà et là les baionnettes de ses soldats" (p. 1134); then, turning his head, "ses *yeux* furent saisis par l'*éclat* extraordinaire de l'Océan" (p. 1135). Here he beholds (il y *aperçut*) a mass of sails, "un *spectacle* ... funeste" by "les *rayons blanchissants de la lune*," though he tries to convince himself that "cette *vision* était un *piège d'optique* offert par les fantaisies des ondes et de la lune." At this point, one of Victor's grenadiers approaches to relate several suspicious *observations:* he has followed someone carrying "une *lanterne* à la main" and comments that "une *lanterne* est furieusement suspecte," for he does not believe that "ce chrétien-là ait besoin *d'allumer des cierges* à cette heure-ci." As a terrible cry echoes through the town, "une *lueur* soudaine *éclaira* le commandant" and "un *feu* de paille et de bois sec *brillait* comme un *incendie* à dix pas du jeune homme" (p. 1135).

These various images of light and vision continue and reflect

the original luminous vista which Victor overlooks in the first
paragraph of the text, the contemplation of which distracts him
from his surveillance duties and allows the Spanish insurrection
to begin undetected. So his crime is essentially one of vision, of
seeing so much light that his sight is obstructed.

But we need to look more closely at this scene of panoramic
contemplation. For we learn the following:

Pendant toute cette soirée, l'aînée des filles avait regardé l'officier avec
un intérêt empreint d'une telle tristesse, que le sentiment de compassion
exprimé par l'Espagnole pouvait bien causer la rêverie du Français.
Clara était belle. [pp. 1133–34]

[During this entire evening, the elder daughter had watched the officer
with an interest tinged with such sadness, that the Spanish woman's
expression of compassion might well have caused the Frenchman's revery. Clara was beautiful.]

It becomes apparent not only that Victor's distraction is the result of the meditation inspired by the marquis's daughter, but
also that the alluring illuminated landscape is in effect a rhetorical projection which might be termed an onomastic fallacy: that
is, a metonymic diffusion of the woman to the landscape through
the semantic characteristics of her name, Clara.

So Victor Marchand's visual preoccupation is more fundamentally an erotic one. A close examination of the narrative discourse makes this increasingly evident, for the scenic description
abounds in feminine metaphors. We note that "la *douce* lumière
de la lune éclairait une *vallée délicieuse* qui *se déroulait coquet-
tement* à ses pieds" (p. 1133 [emphasis added here and below];
the *soft* moonlight lit a *charming valley* which *stretched out co-
quettishly* at his feet). The phrase that tells us: "il apercevait la
mer, dont les *eaux* brillantes *encadraient* le paysage d'une large
lame d'argent" (p. 1133) presents a striking uterine image. The
text once again registers the woman's metaphoric trace in the
following fragment: "Enfin les jardins étaient plantés d'arbres si
odoriférants et de fleurs si suaves, que le jeune homme se trouvait
comme plongé dans un bain de parfums" (p. 1133; And the gar-

dens were planted with such fragrant trees and such sweet-smelling flowers, that the young man felt as if he had plunged into a perfumed bath).

Thus later, in the midst of the "real" story, it is no revelation that Victor, as he releases Clara from her fetters, "ne put s'empêcher d'effleurer les bras de la jeune fille, en admirant . . . sa taille souple" (p. 1139; could not help brushing against the young woman's arms, as he admired her graceful figure). It is rather a deferred avowal of an erotic element which the rhetoric of the text has already disclosed in spite of itself. Furthermore, if the opening vista is sexualized through the language that describes it, so too are the viewer and the process of viewing.

But an evaluation of this scene, and the understanding of its import for the drama it launches, here necessitate a digression. While Victor is surveying the vista at his feet we must momentarily leave him in order to observe another drama of viewing which unfolds in *Facino Cane,* for it is not without significance for the comprehension of *El Verdugo.*

The narrator of *Facino Cane* presents himself as a writer dominated by a single passion: the intuitive observation of other individuals, the *penetration* of their lives. Creating narratives ("chefs-d'oeuvre *enfantés* par le hasard";[10] masterpieces *engendered* by chance) is, for him, a monomania expressed in sexual terms: "En entendant ces gens, je pouvais *épouser* leur vie . . . mon âme *passait dans* la leur" (p. 1020 [emphasis added]; As I listened to these people, I found myself *wedded* to their lives . . . my soul *passed into* theirs). He is endowed with an unusually acute power of observation, which, he tells us, "pénétrait l'âme sans négliger le corps" (p. 1019; penetrated the soul without neglecting the body). Narrating involves both a literal descent (he is obliged to come down from his attic abode to fuse with his potential subjects, the passersby in the street) and a figurative one, a descent beneath the surface of appearances to discover stories which are "buried" (p. 1021), "lost," or "forgotten" (p. 1020): "il faut descendre trop bas pour trouver ces admirables scènes" (p. 1020; to find these wonderful scenes, one must go down too deep). This gift of penetration, however, carries with it a great anxiety. The narrator is obsessed with the fear that his powers might be "une seconde vue . . . une de ces qualités dont l'abus mènerait à la folie" (p. 1020; a kind of second sight . . . the kind of quality which, if abused, could lead to madness).

Having explained his ability to live the life of another, to substitute himself for another, the narrator begins to relate the tale of his encounter with the blind musician Facino Cane, an aged Italian expatriate. This intermediary section of the text dramatizes the narrator's powers of penetrating vision: we see his impassioned imagination give form to the character Facino Cane. Once the narrator's soul has passed into the body of the musician, the narrative substitution is realized, and Facino Cane becomes narrator in turn, delivering a story that is nothing less than the metaphoric reenactment of the narrator's discourse.

His autobiographical narrative begins by informing us that he, like the first narrator, is dominated by a single passion. He intuitively senses gold: "Je sens l'or" (p. 1027). Just as the original narrator's visionary power "saisissait si bien les détails extérieurs, qu'elle allait sur le champ au-delà" (p. 1019; grasped external details so well that it immediately went beyond), Facino Cane's senses know no barriers: "Je verrai l'or à travers les murailles," he maintains (p. 1030; I will see gold through walls). His passion, like the narrator's, is monomaniacal, a kind of intoxication: Facino Cane's "fièvre de l'or" (p. 1029) corresponds to the narrator's "ivresse des facultés morales" (p. 1020). Facino's passion, like the narrator's, involves a descent, this one quite literal. In his youth, when he was twenty (the narrator's age at the moment of the narration), he was imprisoned in a Venetian dungeon for the murder of his lover's protector. Here he discovers a buried treasure—buried like the stories exhumed by the narrator—and digs up the floor of his cell to reach it.

But the discovery of this treasure leads to a loss, for five years later Facino Cane is struck by blindness. And he suggests that his ability to see gold was "un abus de la puissance visuelle qui me prédestinait à perdre les yeux" (p. 1030; an abuse of the power of sight that predestined the loss of my eyes). It is evident that Facino Cane's loss of sight, as retribution for excessive visual activity, translates the narrator's fear of madness (losing his senses) as punishment for the abuse of his powers of second sight. The analogy between madness and blindness is reinforced by the fact that Facino Cane was held for two years at Bicêtre (an asylum for the insane) before entering Les Quinze-Vingts (an asylum for the blind).

Thus the narrator's story and Facino Cane's are metaphorically related, and an analogy is established between writing and looking, narrative and buried treasure or gold. The unstated common denominator, the common crime or abuse of the two parallel stories is sexual; the unstated common punishment, castration. We have seen the sexual terminology which defines the narrator's literary activity; Facino Cane's gold-digging is similarly defined. For the gold which is the object of his fascination is continually associated with a woman, as the loss of his fortune is related to erotic loss. Bianca, the object of Facino's first erotic passion, becomes a substitute for gold, for Facino recounts: "Quand je n'eus plus de fortune, je fus pris par la rage de voir Bianca" (p. 1027; When my fortune was gone, I was seized by a mad desire to see Bianca). While he explicitly names his infatuation with gold as his downfall ("Cette passion m'a perdu," he states [p. 1027]), he also mentions: "J'ai commencé par la première des folies, par l'amour" (p. 1026; I began with the greatest folly, love), and it is the indulgence of this passion which leads to the first catastrophe, his incarceration. Moreover, Bianca's death and Facino Cane's loss of sight are synchronically narrated (p. 1030), so that the advent of blindness is indirectly linked to eros.

Blindness, then, is only a metaphoric token of the loss incurred by Facino's overindulgence, as gold is the metaphor coined to represent eros. The mere tone of Facino's voice announces to the narrator "que ses regrets ne portaient pas seulement sur la perte de sa vue, mais sur quelque grand pouvoir dont il aurait été dépouillé" (p. 1024; that his regrets extended not only to his lost sight, but to some great power which had been stripped from him). Facino's tone of voice seems rather scanty motivation for this periphrastic revelation; I think we must instead attribute it to a projection on the part of the narrator, which allusively points to castration as the unspoken standard alternately represented by blindness and madness, the unmentionable tax levied on the writer.

Facino Cane holds a unique position in the *Comédie humaine,* because it is the text that deals most directly with the figure of the writer. Paradoxically, the significant part of what it has to say about writers and writing is most indirect, displaced by a substituted story and disguised by a network of metaphor. The relative silence that shrouds the theme in general, and the textual reticence that envelops it in this particular story, are both traceable to a fundamental perception of writing as a forbidden erotic activity. We will find that the motif of writing is not in fact absent, only disguised, in other texts, where dispersed metaphoric fragments can be significantly reconstructed by referring to the patterns uncovered in *Facino Cane.*

When we return to *El Verdugo* and Victor Marchand, we find him "*abîmé* dans une contemplation . . . *profonde*" (p. 1133 [emphasis added]; *sunk* in deep contemplation); standing on a parapet, he looks down at Menda, "à cent pieds au-dessous de lui" (p. 1133; a hundred feet below him). Having unveiled the sexual connotation of the penetrating look as well as of that form of observation which plumbs the depths in *Facino Cane,* we are now prepared to appreciate that the nature of Victor's gaze is rhetorically betrayed. That his contemplation is in fact an erotic absorption is confirmed by the statement that he finds himself "comme *plongé* dans un bain de parfums" (p. 1133 [emphasis added] as though plunged in a perfumed bath), which metaphorically translates an imagined erotic involvement with Clara.

Both the rhetoric and the plot of this text represent Victor's erotic interest in Clara as a crime. Victor Marchand, the son of a petit-bourgeois father (as his patronym emphatically reflects) does not have the right to covet a Spanish noblewoman: "Mais comment *oser* croire que la fille du vieillard le plus entiché de sa grandesse qui fût en Espagne, pourrait être donnée au fils d'un épicier de Paris!" (p. 1134 [emphasis added]; But how could he *dare* believe that this daughter of an old man more infatuated with his nobility than any other in Spain might be given to the son of a Parisian grocer!). The verb *oser* marks the transgression.

Moreover, the Spanish insurrection (itself a transgression of the French masters' authority) is a result of Victor's inattention to his surveillance duties. This manifestation of the erotic crime arouses a sense of guilt and a fear of punishment in Victor:

"Il était sans épée. Il comprenait que ses soldats avaient péri et que les Anglais allaient débarquer. Il se vit déshonoré s'il vivait, il se vit traduit devant un conseil de guerre." [p. 1136]

[He was swordless. He realized that his soldiers had perished and that the British were about to land. He saw that he would be dishonored if he lived, he saw himself court-martialed.]

When he arrives at his general's quarters, Victor, sure of his doom, announces: "Je vous apporte ma tête!" (p. 1136; I bring you my head!), whereupon his superior assures him that when the emperor is made aware of his fault, "il voudra vous faire fusiller" (p. 1136; he will want to have you shot). Ultimately, Victor is not court-martialed, beheaded, or shot. But his chastisement, obedient to talion law, corresponds to both the manifest and the latent crime, simultaneously punishing the transgression of vision and the erotic transgression.

A familiar metaphoric chain that establishes a continuity of the concepts of sight, light, the sun, and fecundation at first glance seems to elucidate the textual association of vision and eros. But a curious problem arises at this point: the text assigns Victor a male erotic role (whereby he is figuratively a generator, the sun, a source of light), but the light that suffuses the text is clearly generated by Clara's name. Thus there appears to be a confusion of male-female roles in this first section of the narrative. The paradox is dispelled, however, when we recall that the light that bathes Victor's meditation is moonlight, a "clair de lune" induced, as we have seen, by "Clara." Just as the moon's light is derived from the sun, Clara functions as a reflective surface for Victor, intensifying his self-image (affirming his male role) by reflecting it, by recognizing or *regarding* him. We remember that the immediate cause of Victor's revery is Clara's continuing gaze. In this context, we must also anticipate that later moment when Victor procures a conditional pardon for Clara. This pardon, contingent upon Clara's recognition of Victor as husband, is one more indication of her mirroring function in the text; her life depends on her acceptance or rejection of this role.

Lest we forget, in this discussion of light and its refraction, the chiaroscuro contrasts of the first part of the text (all the play of light occurs at midnight), we ought briefly to turn our attention to the peculiar choice of the name Clara for the love-object of this rather "ténébreuse affaire." Indeed, this name might almost be termed a misnomer. For despite the semantic charge of her name, despite the projection of her name in images of brightness and illumination, we learn much later on that Victor admires "sa chevelure noire" (her black hair), that she is "une véritable Espagnole: elle avait le teint espagnol, les yeux espagnols, de longs cils recourbés, et une prunelle plus noire que ne l'est l'aile d'un corbeau" (p. 1139; a true Spanish woman: she had a Spanish complexion, Spanish eyes with long wavy lashes, and pupils blacker than a raven's wing). So, if Clara refracts light, she also augurs darkness. As the shattering of a mirror necessarily has grave consequences for the reflected image, so Victor's fate is to a large extent dependent on Clara's.[11]

In the myth of Diana and Actaeon, the young man is caught spying upon the moon goddess at her bath; as punishment for this affront to her chastity, she changes him into a stag. Victor's crime of contemplation, similar to Actaeon's, provokes a retributive alteration analogous to Actaeon's metamorphosis. This fate is alluded to early in the text, for when Victor perceives the British sails in the distance, "il tressaillit, et tâcha de se convaincre que cette vision était un piège d'optique offert par les fantaisies des ondes et de la lune" (p. 1135; he started, and tried to convince himself that what he saw was an optical illusion produced by the caprices of the waves and the moon). As in the story of Diana and Actaeon, the moon is the source of transformation and alteration. The fantasy it (she) inspires in Victor is a quite literal "piège d'optique," an optical trap that is alluringly baited to distract him, to entice him, and from which he will not escape unscathed. His mistake, which testifies to the moon's powers of illusion—and for which he will pay dearly—is that what he names "fantasy" (the sails) is real, while the object of his vision (the imagined erotic tableau) is fantasy.[12]

III

> *Jocasta.* As to your mother's marriage bed,—don't fear it.
> Before this, in dreams too, as well as oracles,
> many a man has lain with his own mother.
>
> SOPHOCLES, *Oedipus the King,*
> trans. David Grene

> Dieu seul sait le nombre de parricides qui se commettent par la pensée.
>
> BALZAC, Preface to *L'Elixir de longue vie*

It appears, then, that the two halves of this text juxtapose an erotic crime and a parricide. In order to understand how these two potentially discordant parts of the text are related, we need to turn to a close examination of the parricide.

The crime provokes a mixed reaction on the part of the reader. The various critical introductions to the story speak of the horror and cruelty of the crime, but this aversion is tinged with not a little admiration.[13] The reader's ambivalence echoes Balzac's summary of the crime as an "admirable forfait" (p. 1143); the oxymoron reflects the fact that the plot is ambiguously structured. Juanito's parricide is ordered by his father; the most extreme expression of filial revolt here coincides with the most absolute form of filial obedience.

Lest we lend too much credence to what the text, for its own purpose of dissimulation, would have us believe, we should regard the paternal command with a healthy dose of skepticism. We can read this apparent contradiction as a textual compromise, as the sign of a conflict between the story attempting to surface and the forces of censorship striving to repress it; as such, this paradox marks a significant affective node of the intrigue.[14]

By analogy with the dream-work, which strives to disguise its disturbing or forbidden content, the act of writing, as it works to conceal what is actually the son's parricidal desire, makes of desire a necessity. It transforms the paternal prohibition into its opposite: a paternal command.[15] That the French pronunciation of Menda—the site of this drama—makes it the homonym of *mandat,* or mandate, is no accident; every effort is being made to legitimize the crime that occurs here. The reversal is further emphasized by a description of the father in a supplicant pose before his son: "Le jeune comte restant immobile, son père tomba à ses genoux. . . . 'Mon fils. . . . Veux-tu me laisser long-temps à genoux?" (p. 1140; When the young count did not move, his father fell to his knees. . . . "My son. . . . How long would you have me kneel before you?"). Paternal authority is expressed as submission, and filial transgression is dissimulated as obedience.

But to attribute the expression of supreme revolt as absolute obedience purely to a concealment attempt oversimplifies a jux-taposition which is dually determined. We should also consider that the son's desire to efface the father, to replace him, has its roots not only in rivalry but in a sense of admiration for the father and of identification with him.

It becomes evident that we are dealing with an oedipal crime, whose erotic component has been expurgated from the "real" story and displaced to the "background" region of the first part of the text. This technique of dividing the crime into two thereby attenuated components, each attributed to a differ-ent character (as if to prevent the crime from bursting forth in all its unmitigated horror) is strikingly similar to the dramatic device used by Corneille in his *Oedipe*. Corneille, however, splits the crime in two (assigning parricide to Oedipe, incest to Thésée) only temporarily; he eventually reunites the two crimes, reas-signing both to Oedipe. We are then led to ask whether *El Ver-dugo* contains the possibility of a similar reintegration of its di-vided crime, or whether, on the contrary, its diptych structure resists such a unification attempt, relegating Victor and Juanito to their separate domains.

The erotic component is in fact not wholly consigned to Victor's story: Victor's erotic transgression (though to a certain extent veiled) is only more overtly expressed than Juanito's. Juanito's rapport with his sister is, to say the least, equivocal:

Clara vint s'asseoir sur ses genoux, et, d'un air gai: —Mon cher Juan-ito, dit-elle en lui passant le bras autour du cou et l'embrassant sur les paupières; si tu savais combien, donnée par toi, la mort me sera douce.

Je n'aurai pas à subir l'odieux contact des mains d'un bourreau. Tu me
guériras des maux qui m'attendaient, et . . . mon bon Juanito, *tu ne me*
voulais voir à personne, eh! bien?
    Ses yeux veloutés jetèrent un regard de feu sur Victor, comme pour
réveiller dans le coeur de Juanito son horreur des Français. [p. 1140;
emphasis added]

[Clara came and sat in his lap, and, as she put her arm around his neck
and kissed his eyelids, said cheerfully: "If you only knew how sweet
death would seem to me, if it were given by you. I won't have to bear
the abomination of an executioner's hands. You will cure me of the evils
awaiting me, and . . . my dear Juanito, *you didn't want me to belong to*
anyone, so . . . ?"
    Her velvety eyes cast a fiery glance at Victor, as if to reawaken in
Juanito's heart his horror of the French.]

    Clara's plea for death is an appeal to her brother's posses-
sive love for her. The nature of this love is elucidated by a scene
from *Béatrix* that depicts a lovers' dialogue culminating in a
murder attempt. The protagonist, Calyste, asks the woman he
adores if she will return to her former lover. Béatrix replies that
she must. Whereupon: *"Tu ne seras donc jamais à personne,* dit
Calyste en poussant la marquise avec une violence frénétique"[16]
(*"You will never belong to anyone,"* said Calyste as he pushed
the marquise with the violence of a madman). Moreover, we are
told a bit later on that "une femme ne pouvait être qu'heureuse
et flattée dans toutes ses vanités d'avoir été l'objet d'un crime"[17]
(to be the object of a crime could only make a woman happy,
flatter her vanity). Calyste's words ("Tu ne seras donc jamais à
personne") echo Clara's appeal to her brother ("tu ne me voulais
voir à personne") and assimilate the Clara-Juanito relationship
to the Béatrix-Calyste relationship. The murder of Clara, like the
attempted murder of Béatrix, is thus a lover's crime—the difference being that Juanito is both less and more than a lover to
Clara.
    It is striking that the rationale behind Clara's death-plea to
her brother (which might be paraphrased as, "Since you can't
have me, kill me so that no one else can") is repeated by the

conditional pardon that Victor Marchand extends to Clara. He offers her life in exchange for the gift of her person, which is tantamount to saying, "If I can't have you, you will die so that no one else can."

Victor and Juanito, by the analogy of their similar erotic relationship to Clara, are thus doubles—the difference being, of course, that Juanito is her brother as well. Several additional factors reinforce this identification. The title accorded Juanito at the story's end, "El Verdugo," alliteratively identifies him with Victor. Victor and Juanito are close in age. Victor escapes from the scene of his crime on Juanito's horse, which serves as a metonymic vehicle connecting the two. Clara is the common denominator; it is Clara who offers Victor her brother's horse, Clara who, rousing her brother's jealousy of Victor, places the two men in a structure of equivalence by making them rivals in love. Perhaps the most revealing link is suggested by a train of ocular associations. We recall that the manifest sign of Victor's erotic crime was a forbidden contemplation, a misplaced glance. Now, when we turn to Juanito, we find that his eyes are the erotic focus of his sister's and mother's attention. While the family members attempt to convince Juanito to serve as their executioner, Clara bestows kisses on his eyelids and turns her ardent gaze upon him, and these rather intimate gestures are echoed by the mother's act of reading his assent "en voyant Juanito faire un mouvement des sourcils *dont la signification n'était connue que d'elle*" (p. 1140; emphasis added; upon noticing a movement of his brows *whose meaning she alone knew*). As vision is once again associated with erotism, Victor and Juanito's status as textual doubles is confirmed.

Now, if we superimpose the two characters, the one (Victor) erotically linked to Clara, the other (Juanito) related to her by blood, the pattern that emerges is one of vicarious incest. Since Victor and Juanito reduplicate each other, each completing the other's erotic crime, it comes as little surprise that Victor's story includes a figurative parricide. We recall that Victor's early scene of contemplation (the representation of his desire for Clara) was punctuated by a reflection on his petit-bourgeois origin ("Mais comment oser croire que la fille du vieillard le plus entiché de sa grandesse qui fût en Espagne, pourrait être donnée au fils d'un épicier de Paris!" [p. 1134]). This evident contempt for his humble birthright betrays a symbolic rejection of his father, who is clearly the obstacle that prevents him from attaining Clara.

Having nonetheless committed the forbidden act, having foiled the paternal prohibition carried in his very name, Marchand, by rhetorically enacting the erotic transgression, Victor appropriately seeks punishment from two father-surrogates: first "le terrible général" and then Napoleon: "Quand l'Empereur saura cela!" (p. 1136; When the Emperor finds out!).

His paternal repudiation is in fact not confined to the verbal rejection. There is a (displaced) passage from the word to the deed, because Victor's erotic crime (his contemplation) leads to neglect of his surveillance duty, making him a traitor to his general and emperor, and abetting the Spanish insurrection. Victor's negligence culminates in the punishment meted out to the rebels, and so he is indirectly responsible for Juanito's parricide.

The Victor story and the Juanito story stand, like a photograph and its negative, in an inverted relationship to each other. We can trace a *chassé-croisé* pattern according to which the oedipal crime is divided and distributed:

	Victor	Juanito
manifest	eros	parricide
latent	parricide	eros

The two components of the crime—the erotic and the parricidal—are dissociated, but each retains latent elements of the other, so that the two parts of *El Verdugo* ultimately correspond to a disguised retelling of the same tale.

Now we begin to understand what it means to commit "tous les crimes en un seul." The expression is a euphemism for the two crimes of Oedipus, who killed his father and married his mother.[18] The hyperbole is well taken, masking as it does the double transgression of the most fundamental law upon which civilization is based.

IV

At the origin of this divided text there is an imaginary cohesive story which, though unwritten, can be more or less (but never entirely) reconstructed. If we can never precisely locate the origin, this is because the only "real" story is the one that never has been (and perhaps never can be) written, for as soon as the writing process begins, so too begins a process of association, dissociation, and dissimulation. We have seen that Juanito's story repeats Victor's, transforming the word of parricide into the deed, copying the erotic letter with a fainter trace. This suggests that Victor's story, as the more occulted one, might yield a clue about the original story, original understood here as virtual, or unwritten.

As we reintegrate the two crimes and the two stories, it is important to remember that Victor's meditation, with its conspicuous "confession" of a hostile son, launches the Spanish uprising and eventually creates Juanito's drama: it is the triggering element of the ensuing text. The castle of Menda, then, is a synonym for Victor's "château en Espagne," and the drama which unfolds there can be read as his "family romance," a projection of his desire for self-authored origins. We note the transformation of his "marchand" father, a petit-bourgeois Parisian grocer, into a Spanish marquis; we see his rebelliousness dramatically translated into Juanito's parricide.[19] Victor's narratorial status, however, is beset by contradictions.

Although this is a third-person narrative delivered by an anonymous narrator, there is a narrative investment in Victor: we read from his perspective, and he is the figure with whom the narrator identifies. Until the penultimate narrative moment, Victor is an omnipresent figure in the text, first as protagonist of his story, later, somewhat attenuated, as bargaining agent or "marchand." He does not leave the scene of the tale until shortly before its close; his disappearance in fact seems to precipitate the tale's end. And yet it is only after his exit that a soldier's passing remark attributes a narratorial role to Victor: "'Mon général, dit un officier à moitié ivre, *Marchand vient de me raconter* quelque chose de cette exécution, je parie que vous ne l'avez pas ordonnée'" (p. 1142 [emphasis added]; "General," said a half-drunken officer, "*Marchand just told me part of the story* of this execution; I'll bet you didn't order it"). Even then, the remark is doubly depreciated because it is more precisely an *allusion* made by a *drunken* (and therefore implicitly unreliable) speaker.

We have seen, however, that the narrative rhetoric of the opening paragraph betrays Victor's erotic act; more crucially, it betrays the erotic attitude of whoever is delivering the narrative, whoever is performing the narrative act. Victor's contemplation, his lapse of attention, is matched by a rhetorical lapse. The erotic turn of the opening reveals that the narrator, like Victor, has a vested interest in Clara, or in the eros she represents. So if Victor cannot technically be classified as narrator, he is nevertheless the substitute for a narrator under cover. Victor's erotic transgression (already concealed behind a crime of vision) in turn conceals a narrative transgression. The meaning of this three-tiered system of disguise (vision : sexuality : narration) can be elucidated by once again referring to the similar but more overtly elaborated metaphoric structure of *Facino Cane.*

In *Facino Cane,* the narrative act is explicitly represented as a criminal deed susceptible to punishment by madness. The crime and punishment are then metaphorically projected as a crime of excessive vision (seeing too much gold) punishable by blindness. The two series are linked by a mediating rhetoric of sexuality and castration. Thus, a metaphorical chain of punishment (blindness : castration : madness) corresponds to a metaphorical chain of crime (vision : sexuality : narration, or writing). The text of *Facino Cane* is tightly forged by this tripartite chain; one link always involves the simultaneous operation of the other two. The pattern is apparent from the very first reference to storytelling, described as "a single passion": "Chez moi l'observation était déjà devenue intuitive, elle pénétrait l'âme sans négliger le corps" (p. 1019; For me observation had already become intuitive; it penetrated the soul without neglecting the body).

When we then read in *El Verdugo* that Victor is "abîmé dans une contemplation ... profonde" (p. 1133), we recognize the same eroticized pattern of penetrating observation attributed to narration by the narrator of *Facino Cane,* except that the third link of the chain of transgression (narration) is suppressed in *El Verdugo,* as is the narrator, the double of an author for whom writing is a culpable occupation.[20] Turning now to the chain of punishment, we will see that the corresponding link suffers a similar fate.

When the drama intensifies (in the second part of the text) Victor begins to fade, and he disappears entirely when catastrophe strikes the dénouement. In his absence, the narrative briefly wanders from voice to voice, then ends abruptly in an anonymous and atemporal epilogue:

Malgré les respects dont il est entouré, malgré le titre d' *El Verdugo* (le Bourreau) que le roi d'Espagne a donné comme titre de noblesse au marquis de Léganès, il est dévoré par le chagrin, il vit solitaire et se montre rarement. Accablé sous le fardeau de son admirable forfait, il semble attendre avec impatience que la naissance d'un second fils lui donne le droit de rejoindre les ombres qui l'accompagnent incessamment. [pp. 1142–43]

[Despite the respect which surrounds him, despite the title *El Verdugo* (the Executioner) that the King of Spain has given the Marquis de Léganès as a title of nobility, he is consumed by grief; he lives a solitary life and is rarely seen. Overwhelmed by the burden of his admirable crime, he seems to be waiting impatiently until the birth of a second son gives him the right to join the shades that are constantly with him.]

No mention is made of Victor's fate; he seems to have retired into the shadows that cover Juanito.

We can, however, locate Victor's path of exit from the text if we reenact his last appearance. He arrives at the scene of the execution in time to see Clara kneeling beneath her brother's sword. Rushing toward her, he proposes to save her in exchange for marriage. In response, "L'Espagnole lança sur l'officier un regard de mépris et de fierté. 'Allons, Juanito,' dit-elle d'un son de voix profond" (The Spanish woman flashed a glance of proud contempt at the officer. "Let's go, Juanito," she said in a firm voice). And then: "Sa tête roula aux pieds de Victor" (p. 1142; Her head rolled at Victor's feet).

We hear no more of Victor. It is at this point that the narrative voice changes, seems to become detached from the tale it relates. Clara's death, Victor's expulsion from the text, and a break in the narrative voice all correspond. In a sense the penalty represented by Clara's death has already been metaphorically inflicted, for the sentence in which Victor last appears, "Sa tête roula aux pieds de Victor," echoes the words with which Victor surrendered to his general after his blinding erotic contemplation: "'*Je vous apporte ma tête!*' s'écria le chef de bataillon en apparaissant pâle et *défait*" (p. 1136 [emphasis added]; *I bring you my head!*' cried the battalion commander, as he arrived looking pale and *discomposed*). In both passages, the stroke of the sword is elided (and the elision is repeated, on a grander scale, by the averted matricide). This is hardly surprising. Since Clara was light, eros, the reflection of Victor's sexuality, her death will mean the deprivation of light, the eclipse of sexuality. As Oedipus accepts the Law—as Juanito seeks retribution in shadow—so Victor beholds his shattered image and figuratively blinds himself. Like Juanito's, his fate is darkness: he enters the deepest shadows of occultation.

It is this darkness that elucidates the change of narrative voice. As the narrative transgression was veiled by metaphors of eros and of light, so, too, is the punishment meted out for the transgression. Clara's death means blindness and castration, but it also implies deprivation of narrative power. As Victor, stricken powerless by the knowledge of his transgression, relinquishes his authority and silently fades from the text, the narrative circulates among disparate voices (the soldiers, the general, the anonymous final voice). The crime and punishment spread to the feasting soldiers, whose banquet in fact resembles a totem meal, a festival whose coincidence with the Léganès murder suggests a scandalous and transgressive celebration. However, if this banquet, marked by "le bruit du festin et les rires joyeux des officiers" (p. 1142; the sound of festivities and of the officers' merrymaking) indicates a contagious parricidal rejoicing, it quickly receives the impact of the inflicted retribution, for when the general corroborates the massacre report, "il ne se trouva personne, pas même un sous-lieutenant, qui osât vider son verre" (p. 1142; not a single person, not even a sublieutenant, dared to empty his glass).

Thus the concept of a "real story" confinable to a limited portion of the text, to be identified solely with Juanito's saga, once again proves to be illusory. We read in *El Verdugo* a story preoccupied with the drama of its own narration and the fate of its would-be narrator.

Despite Balzac's obvious reluctance to assign him an overt narrative role, Victor Marchand leaves his signature on the text in the form of a series of "marchandages," or bargainings. The second part of the text, marked by a transition from Victor's story to Juanito's and by a concomitant shift from an internal to an external perspective (Victor's thoughts and sensations are no longer made known to us) nevertheless retains Victor's influence by materializing his name.

The first exchange takes place at the end of what I have labeled the first part of the narrative, in the transitional phase between Victor's story and Juanito's. The language of bargaining is readily perceptible:

Les assassins des Français, prévoyant, d'après la cruauté connue du général, que Menda serait peut-être livrée aux flammes et la population entière passée au fil de l'épée *proposèrent* de se dénoncer eux-mêmes au général. *Il accepta cette offre, en y mettant pour condition* que les habitants du château ... seraient mis entre ses mains. *Cette capitulation consentie, le général promit* de faire grâce au reste de la population. [p. 1137; emphasis added]

[Knowing the general's reputation for cruelty, the Frenchmen's murderers anticipated that Menda might be set on fire and the entire population put to the sword, and so they *proposed* to give themselves up to the general. *He accepted this offer, on the condition* that the château's inhabitants would be put in his hands. *When they consented, the general promised* to spare the rest of the population.]

The second transaction explicitly assigns Victor the role of mediator, or "marchand." Speaking for the marquis, he asks the general for three graces: a change from hanging to an honorable death by decapitation, religious succor in exchange for a promise not to flee, and, most notably, the pardon of one of the sons, in return for which the marquis will give his entire fortune. The general's reply is striking:

"Eh! bien, *qu'il achète l'éternité de son nom,* mais que l'Espagne se souvienne à jamais de sa trahison et de son supplice! Je laisse sa fortune et la vie à celui de ses fils qui remplira l'office de bourreau." [p. 1138; emphasis added]

["Very well, *let him buy the eternity of his name,* but let Spain forever remember his treason and his punishment! I will grant life and fortune to whichever one of the sons will serve as executioner."]

The text labels this transaction quite clearly: "Le jeune officier hocha la tête, en désespérant de voir accepter par un de ces quatre personnages *le marché* du géneral" (p. 1139 [emphasis added]; The young officer shook his head, for he despaired of seeing one of these four people accept the general's *bargain*).

Victor's success as mediator in this bargaining process is crowned by the role exchange he negotiates: "Le bourreau comprit, comme tout le monde, que Juanito avait accepté sa place pour un jour" (p. 1141; The executioner understood, as everyone did, that Juanito had taken his place for a day). Having fulfilled these public mediating functions, Victor fails in his attempt to strike a personal bargain with Clara, in which her life is the object of barter: "Le général t'accorde la vie si tu veux m'épouser" (p. 1142; The general will spare your life if you will marry me).

I want to argue that each of these "marchés" refers to a more significant *narrative* transaction: the exchange of Balzac's story for Victor's, and Victor's story for Juanito's. It is in this context that Victor Marchand's mediating function becomes essential. For his role, as suggested by his patronym, is to *donner le change*, to lure the reader toward another's story—the Other's story—which is given in exchange for Victor's own, to fool the reader into accepting this story as the "real" one when it is in fact a substitute, a projection of Victor's story, of the narrator's: the story of narrative, of writing.[21]

V

Je dis: une fleur! et, hors de l'oubli où ma voix relègue aucun contour, en tant que quelque chose d'autre que les calices sus, musicalement se lève, idée même et suave, l'absente de tous bouquets.

MALLARMÉ, "Variations sur un sujet"

At the core of this imbricated structure of exchange is the verbal merchandise mediated by the text. The Léganès story represents a series of linguistic transactions, of name exchanges, as the son's name, Juanito (already a diminutive of the father's name), is exchanged for the father's, the Marquis de Léganès, which is replaced by El Verdugo, which in turn gives way to a translation, le Bourreau.

Within the execution scene we can find the standard of exchange, for this scene is a spectacular representation of a passage from the flesh and blood father to the father's name. The marquis dies so that his name may be perpetuated. There is an exchange of blood for language, father for name, real for symbolic. It is of no small significance that commentators stress a lack of character delineation in this text.[22] If these characters are so little developed, it is because they are, in the most literal sense, *des porte-parole*. They exist to carry the word—the word being the name, "Léganès,"—and they are effaced to preserve their subordination to the name. The patronym Juanito inherits through his father's death has as its root the Spanish verb *legar,* derived from the Latin *legare* (*léguer* in French), "to bequeath," "to leave a legacy." Since one must die in order to make a legacy effective, the father's death gives meaning to his name, makes his name signify. By dying, the Marquis de Léganès makes his name a proper one, which subsequently becomes replaceable by a metaphor: El Verdugo.

Thus the father's death opens the possibility of language as signification, as symbolization. The end of the story refers us to the beginning of the Text, for it represents the a priori foundation of writing: the substitution of the semantic illusion (the belief in a natural relationship between signifier and signified) for the referential illusion (the belief in the identity of signified and referent).[23]

The rapport between language and the father, narrative and death, is very much the same for Balzac as for the fictional characters he creates in Juanito and Victor; this is a kind of external evidence that the text reflexively represents its own generative principles. *El Verdugo*, Balzac's first tale of parricide, was written in October of 1829, four months after the death of his father. It is the first text signed "H. de Balzac" by the writer, who here appropriates the particule which Bernard-François, his father, assigned himself. Here, then, Balzac accedes to the patronym. It is also among the very first of the texts that were to figure in the *Comédie humaine*.

The text reposes on a lack which is at the same time a plenitude: the real father dies, but his death guarantees his legacy, which is his name, his name which is his legacy, his law which establishes a symbolic order capable of generating an infinite series of substitutions. The chain that leads from the dead father, the Marquis de Léganès, to his successor, Juanito, the new Marquis de Léganès, to his title, El Verdugo, and then to le Bourreau, culminates in *El Verdugo*—the text. The symbolic order—a precondition for the generation of the literary text—is attained through the father's name once his literal presence is annihilated. The narrative closes upon itself like a Möbius strip, for its fictional pretext plays out its textual conditions of being: death makes life narratable.

My claim that the origin of narrative is death, and its foundation an absence, needs to be qualified by a critical distinction between two very different kinds of literary murder. Both are parricides (at least, figuratively so) but one—the one I have been referring to—nevertheless consecrates paternity as the fundamental ordering source (of families, societies, economies, and also of signs and texts), while the other nullifies it utterly. In the first case we are talking about effacing the father as image (and this kind of absence actually tends to sanctify paternity by calling attention to the empty position, much as transgression strengthens the law it violates). In the second case, we mean that the paternal symbol is effaced. The latter case has more far-reaching consequences, for, in contrast to the former situation, in which an individual is absent from the father's position, it is here the father's *position* which is absent, nonexistent: all signifying sys-

tems are endangered, because the ultimate signifier has come undone. Putting it another way, we might say that the father has
never assumed his name and his nominating functions. These are
Foucault's terms (which lean heavily upon Lacan's), and I would
like to quote directly from his very cogent argument:

Ce n'est . . . pas dans les termes . . . fonctionnels de la carence qu'il faut
penser une lacune fondamentale dans la position du Père. Pouvoir dire
qu'il manque, qu'il est haï, rejeté ou introjecté, que son image passe par
des transmutations symboliques suppose qu'il n'est pas d'entrée de jeu
"forclos," comme dit Lacan, qu'en sa place ne s'ouvre pas une béance
absolue. Cette absence du Pére, que manifeste, en s'y précipitant, la
psychose, ne porte pas sur le registre des perceptions ou des images,
mais sur celui des signifiants. Le non par lequel s'ouvre cette béance
n'indique pas que le nom de père est resté sans titulaire réel, mais que
le père n'a jamais accédé jusqu'à la nomination et qu'est restée vide
cette place du signifiant par lequel le père se nomme et par lequel, selon
la Loi, il nomme. C'est vers ce "non" qu'infailliblement se dirige la
droite ligne de la psychose lorsque, piquant vers l'abîme de son sens,
elle fait surgir sous les formes du délire ou du fantasme, et dans le dés-
astre du signifiant, l'absence ravageante du père.[24]

[It is not in . . . functional terms of deficiency that we understand the
gap which now stands in the Father's place. To be able to say that he is
missing, that he is hated, excluded, or introjected, that his image has
undergone symbolic transmutations, presumes that he is not "fore-
closed" (as Lacan would say) from the start and that his place is not
marked by a gaping and absolute emptiness. The Father's absence, manifested in the headlong rush of psychosis, is not registered by perceptions or images, but relates to the order of the signifier. The "no"
through which this gap is created does not imply the absence of a real
individual who bears the father's name; rather, it implies that the father
has never assumed the role of nomination and that the position of the
signifier, through which the father names himself and, according to the
Law, through which he is able to name, has remained vacant. It is toward this "no" that the unwavering line of psychosis is infallibly directed; as it is precipitated inside the abyss of its meaning, it evokes the
devastating absence of the father through the forms of delirium and
phantasms and through the catastrophe of the signifier.]

Although I want provisionally to situate the *El Verdugo*
parricide under the influence of benign paternal absence (of pa-

ternal order upheld) I want also to emphasize how precarious this position is. The other texts I will turn to provide increasing evidence of the father's "devastating absence" and exhibit a resultant signifying catastrophe. *El Verdugo* is exquisitely balanced between the paternal order it so steadfastly maintains and the impending doom of this order. I say this not so much because of its place in intertextual chronology but because it shows internal signs of a yet unconscious doubting of the father's law and its power to regulate. Although this law is elaborately staged through the juxtaposition of the father's death and the transmission of his name, I think we shall find some curious technical flaws in the representation.

Juanito's agreement to serve as executioner is a capitulation to his father's will; it is specifically expressed as the son's acknowledgment of his biological filiation.[25] For when Juanito at first refuses to comply, his father turns to his mother and asks: "Est-ce mon fils, madame?" (p. 1140; Is this my son, madame?). It is the possibility of nonrecognition (of sonhood, of fatherhood, of the generational bond) that determines Juanito's parricide: in killing the marquis, Juanito answers that he *is* his father's son, and in so doing acknowledges the marquis's fatherhood. The murder which we might otherwise expect to clear access to the mother here becomes an act of renunciation, for in giving death to his father, Juanito takes on the patronymic legacy, recognizes the Law in the transmitted name.

The Law is the law of generations; recognizing it means deferring desire, accepting a (deferred) substitute in the mother's place, moving from the oedipal triad to the generational triad and then to a *new* oedipal triad—in short, living in time. The epilogue of the text implies Juanito's observance of these conditions. Having murdered his father, he chooses a punishment befitting the crime. Like the archetypal parricide, he flees the light: "les ombres . . .[de sa famille] l'accompagnent incessamment" (the shades . . .[of his family] are constantly with him). But death, this final retreat into the shadows, is forestalled by the law transmitted in the dead father's name. The new marquis must wait until the advent of a new generation gives him the right to die: "Il semble attendre avec impatience que la naissance d'un second fils lui donne le droit de rejoindre les ombres" (p.

1143; He seems to be waiting impatiently until the birth of a second son gives him the right to join the shades). This last sentence is worth noting, because it juxtaposes three generations (the shades, Juanito, a son). The son has become the father; the law of generations, represented symbolically by transmission of the father's name, has become the Law. Crime is punished, son replaces father, life redeems death. All seems happily recuperated within the paternal economy.

Balzac is playing a game of *fort/da* here, killing the father and retrieving his authority. Like the child Freud tells of who acts out his mother's anxiety-provoking departure by controlling the disappearance and return of a toy, Balzac is miming a loss he can recover so that he may thereby feign mastery.[26] But there is a margin of loss that falls outside his game plan and escapes his control. I am referring to the anonymous epilogue detached from the identifiable narrative flow, and to a number of logical inconsistencies and formal curiosities within it.

With this last paragraph we pass abruptly from the past tenses of the rest of the text into the present tense. The passage, in its entirety, reads as follows:

Malgré les respects dont il est entouré, malgré le titre d'*El Verdugo* (le Bourreau) que le roi d'Espagne a donné comme titre de noblesse au marquis de Léganès, il est dévoré par le chagrin, il vit solitaire et se montre rarement. Accablé sous le fardeau de son admirable forfait, il semble attendre avec impatience que la naissance d'un second fils lui donne le droit de rejoindre les ombres qui l'accompagnent incessamment. [pp. 1142–43, trans. above]

There is no indication of the amount of time elapsed since the execution; nor is the epilogue itself marked by any time divisions. There is no sense of time passing or to come: the clock seems simply to have stopped. We are left in an eternal present further suggested by the verb *attendre* (to wait). The only temporal distinction is an implied future time in which Juanito will be allowed to merge with the shades which already surround him. Present and future are, then, "shadowed" by the past; the only possible movement in time is this ghostly return to (of) the past.

We are told that the birth of *a second son* will permit Juanito's death. Since by convention fathers wait for a first son and heir to carry on the name, the emphasis on a second son strikes an odd note. Odder still is the fact that although the mention of a second son obliquely introduces a wife and first son, we are told that Juanito lives in isolation ("il vit solitaire" [p. 1143]). Together with wife and son Juanito would have constituted a renewed triad representative of his passage from son to fatherhood. With wife and son suppressed, it is as if Juanito is still the son, still bound primarily to the shadows of his past, which are his ceaseless companions.

All this suggests that Juanito has accepted the law of generations in name only, and that this name, Léganès, is an empty form. Now if the father has been designated as nominating source, and if the father's own name cannot support the charge of meaning invested in it, the entire system of nomenclature begins to crack.

Victor Marchand, pretended merchant of Menda, agent of exchange, is, in the course of the narrative, reduced to nothing. Victim of his vision, blinded to his duty, he is left "sans épée" (p. 1136). When we recall the boast Balzac had inscribed on his bust of Napoleon—"Ce qu'il n'a pas pu achever par l'épée, je l'accomplirai par la plume"[27] (What he could not finish with the sword, I will complete with the pen)—we can appreciate what metaphoric implications this swordlessness has for the text, what narrative story is being told (or exorcised) through this soldier's vignette. Deprived of his honor, his woman, his sword, and his pen, Victor is perhaps more a beggar than a merchant. Since the exchange of Victor's story for Juanito's in effect trades same for same, it yields a repetition, a duplication of loss in which more turns into less, and excess becomes lack. The narrative, tautologically produced, relinquished rather than exchanged, becomes a gratuitous act, and the narrator, would-be seller of tales, a "victor" ironically "vanquished" by his own narration.

In much the same way the text ironically subverts the Cratylistic basis—or bias—upon which it seems to be constructed. The plot is structured upon a metonymic and metaphoric scaffolding which extends the Cratylistic project in two directions: horizontally, through the drama which unfolds as an acting out (and hence a realization) of names (Clara, Victor, Marchand, Menda, El Verdugo), and vertically, via the genealogical playing out (and once again, realization) of proper naming (Juanito's inheritance of the patronym). But the dynamics of plot reshape and displace its foundations. Just as Victor is vanquished, Clara, the purported emblem of light and brilliance, becomes the portent of death and darkness. (She augurs Juanito's early retreat into shadow as well as Victor's disappearance.) The "mandate" of Menda is more accurately an arrogation, an illegitimate presumption, and El Verdugo, Juanito's "title of nobility," is more evidently a title of infamy. So the metonymic representation reveals the noncorrespondence of name and named, the radical impropriety of proper names. We have seen that the metaphoric play fares no better. Juanito's "proper" name is (both literally and figuratively) only nominal; it is the appropriated name of another which becomes his property only when that other (the father, the official name-bearer) is obliterated—at which point it is no longer proper, but figurative.

Juanito's title (and by extension, the text's) rests on equally uncertain authority. In fact he has two titles of nobility: the one, Marquis de Léganès, is patrilineal, the other, El Verdugo, is decreed. It is puzzling that of the two, the one taken as title for this story of succession and transmission is not the birthright but the earned acquisition.

All of these examples are bound by a common thread of perversity running through the text: that is, it persistently makes known the fragility of the order of names it has methodically constructed. It is hard not to recognize in this internal paradox the rehearsal of a suppressed contradiction between textual and extratextual situations.

If we place Juanito's Spain against the (absent) background of Balzac's France, two acutely divergent social contexts emerge. In Spain, we focus on a marquis infatuated with his title—a patriarch whose primary concern is to guarantee the immortality of his name. In France we are only months away from the "bourgeois monarchy." The aristocracy of birth is increasingly doubled by an aristocracy of wealth. There is no longer any need to be born into nobility, for one can earn one's way in. Names and titles are rapidly becoming empty signifiers, commodities irreflective of genealogy.

At a time when traditional sources of authority are failing seriously in France, Balzac turns to Spain to authorize a powerful fantasy of dynastic grandeur. But it is as if some secret knowledge that this is a vision of a dying world were working behind the scenes to mark the representation, to cast doubt on its authority, and to announce the erosion of an apparently triumphant social and textual order.

CHAPTER TWO

Thrice-Told Tale
Une Passion dans le désert

Blinded, and sick with pain from his head wound,
the master stroked each ram, then let it pass,
but my men riding on the pectoral fleece
the giant's blind hands blundering never found.

HOMER, *The Odyssey* (Book IX),
trans. Robert Fitzgerald

 WELL-KNOWN episode of *The Odyssey* draws us into the cave of the barbarian Polyphemus, where Odysseus, imprisoned with his men, first blinds the Cyclops and then drafts a plot designed to outwit him so that the Danaans, undetected, may be led to safety. Trapped in the cave with his own men and the Cyclops's flock of sheep and goats, Odysseus initiates his scheme by putting out the Cyclops's eye with a burning poker. It is hardly a coincidence that Polyphemus is subsequently unable to perceive linguistic difference, unable to detect a linguistic trick; he cannot discern the semantic plenitude disguised within the proper name "Nobody," apparently devoid of semantic content. The presence of Odysseus, who has cunningly taken on the alias "Nobody," is therefore not disclosed to the neighboring Cyclops, for when questioned, Polyphemus responds that Nobody has tricked him. Blinded, Polyphemus cannot "read" language.

Next Odysseus straps each of his comrades, and finally himself, to the underside of a ram. The rams—which in this case may be translated as (scape)goats—are eventually let out to graze, vehicles for a human cargo hidden from their master, Polyphemus. Though his fingers comb the woolly back of every ram as it leaves the cave, the Cyclops seeks no further, so he does not recognize that these are beasts of burden.

The Polyphemus story is a cautionary introduction to Balzac's account, in *Une Passion dans le désert,* of a soldier's highly suspect adventure with a panther. The stratagems employed by Odysseus against the Cyclops (from the blinding scene and its repercussions to the escape ruse) may be read as an allegory of rhetorical and structural strategies deployed by the Balzacian narrator in an effort to "blind" the naive reader, to direct the reading in such a way as to delimit—and thus to limit—the interpretative field.

As readers of this text, we should recognize the irony of playing a Polyphemus-like role of master to the narrator's Odysseus-like plotter, who is unceasingly occupied with eluding our surveillance, thwarting our control in order to preserve the often forbidden content of the text by subverting our reading. If we are to maintain our textual insight, several precautions are in order. We have to be on the lookout for narrative structures which channel our energy toward the solution of minor questions so as to divert it from approaching thornier problems that could snag the superficial textual pattern. We must be wary of literary vehicles whose burden is concealed or obscured, whose figurativeness is disguised as literality. And, as we turn our attention to *Une Passion dans le désert,* we should remember that panthers, like rams, are sometimes also scapegoats dispatched by a cunning plotter to pull the wool over the eyes of an unsuspecting "master."

I

> *Oedipus.* What trouble was so great to hinder you
> inquiring out the murder of your king?
> *Creon.* The riddling Sphinx induced us to neglect
> mysterious crimes and rather seek solution
> of troubles at our feet.
>
> SOPHOCLES, *Oedipus the King,*
> trans. David Grene

A linear plot summary of *Une Passion dans le désert* is an impossibility. We are dealing with a tale which has trouble getting told, trouble finding a teller who will take it to its end, and trouble locating a medium in which to be communicated. It circulates among three potential narrators, plays itself out in alternating written and spoken discourse, and ultimately opts for silence, alluding rather than stating, interrupting phrases rather than carrying them to completion, suppressing certain elements of the story which are introduced only to be suspended and ignored as the text advances.

Reconstructing the plot entails transcending the narrative reticence, filling in a good number of blanks in the text. Any such reconstruction necessarily contains an element of construction, or composition. The reader is in this way implicitly invited to co-author the text; however, the proffered freedom is more pretense than actuality, since foundations for the text's completion have been laid with such care that one tends to build the missing portions upon them unawares.

In an effort to resist such a prestructured reading, the two principal variants established by critical reaction can be compared with Balzac's "unfinished" text, with a view toward disengaging those problems and questions in the original text which are muted or ignored in the "completed" versions. This will lead to an alternative reading of the text, one that allows the previously silenced elements to voice the reasons for their suppression.

We can begin, however, with a brief sketch of what is unambiguously known about Balzac's text. *Une Passion dans le désert* originally appeared in December, 1830, in the *Revue de Paris;* and was published with various revisions and additions in 1837 and 1844. The "Catalogue des ouvrages que contiendra *La Comédie humaine*," compiled in 1845, included *Une Passion dans le désert* among twenty-three titles projected for the *Scènes de la vie militaire;* it was indicated as the third episode of a trilogy to be entitled *Les Français en Egypte.* The first two, however, were never written, and *Une Passion dans le désert,* together with *Les Chouans,* constitute the sole military scenes of *La Comédie humaine* where we find the definitive version of our text, in the Furne edition of 1846.[1]

The text occupies twelve pages in the Pléiade edition, and is divided into three sections. The first and the last fill approximately one page each and frame the ten-page central portion, in which an anecdote is recounted. This middle section represents a written text, while the two outer sections report spoken dialogue.

The opening frame is situated at a menagerie show, where the narrator and his female friend are watching a wild-animal tamer at work with his hyena. The woman's incredulous reaction leads the narrator to recollect his own disbelief when he first witnessed such a demonstration, and this leads him to recall that a fellow spectator (a former soldier) dispelled his incredulity by relating a personal anecdote which demystified wild-animal taming for him. The very end of the section abruptly switches to the woman's home; curious about the soldier's allusions, she wheedles and cajoles until she obtains the narrator's promise to draft the soldier's story for her. She receives the manuscript the following day; whereupon, a blank in our text, and the beginning of the middle section of *Une Passion*.

This middle section is, then, the narrator's written account based on the soldier's verbal narration of his ambiguous adventure with a female panther who befriends and protects him when he is stranded in the Egyptian desert. The narrator writes in the third person, though the internal focus of narration (fixed upon the soldier) suggests an identification with the other's story. After describing the soldier's first encounter with the panther and his growing affection—mixed with a strong dose of hostility—for her, the narrator's text trails off abruptly, in the midst of relating a scene of apparent communion between man and beast. Three dots and a blank replace the missing denouement of this manuscript, and we are forced to substitute the juxtaposed verbal exchange of the closing frame for the absent written conclusion of the narrator's text.

Thus, at an unspecified time and place, when prodded by his lady, the obviously embarrassed narrator falteringly finishes his story aloud, this time citing the soldier's discourse directly, echoing the dialogue which transpired between them, and ostensibly repeating the soldier's conclusion verbatim. According to the soldier, the panther, as if hurt, suddenly turned upon him, seized his thigh in her teeth, and bit him; at this point, to avoid being devoured, he plunged his dagger into her neck. The

panther expired, leaving behind the tearful and remorseful soldier, who has ever since nostalgically remembered the desert.

Two alternative readings of *Une Passion dans le désert* are
readily perceptible. As reader, one can accept the text as is, complete with (or in spite of) its ellipses. One can, that is, adopt the
philosophy that "nothing will come of nothing," and, accordingly not worry about what the suspension points omit or what
the blanks and dashes obliterate. In this case, *Une Passion* becomes the rather trivial story of an exotic friendship.

Alternatively, one can opt to accept Balzac's challenge to a
game of filling in blanks and connecting points. The emergent
pattern reveals the rather thinly veiled erotic nature of this "exotic friendship"; more specifically, the fact (tactfully formulated
by Félicien Marceau) that "les liens entre le soldat et la panthère
sont d'une nature que celle-ci réprouve"[2] (the bonds between the
soldier and the panther are of a nature that Nature condemns).
While the first reading appears overwhelmingly naive in this
more worldly light, it cannot be so easily dismissed, for the second reading incorporates it. The two readings are in fact coop-
erative. The game written into its structure is one of discovery;
it depends upon a passage from naiveté to knowledge, a movement from one reading to the next.

It readily becomes apparent that the text is programmed to
elicit certain predicted responses from the reader through a network of clues. The reader in turn produces a preordained reading
whose very resoluteness is problematic. The second-level reading
is the way we are *supposed* to read; it induces a sense of having
found an answer, the right way to read this text. All this positiv-
ism suggests that there may be a third reading which is *not* supposed to emerge.

Before exploring such a possibility, I want to examine the
mechanisms by which the second reading imposes itself on the
text and the reader, to understand how it works and how it does
not. I will take as a model second reading Léon-François Hoffmann's perspicacious analysis of the manner in which a series of
clues permits the reader to decipher the text.[3] My purpose in so
doing is to consider Balzac's projected reading of his text.

Hoffmann seeks to demonstrate that the narrative frame
constitutes a metatext whose function is to indicate to readers

how they should understand the romance of soldier and panther. The narrator, his lady, and the allusions to their liaison serve several strategies formulated to direct our interpretation of the central anecdote. The narrator's role was invented, suggests Hoffmann, to replace the soldier's, and the indirect narration of the desert friendship indicates its scabrous nature. The erotic tone is heightened by the fact that the narrator agrees to write rather than to tell the story, thus assuring himself time for reflection and the protection of rhetorical evasiveness. And even then, the written account breaks off "au moment critique"[4]—after describing a caress and a knowing look exchanged between man and beast.

The woman's role, continues Hoffmann, is to introduce a need for modesty and to motivate the use of tact and indirection. Also, the allusion to a scene in which the woman induces the narrator (perhaps by seducing him) to deliver the soldier's tale is a sexual marker whose function is to tinge the atmosphere of the entire text with an erotic glow.

Less immediately available to modern readers is a clue contained in the fact that the opening scene of the frame is set at "la ménagerie de M. Martin" (p. 1219), as is the narrator's encounter with the soldier. The animal tamer Henri Martin opened in Paris in December 1829 and became an overnight celebrity. It was widely rumored that he owed his success to his habit of sexually sating the animals before the performance.[5] The allusion to Martin would have been a useful orientation device for the reader of 1830.

While Hoffmann concentrates on metatextual elements in the frame, he also discusses the sustained application to the panther, in the middle section, of metaphors better suited to a woman than a beast and links this technique to the sexualization of the soldier's friendship with her.

Since many of these structural and rhetorical devices were not present in the first version of Balzac's text, Hoffmann maintains that they represent a deliberate effort on the part of the writer to "load" the text, to lead us to a very specific reading of it. For Hoffmann, the ultimate interest of this text lies less in the erotic reading of the anecdote than in the narrative techniques used to induce us to read it as erotic: "Je dirais même qu'ici l'anecdote est au service de l'écriture, et non pas le contraire"[6] (I would even say that the anecdote is in the service of the writing, and not the other way around).

That Balzac constructed a set of clues for the reader I think is indisputable. More open to question, however, is the motivation Hoffmann attributes to this design. His explanation of the text's strategic system assumes that the anecdote is subordinate to the narrative discourse, and thus reduces the text to a bout of textual pleasure, or play. But this view sustains what seems to me an unnecessary—and false—polarization of story and discourse (despite Hoffmann's inversion of the traditional hierarchy, wherein story is privileged and discourse subordinated to it). I would suggest a more continuous theory of textuality, according to which discourse and story (roughly equivalent to frame and anecdote, in this case) have equal status and are inherently bound by a metaphoric and metonymic complicity.

I would also argue that the very insistence of Balzac's system of textual indices makes the textual game-playing thesis liable to suspicion. Hoffmann's resolution is neat. With a deft touch, he unveils all that Balzac (with the imputed intention of making his reader play detective) has methodically (though lightly) veiled. He adds up the clues and deduces the corresponding erotic plot. Realizing, however, that the gravity of the "crime" (the enigmatic anecdote) does not quite measure up to the overwhelming array of clues provided for its solution, he concludes—too neatly—that it is in fact a kind of exercise in detection.

We are less gullible when we read detective novels. We know that one (often facile) solution to the crime is frequently given as a decoy in the opening chapters to prevent the reader from seeking a more tangled truth. The precipitous first explanation invariably has cracks in it which, when perceived, become clues that lead toward a less evident solution.

By analogy, I suggest that in *Une Passion dans le désert*, Balzac holds out a series of systematically prepared clues conceived to lead us to a false sense of discovery; he allows us to discover one "crime" set in our path as a lure to divert our investigatory or interpretative instincts and to prevent the uncovering of a deeper "crime." But there are cracks in Hoffmann's interpretation, or, more accurately, in Balzac's carefully prepared reading of *Une Passion dans le désert*, and a look at these cracks

will indicate what direction our investigation of an alternative
plot should take.

II

The Truth must dazzle gradually
Or every man be blind—

EMILY DICKINSON (#1129)

One of the more puzzling aspects of this text is its fragmentation:
details mentioned once and then left dangling, allusions which
are never clarified, missing or severed links which distort or obscure textual associations. The general narrative malaise referred
to earlier suggests that there may be more behind this stylistic
awkwardness than the mere carelessness of a young author yet
unskilled in his craft. When the loose ends are gathered and re-
connected, we may find that they have been severed and displaced in a most significant way.

Before the narrator mentions the anecdote which forms the
core of this text, he reveals an interesting fact about the Provençal soldier who is both subject and original narrator of this
anecdote. Relating his encounter with the soldier, he describes
him: "Je me trouvais alors près d'un ancien militaire *amputé de
la jambe droite* entré avec moi" (p. 1219 [emphasis added]; I
found myself next to an old soldier *whose right leg was amputated,* who had come in with me). This rather dramatic detail has
no apparent suite. We do, however, find an allusion to a leg in-
jury at the end of the text, when the narrator directly quotes the
soldier's conclusion to his tale:

"Je ne sais pas quel mal je lui ai fait, mais elle [la panthère] se retourna
comme si elle eût été enragée; et, *de ses dents aiguës, elle m'entama la
cuisse,* faiblement sans doute. Moi, croyant qu'elle voulait me dévorer,
je lui plongeai mon poignard dans le cou." [p. 1232; emphasis added][7]

["I don't know how I hurt her, but she [the panther] turned around as
if she were enraged; and, *with her sharp teeth, she bit into my thigh*—
no doubt gently. And I, thinking she would devour me, plunged my
dagger into her neck."]

We are not told how or why the soldier lost his leg; neither
are we informed about the outcome of the panther's attack on

the soldier's thigh. Nevertheless, it is difficult not to associate these two items and not to attribute the amputation (directly or indirectly) to the panther bite. Thus it is exceedingly strange that no connection is made or even hinted at by the narrator, and stranger still that the soldier's account of his post-desert experience seems deliberately to obviate the possibility of such a connection: "—Eh bien, monsieur, reprit-il après un moment de silence, j'ai fait depuis la guerre en Allemagne, en Espagne, en Russie, en France; j'ai bien promené mon cadavre" (p. 1232; Well, sir, he continued after a moment's silence, since then I've fought in Germany, Spain, Russia, and France; I've hauled my carcass around quite a bit). The logical challenge to an already obscured textual connection suggests that the text is resisting any coherent formulation of the amputation-panther correlation. But the voice of incoherence calls attention to a text divided against itself, guarding against internal leaks.

The narrator's manuscript introduces another enigmatic incident. In the middle of the desert, the soldier has found a grotto which will shelter him for the night. Anxious to protect himself against marauding animals, he fells a date palm which he wants to use as barricade:

Malgré son ardeur, malgré les forces que lui donna la peur d'être dévoré pendant son sommeil, il lui fut impossible de couper le palmier en plusieurs morceaux dans cette journée; mais il réussit à l'abattre. Quand, vers le soir, ce roi du désert tomba, le bruit de sa chute retentit au loin, et ce fut comme un gémissement poussé par la solitude; le soldat en frémit comme s'il eût entendu quelque voix lui prédire un malheur. [p. 1223]

[Despite his eagerness, despite the strength given him by the fear of being devoured in his sleep, he was unable to cut the palm in pieces during the day, but he did manage to chop it down. When, toward evening, this king of the desert fell, the noise of its fall echoed far and wide, as if solitude were moaning; the soldier shuddered as if he had heard a voice predicting misfortune.]

The noise made by this tree falling is metaphorically compared to a prediction of calamity uttered by some unknown voice: in other words, to an oracle. The prophesied "malheur" is fulfilled by the double violence at the text's end: the murder (and loss) of the panther, the wounding (and loss) of the soldier's leg. But it is hard to know what to make of this oracle in the middle of the desert. If the prediction is, as it appears to be, a punishment for cutting down the tree, what vengeful god has been offended? Why is the entire episode suspended as soon as it has been evoked? If we knew why the tale of the felled tree were cut short, might we also be able to explain why the amputation story is elided? That is, could it be more than a coincidence that the reader is doubly "stumped" by these two truncated accounts?

With these questions in mind, we need to reexamine the erotic plot which Balzac has arranged for us to uncover like a secret buried in the text. The soldier's zoophilic perversion seems a rather simplistic secret core of this text. Such a solution ignores the problems mentioned above and leaves a myriad of other questions unaddressed as well. It does not consider the two peculiarly antithetical threads of the erotic plot, which is as much zoophobic as zoophilic. It overlooks the very aggressive nature of the soldier's affection, expressed in dagger-blade caresses and assassination projects, and does not deal with the panther's reciprocal display of tenderness, enhanced by the ever-present threat of devouring or dismembering, and is thus at a loss to follow the two threads to the point at which they merge in the violent consummation of the text, bound in an embrace which juxtaposes orgasmic tremors and death throes.

We need to take another look at the connection between the story and the frame. Is the exotic scandal sufficient explanation for the fluctuating modes of discourse (writing, speaking in monologue, dialogue, and citation) which seem necessary to overcome the narrator's reluctance to transmit the story? On the other hand, can the frame be neatly dispensed with as an erotic clue which is not an integral part of the story? We should consider the possibility that the erotic components of frame and anecdote are reciprocally referential, that the erotic adventure is "framed" by the narrative structure to protect another scandal lurking in the background.

We should reflect upon the significance of embedding a text within a text, and recognize the difficulty of distinguishing between story and frame, especially in this case where the inner text cannot be contained by its own textuality, and, taking an oral form, flows over its bounds into the frame. So we must consider story and frame, tale and telling, as an integral unit, ever asking, "How can we know the teller from the tale?" and ever answering that we cannot.

Finally, we should carefully examine the sustained feminine metaphor applied to the panther, which extends to the point of our being told that the soldier names the beast Mignonne after his first mistress. Several explanations of this panther-woman assimilation have been offered. As mentioned earlier, Hoffmann attributes the progressive metamorphosis of the animal to the gradual eroticization of the friendship, coupled with the onset of a hallucinatory state caused by the soldier's solitude, his exposure to the blazing sun, his lack of human contact. According to this theory, the multiplication of feminine metaphors is dually determined: it is an allusion to the zoophilic plot, but even before that, a symptom of mental derangement. Such an interpretation grants the hallucination a primacy which both causes and excuses the erotic aberration.

Another possible explanation is suggested by Patrick Berthier, in his introduction to *Une Passion*:

Il faudrait pointer tous les mots par lesquels Balzac, plus ou moins innocemment, force la vraisemblance animalière: bracelets, fourrure, robe, pierreries et même "simarre", et aussi les gestes de tendresse, l'attitude à la toilette, etc. Peut-être pensait-il que plus Mignonne serait femme, moins son aventure, même suggérée, paraîtrait scandaleuse? [p. 1217]

[We ought to note all the words by which Balzac, more or less innocently, strains the limits of animal description: bracelets, fur, robe, jewels, and even "simar"; and also all the gestures of tenderness, all the poses "à la toilette," etc. Perhaps he thought that the more Mignonne seemed a woman, the less scandalous her adventure (although only alluded to) would appear?]

Each of these hypotheses argues a similar point, from slightly differing perspectives. That is, the feminine comparisons are intended to attenuate the scandal of this adventure. I would argue that the result is just the opposite; the more the panther takes on a feminine identity, the more profoundly scandalous this text becomes.

The metaphorical fabric bears a curious pattern. In repeated cases, the features of the panther that elicit female personification or summon visions of the soldier's former mistress are not arbitrary; on the contrary, such comparisons seem to be motivated by a limited field of observed traits. More specifically, the language of resemblance tends to be activated by the soldier's various perceptions of the panther as ferocious, predatory, menacing, cruel, rigorous, jealous, demanding, imperious, and guileful.

Now metaphors are not unidirectional. When we compare Achilles to a lion, not only are we saying that Achilles possesses a certain quality (courage); we are implicitly selecting or confirming this particular quality as that which determines "lionness." Thus we inevitably reveal our conception of the comparing term, or vehicle, as we express an idea about the term compared, or subject.

So the feminizing rhetoric of this text speaks as much of the narrator's image of women as of his feelings toward panthers. The description of the soldier's first sight of the panther (where we find the first flagrantly feminine reference) is a case in point:

Enfin elle baîlla, montrant ainsi l'épouvantable appareil de ses dents et sa langue fourchue, aussi dure qu'une râpe. *"C'est comme une petite maîtresse! . . ."* pensa le Français en la voyant se rouler et faire les mouvements les plus doux et les plus coquets. Elle lécha le sang qui teignait ses pattes, son museau, et se gratta la tête par des gestes réitérés pleins de gentillesse. [p. 1225; emphasis added]

[At last she yawned, displaying the terrible apparatus of her teeth and her forked tongue, rough as a file. "She's like a charming mistress! . . ." thought the Frenchman as he watched her gentle and coquettish way of rolling about. She licked the blood that stained her paws and her muzzle, and scratched her head with repeated gracious movements.]

It is a bit disconcerting to locate the context of the soldier's comparison. For his silent exclamation of recognition, "C'est comme une petite maîtresse!" follows his first view of the panther's terribly equipped mouth, her teeth, her blade-like forked tongue. It is logical to assume that this awesome cutting edge is the rather curious tenor of the metaphor, the common property which allows one term (mistress) to replace the other (panther). This is so despite the fact that the comparison is grammatically linked to a less startling observation: ". . . pensa le Français *en* la voyant se rouler et faire les mouvements les plus doux et les plus coquets" (emphasis added). The panther's dreadful weapon spontaneously inspires the feminine metaphor, which metonymically generates the description that *retroactively* justifies the metaphor. In the next sentence, the nominally gentle, flirtatious gestures ("doux," "coquets") are revealingly detailed: "Elle lécha le sang qui teignait ses pattes, son museau. . . ." The mention of the bloodstained paws and muzzle returns us to the original implied tenor of savagery and menace. In view of the back-and-forth pattern of implication and denial which is emerging, it comes as no surprise that this connotation is no sooner prepared then denied, again grammatically, by a prepositional clause which explains *how* the panther licks off the blood: "par des gestes réitérés pleins de gentillesse."

Nevertheless, the work of revision does not sufficiently obscure the connection that sparks the metaphor, which recurs too often in this text to be ignored. So we are confronted by still another element which defies the simplicity and integrity of the zoophilia plot it ostensibly serves.

This "official" plot is delineated by a series of allusions, ellipses, and double entendres, which are scattered or "plotted" for the reader like a design of dots which must be connected. If we draw the lines we are meant to draw, we are led to believe that the use of various forms of reticence constitutes a rhetorical strategy designed to the specifications of the bestiality plot, whose unspeakable nature calls for indirection but also indication.

But reticence, like any figure, is two-faced, and is capable of betraying the authorial plotter who depends upon it for strategic purposes. It is by definition unreliable: "La *Réticence* consiste à s'interrompre et à s'arrêter tout-à-coup dans le cours d'une phrase, pour faire entendre par le peu qu'on a dit, et avec le secours des circonstances, ce qu'on affecte de supprimer, *et même souvent beaucoup au delà*"[8] (*Reticence* consists of breaking off suddenly in the middle of a sentence, to make known by the little one has said, and with the help of circumstances, what one pretends to suppress, *and often even much more*). As Fontanier suggests, it is impossible to enforce a distinction between the "pseudo-suppressed" ("ce qu'on affecte de supprimer") and the truly suppressed or repressed ("beaucoup au delà"). Reticence is a kind of Pandora's box which can neither be controlled nor made to release its hidden contents selectively, once opened.

This is why the strategy whose purported function is to mask (and to entice the reader to unmask) scandal also reveals some thematic and narrative elements marginal to the scandal unmasked; the metaphoric feminization of a panther, the enigmatic maiming of a limb, the prophetic felling of a tree, the brutal representation of eroticism, the choppy delivery of a story. Here, I would argue, is the "beaucoup au delà," or the underside, of reticence, the part—supposed to remain hidden—which emerges nonetheless.

The blush of reticence which suffuses the text is more than an indication of excessive modesty and more than a sign of textual pleasure: it is, at its least, a provocative invitation to consider the disavowed plot. I will begin to respond by rereading the rhetoric of femininity and sexuality surrounding the panther, interrogating not only the figure of the woman but the letter of the beast.

III

Down from the waist they are Centaurs, though women all above. But to the girdle do the gods inherit. Beneath is all the fiend's. There's hell, there's darkness, there is the sulphurous pit; burning, scalding, stench, consumption.

SHAKESPEARE, *King Lear*

Very soon after the beginning of *Une Passion,* the narrator describes his first glimpse of the Provençal soldier:

Je me trouvais alors près d'un ancien militaire amputé de la jambe droite entré avec moi. Cette figure m'avait frappé. C'était une de ces têtes intrépides, marquées du sceau de la guerre et sur lesquelles sont écrites les batailles de Napoléon. [p. 1219]

[I found myself next to an old soldier whose right leg was amputated, who had come in with me. This figure/face had struck me. He had one of those intrepid presences/heads stamped with the seal of war, and upon which Napoleon's battles are written.]

It is interesting to follow the shifting nominatives which designate the soldier in these three sentences. He is first named "un ancien militaire amputé de la jambe droite." This descriptive designation next becomes simply "cette figure," and is finally once again extended to yield another description, abstract this time: "une de ces têtes intrépides, marquées du sceau de la guerre et sur lesquelles sont écrites les batailles de Napoléon." Now, "figure" and "tête" quite obviously each denote, by metonymy, "person" or "character." But if we read literally, three parts of the body are indicated here: leg, face, and head, respectively. The upward movement or displacement draws attention away from the (absent) limb toward the head, which has an over-insistent presence: it not only bears the seal of war, but also is a text on which Napoleon's battles are written. Without probing too deeply into how one poor head can carry such a heavy weight of signification, it is important to note that the signified intrepidity is both over- and underdetermined. The narrator metaphorically speaks of the soldier's head (or person) as a text teeming with marks or letters—which by analogy, should correspond to facial (or corporal) traits. Yet the only physical detail we are given is that this soldier has a missing leg. The distinguishing trait, or mark, is an amputation, a lack, an excision; the letter is a blank, a signifying gap inscribed on a human writing surface. In place of writing there is blankness; that is, *writing is this blank*. We read a significant absence, albeit disguised (or displaced) as presence. The superficial textuality imputed to the head in fact represents a trompe-l'oeil attempt to cover up the only described physical trait—the missing one—that matters, because it alone spells out war and Napoleonic battles.

I am suggesting that this rhetorical legerdemain exemplifies the narrative strategy which dominates the text, and consequently that being aware of how it operates in this particular case provides a major clue to how to read the text as a whole. Keeping in mind that the intrepid head/text covered with *letters* is in fact a *figure* ("cette figure"), a presence substituting for an original absence (the severed limb) which is ultimately the signifying source, I think we have to anticipate that what appears to be literal may actually be figurative, and that figurative presence will often replace significant lack or absence. We will then have to seek meaning in the blank spaces of this text, between the lines, in the intertextual interstices, reaching toward an evacuated or decentered generative source.

We have seen that a woman is metaphorically present in *Une Passion*, ostensibly invoked to qualify the soldier's relationship with the panther. But closer contextual examination of some of the comparisons has suggested that the woman's role may be far more complex and much less subordinate than a first reading would have us believe. On the suspicion that metaphorization may turn out to be an attenuated or compromise form of textual occultation, we must pursue the attempt to extricate the grounds of comparison, curious to discover what constitutes femaleness, what constitutes pantherness, and wherein lies the connection.

If we assemble the scattered feminine traits established metaphorically and divide them into three major features, we can begin to compose a working sketch of an elusive female figure. Most striking are the numerous details descriptive of the panther's physical characteristics and accoutrements, which most notably evoke her supple and voluptuous body. The soldier addresses her as "ma petite blonde" (p. 1228); he admires "les lignes moelleuses et fines des contours, la blancheur du ventre, la grace de la tête . . . sa souplesse" (pp. 1230–31; her fine, supple lines, the whiteness of her belly, her graceful head . . . her lithe form); he caresses her as he would "la plus jolie femme" (p. 1226). This physical sensuality is very much dependent on ornamental elegance and luxury: some velvety patches around the panther's paws form "pretty bracelets" (p. 1224); there are numerous ambiguous references to the lushness of her fur and her "robe"; she alternately gleams and glitters like gold and jewels.

A second feminizing attribute is the panther's flirtatiousness, her capriciousness. She is a "courtisane impérieuse" (p. 1226) and resembles "une femme artificieuse" (p. 1227). Her movements are described as "coquets" (p. 1225) and she merits the appellation "la coquette" (p. 1231). She is the soldier's "capri-

cieuse compagne" (p. 1226); we are told that "parfois elle pro-
voquait le soldat en avançant la patte sur lui, par un geste de
solliciteur" (p. 1229; sometimes she provoked the soldier by putting her paw out in a soliciting gesture).

An oxymoronic quality of aggressive seductiveness (or seductive aggressiveness) emerges as the third determinant of the
panther's womanlike nature. She is a "tranquille et redoutable
hôtesse" (p. 1224); a "farouche princesse" (p. 1226); a "terrible
compagne" (p. 1227). As was the case with his first (human)
passion, this bestial passion constantly exposes the soldier to the
danger of attack and mutilation and requires his own aggressive
instincts to be in a perpetual state of alert.

Thus the system of metaphors establishes a consistent series
of traits which delineates the figure of a feminine persona.
Though a literal feminine presence is denied to this text, women
are very much present in Balzac's other works, where they are
not infrequently compared to wild animals. A glance at some
such instances, inversions of the metaphoric beast-woman pattern we have uncovered in *Une Passion,* will facilitate our efforts
to find the woman evacuated from this text, and to understand
why she is so metaphorically insistent in absentia.

La Fille aux yeux d'or presents the most systematized assimilation of a woman to a creature of the wild.[9] Even the Parisian
apartment where the intrigue unfolds recalls the desert seclusion
of *Une Passion,* for the exotic Oriental decor is an oasis-like
enclosure as far from the Parisian mainstream as if one were "au
milieu du Grand Désert"[10] (in the middle of the Great Desert).
This shift of contexts will be of particular interest later when we
find references to France and vestiges of civilized life intruding
into the wilds of the Egyptian desert.

Most striking is the physical resemblance between Paquita
(la fille aux yeux d'or) and Mignonne. Mignonne's feminization
is matched by Paquita's "felinization," and Mignonne's gleaming
golden eyes reappear in Paquita, who has "deux yeux jaunes
comme ceux des tigres"[11] ("two yellow eyes like a tiger's").

Although intriguing, the physical analogy becomes really
useful only when replaced in the larger narrative context, where
it becomes evident that the beast-woman and the woman-beast
play similar roles within their respective texts, for the very reason

that the nature of each of these roles is inherently dualistic. Neither woman nor panther can be conceptualized independently, though each text accords dominant (literal) status to one of the two and subordinates (metaphorizes) the other. Such a relationship of complementarity means that the wild fille aux yeux d'or can tell us something about the woman disguised in panther's clothing.

When considering Paquita Valdès, we cannot avoid observing "la femme" as well as "la fille," for Paquita is symbolically—and almost literally—welded to her mother, an old slave originally purchased "for her rare beauty" but now described as "la terrible harpie" (p. 1081). Despite Paquita's beauty, she is an ironic replica of her monstrous mother. The mother, too, has yellow eyes, eyes in which appear "l'éclat froid de ceux d'un tigre en cage qui sait son impuissance et se trouve obligé de dévorer ses envies de destruction" (p. 1081; the cold glare of a caged tiger who knows he is powerless and is obliged to swallow his hunger for destruction). Her quarters are referred to as her "tanière" (p. 1108; lair). She is "une hyène à laquelle un jaloux a mis une robe" (p. 1065; a hyena upon whom some jealous man has put a dress)—which description carries a very distinct echo of the panther Mignonne.

Never was the question of origins—and of endings—more inescapable. A rendezvous between Paquita and her lover, de Marsay, takes place before her mother's vigilant eyes, and leads to the following reflection, on his part:

Cette femme décrépite était là comme un dénouement possible, et figurait l'horrible queue de poisson par laquelle les symboliques génies de la Grèce ont terminé les Chimères et les Sirènes, si séduisantes, si décevantes par le corsage, *comme le sont toutes les passions au début.* [p. 1080; emphasis added]

[This wasted woman was there like a potential denouement, and called to mind the horrible fish-tail with which the allegorical geniuses of Greece completed their Chimeras and Sirens, whose bodices are so seductive, so deceptive, *just like the beginning of all passions.*]

This rather complicated three-tiered metaphor first tentatively compares Paquita (and the passion she represents) to her mummified mother: "un dénouement possible." The potential outcome of love is figured by this decayed female creature who stands for aging and death. But the metaphor is gripping, because it is doubled by an implicit metonymy; we know that the mother was once beautiful, like the daughter, and she thus represents the continuation of the daughter's life and image. The temporal metaphor is next spatialized, and the original subject and vehicle are conflated to form the subject of the following comparison. Now passion and hag together are likened to "l'horrible queue de poisson" (literally a fish-tail, but figuratively an arbitrary or insignificant ending) attached by the Greeks to "les Chimères et les Sirènes." At this point, an extension of the vehicle (the upper region of the mythical beings whose nether parts figured earlier) quite dexterously turns back to the original subject. Despite their horrible termination, chimeras and sirens are "si séduisantes, si décevantes par le corsage, comme le sont toutes les passions au début." As Paquita and her mother are metonymically related, they together form a Chimera, a Siren, the image of passion's course; as they are metaphorically related, either one of the two figures all the other elements of the chain.

Several points should be extricated from this tangled string of metaphors. We should take special note of the metaphorical and metonymical equivalence of Paquita and her mother; this rapport, coupled with an almost constant spatial proximity, leads to the postulation of a profound primary identity which is only secondarily split or divided into two personae. This means that we, like de Marsay, have to deal with a composite figure which juxtaposes the enticement of beauty and sensuality with the threat of violence and the menace of death.

The queue de poisson metaphor can be singled out and juxtaposed to the similar category of reptilian women so common in Balzac. We find another version of this in the person of Paquita, who seizes her lover's body, "s'entortillant autour de lui comme un serpent" (p. 1083; twisting around him like a serpent). But the queue de poisson metaphor is of particular interest because it presents an internal contradiction. In its literal acceptation, a fish-tail appended to a woman makes a mermaid and creates an alluring visual presence. In a figurative sense, a woman (or a passion) ending "en queue de poisson" amounts to nought, signifies little, evanesces, *entails a lack*. Once again we find presence—very insistent presence—used to express absence.

We can locate another (and ultimately similar) ambiguity in the person of Paquita. The denouement clears up a mystery that has pervaded the text up to this point: that of Paquita's knowing innocence. Paquita is bisexual; she belonged to the marquise and was a woman's erotic slave before meeting de Marsay and being enthralled by a man. This symbolic hermaphroditism defies Henri's sense of his own masculinity and brings about a symbolic castration. In a moment of ecstatic transport, Paquita, the incarnation of female perfection for Henri, cries out to him, *using a woman's name* instead of his own (Mariquita, the marquise's nickname). Thereupon "il reçut au milieu de sa joie un coup de poignard qui traversa de part en part son coeur mortifié pour la première fois" (p. 1102). Using metaphors of emasculation, the text records the dual movement whereby Paquita inadvertently reveals her own ambiguous sexual identity (her Sapphic past) and unwittingly calls into question de Marsay's sexuality:[12]

L'exclamation de Paquita fut d'autant plus horrible pour lui qu'il avait été détrôné du plus doux triomphe qui eût jamais agrandi sa vanité d'homme. L'espérance, l'amour et tous les sentiments s'étaient exaltés chez lui, tout avait flambé dans son coeur et dans son intelligence; puis ces flambeaux, allumés pour éclairer sa vie, avaient été soufflés par un vent froid. [p. 1104]

[Paquita's exclamation was all the more horrible for him because he had been dethroned from the sweetest triumph that had ever inflated his male vanity. Hope, love—all emotions—had been excited in him, his heart and his wit had been ablaze; then these torches, kindled to light up his life, had been blown out by a cold wind.]

Such an itinerary of sexual illusion and loss is traveled many a time by Balzac's characters. Representations of men whose masculinity is compromised by involvement with women whose femininity is both less than and more than it should be (because supplemented by apparently masculine attributes or characteristics) are legion.

Sarrasine presents a similar case. A severe blow is dealt to the protagonist's masculinity when he discovers that the "ideal woman" he has fallen in love with is in fact a castrato:

"Et c'est une illusion!" s'écria-t-il. Puis, se tournant vers Zambinella: "Un coeur de femme était pour moi un asile, une patrie.... Quelle espérance puis-je te ravir pour toutes celles que tu as flétries? Tu m'as ravalé jusqu'à toi. *Aimer, être aimé!* sont désormais des mots vides de sens pour moi, comme pour toi. Sans cesse je penserai à cette femme imaginaire en voyant une femme réelle."[13]

["And it is an illusion!" he cried. Then, turning toward Zambinella: "A woman's heart was a sanctuary, a homeland, for me. . . . What hope can I tear from you for all those that you have blighted for me? You have reduced me to your own level. *To love, to be loved!* These are henceforth empty words for me, as for you. I will never cease to think of this imaginary woman when I see a real woman."]

These lines suggest, as Barthes has pointed out, that castration becomes contagious, and that Sarrasine (the protagonist) is himself contaminated.[14]

   A man desires another man under the illusion that this other is a woman. The revelation of the truth (the beloved is another male) is emasculating, all the more so because it prophetically takes the form of the effect it will produce (the other male is a castrato), so that there is a doubling or mirroring effect. Yet even this is not the real scandal of the text, which does not dare formulate the idea it nevertheless doesn't quite succeed in hiding. "Loving and being loved are henceforth empty words," says Sarrasine. Semantic emptiness clearly reflects the loss or lack effected by castration.[15] "I will never cease to think of this imaginary woman when I see a real woman." The real woman is condemned always to bear the mark (the mark of absence) of the imaginary woman—the castrato, that is. In words which indicate a regression to childhood sexual theories, Balzac's character reveals the belief that woman is but a castrated version of man. As such she carries a vital threat, a warning of potential punishment. *Sarrasine* can be read as an allegory of very basic sexual apprehensions and misapprehensions. It offers an insight into other works which impose various transmutations and revisions upon the original (mis)conceptions.

A vision of woman as creature of the wild dramatically dominates a short text, *Voyage de Paris à Java,* in which sexuality and sex roles are once again put in question.[16] The text is less a story than a mythical treatise on love as epitomized by the Javanese woman; as such, it presents some startling erotic conceptions.[17] The most extraordinary feature of these conceptions is their underlying consistency with innumerable erotic representations of a less hyperbolic nature throughout the *Comédie humaine.*

In Java, love once again reaches its pinnacle at the intersection of seduction and danger. Surrendering oneself to the seductive powers of a Javanese woman is nothing less than "une folie mortelle" (p. 83; a fatal madness). The narrator describes his own surrender:

Quant à moi, j'y ai succombé, malgré l'effroyable avertissement écrit sur le front de ces Javanaises, presque toutes mariées cinq à six fois, et cinq à six fois veuves. Pour un artiste, qu'y a-t-il de plus tentant que de lutter avec ces femmes pâles, frêles, délicates, vampiriques? [p. 84]

[As for me, I succumbed, despite the dreadful warning written on the faces of these Javanese women, almost all married five or six times, and five or six times widowed. For an artist, what could be more tempting then to struggle with these pale, delicate, frail, vampirelike women?]

These vampirelike women are predators—therein lies their glory and their charm.[18] They are praised and desired for their literally consuming passion, which is motivated by an implacable jealousy: "Elles ne vous pardonnent pas même un regard jeté à leur rivale. . . . Leur amour est un feu véritable, il brûle" (p. 86; They don't forgive you for even a single glance cast at their rival. . . . Their love is a real fire, it burns). This is similar to the jealousy which occasions the soldier's assimilation of the panther and his first mistress in *Une Passion.*[19]

In view of the reprise of so many of the character traits associated with the panther of *Une Passion,* it comes as little surprise to note that the Javanese woman is likened to various beasts. Her eyes bear "les langoureuses ardeurs des regards de la

gazelle" (p. 83).[20] The narrator remembers his "blanche Javanaise" (white Javanese woman) as "une biche sur un lit de
feuilles" (p. 103; a doe on a bed of leaves). Even the body movements which typify the Javanese woman are characteristic of a
wild creature: "Le corps d'une Javanaise semble doué de fluidité;
puis il a de ces torsions rapides que nous admirons chez les bêtes
fauves" (p. 84; The body of a Javanese woman seems to flow;
also, it twists rapidly in that way we so admire in wild animals).
It is precisely her resemblance to a beast which makes the Javanese the narrator's sought-after woman: "Ah! les Indes sont la
patrie des voluptés. . . . les Parisiennes pensent, elles font de l'esprit, et la femme de l'Orient est une bête sublime" (p. 104; Oh!
the Indies are the land of sensuality. . . . Parisian women think,
and they are witty, but the Oriental woman is a sublime beast).

As in *Une Passion,* we have here the following rather extended nexus: beast / woman / jealousy / predation / seduction /
mortal danger / mutilation. The reptilian traits which we discovered in *La Fille* are also present, for the Javanese woman "possède les mouvements annulaires des plus gracieux reptiles" (p.
84; has the undulating movements of the most graceful reptiles).
The epigraph of *Voyage de Paris à Java* is in fact a variation of
the "queue de poisson" metaphor applied to Paquita's mother
(and implicitly to woman in general) in *La Fille:* "Je supplie
Votre Majesté d'examiner ces arabesques, qui commencent par
une tête de femme et finissent en queue de crocodile" (p. 78; I
entreat Your Majesty to examine these arabesques, which begin
with a woman's head and end in a crocodile-tail). The unexpected substitution of "crocodile" where the idiom would place
"poisson" has the effect of concretizing the expression while retaining an element of the figurative meaning. The epigraph is
rather overdetermined; it can be traced to at least three motivating sources. First, and quite literally, it is a thumbnail sketch of
the text which, soon after its introduction, is devoted to a rather
lengthy discourse on women, then goes on to discuss the flora
and fauna indigenous to Java, skipping from birds to flowers to
poison trees to monkeys, and eventually mentions the narrator's
introduction to a colony of crocodiles.

Alternatively, we may read the epigraph as a punning commentary on this Javanese voyage which is in the end revealed to

be an illusion of sorts; unbeknownst to the reader, there has been a midstream shift in narrators, so that the original narrator has in fact never accomplished this voyage. His tale is a mixture of fantasy and second-hand account, and as such constitutes a deception. When the text finally "confesses" the sleight-of-hand and disabuses the reader, it in effect ends "en queue de poisson." A bit of diegetic word-play transforms it into "queue de crocodile." However, it would be careless not to recognize the paradox which consists of repeatedly appending a tail to a woman while simultaneously asserting that there is nothing of any significance there.

This contradiction must be read in the light of the lesson of *Sarrasine*. If every woman is perceived as an imaginary woman (that is, a castrated man) who makes love an empty—and thus impossible—word, then restoring meaning—and possibility—to love necessitates restoring the woman's lost object, that is, denying castration (sexual difference). Thus the fish-tail and crocodile-tail represent a compromise formation whose fetishistic purpose is to recognize the absence of a female phallus while preserving it in another form. Not surprisingly, the horror engendered by the real female genitals is only displaced, rarely banished from the text. Thus the Javanese women are described as devouring; they consume men; their love is voracious. The crocodiles which appear near the end of the text are "horribles animaux"; the narrator knows nothing "de plus effrayant que leurs gueules béantes" (p. 101; more frightening than their gaping mouths). The attitude of horror inspired by the disavowed female genitals extends to the fetish, which consequently admits what it denies, as in those cases mentioned by Freud where "both the disavowal and the affirmation of the castration have found their way into the construction of the fetish itself."[21]

Images of a combined woman-beast figure are frequent and widely dispersed in the Balzacian corpus, though I have only examined extended cases, where the metaphor is almost systematized.[22] The repeated use of this configuration, which is consistently endowed with markedly phallic attributes, suggests a fetishistic creative activity. Specifically, the beast constitutes a narrative fetish whose inclusion is necessary to an integral female representation.

IV

Les glaives sont brisés! comme notre jeunesse,
Ma chère! Mais les dents, les ongles acérés,
Vengent bientôt l'épée et la dague traîtresse.
—O fureur des coeurs mûrs par l'amour ulcérés!

BAUDELAIRE, "Duellum"

La femme a un duel avec l'homme, et, où elle ne triomphe pas, elle meurt.

BALZAC, *Letter to Mme. Hanska*

The official version of the scandal represented in *Une Passion* is that a man becomes sexually involved with a panther. The metaphors of femininity applied to the panther (so the report continues) rhetorically effect a transmutation of panther into woman and thus attenuate the impression made on the reader by this heinous crime against nature. But the fact that wild beasts and women are consistently linked in a rhetorical relationship which is the inverse of this one gives us pause for thought.

In "The Purloined Letter," Poe writes of a letter astutely hidden by being left out in the open. A similar technique acts as a cover-up for a troubled and troubling attitude towards women in *Une Passion dans le désert*. The beast, which in numerous other contexts acts as a figure used to describe or qualify a woman, here changes place with the woman (who receives figurative status), and goes on to become a letter which is conspicuously displayed the better to escape detection. This inversion of figurative and literal has the advantage of masking the greater scandal (the systematic abolition of sexual difference) by a lesser scandal (an account of an isolated incident of bestiality). Flipping the metaphor back again unmasks the guarded secret that "la belle *est* la bête" (beauty *is* the beast).

The motivation for reinverting the metaphoric structure of this text (that is, restoring its original position) is threefold. Fundamentally, it has become evident that the authorized interpretation of a literal panther that is figuratively feminine does not provide a sufficiently coherent reading of the text. Next, the juxtaposition of intertextual variants of the beast-woman configuration has strongly suggested that the inverted form found in *Une Passion* is exceptional and constitutes a transformation or revision of an unacceptable primary content into a more permissible (because disguised) form. Finally, this hypothesis receives unspoken textual confirmation through a peculiarly phrased statement which functions as a clue. Leaving M. Martin's menagerie after watching the trainer work with his hyena, the narrator and his friend discuss the act; he tries to diminish her incredulity: "—Vous croyez donc les bêtes entièrement dépourvues de passions? lui demandai-je, apprenez que nous pouvons leur donner tous les vices dus à notre état de civilisation" (p. 1219; "So you think that animals are completely lacking in passion?" I asked her. "Learn that they are subject to all vices resulting from our state of civilization"). This represents a rather unexpected inversion of a truism which maintains that civilized beings are susceptible to all the passions and vices commonly attributed to savage creatures. To state that beasts are subject to all the passions of humans is to bring about a curious reversal of an *idée reçue*, a reversal which reflects the inverted structure of the text. Once we recognize that *Une Passion* is an allegory of a particular conception of femininity, we can admit the panther's vehicular function, and begin to unload its occulted feminine cargo.

The woman bound to the beast is alternately "reine," "sultane," "petite maîtresse," "femme," "courtisane," "petite blonde," "coquette," "compagne." So when one takes a closer look at the physical traits which constitute her femininity, it is discomfiting to discover that a large proportion of them are masculine or connote masculinity. They range from isolated details ("ces barbes rares et droites," [p. 1225]; her sparse, straight whiskers) to reappearing motifs.

One of the most revealing references describes the panther's voice. A mere murmur passes through "un gosier si puissant et si profond, qu'il retentit dans la grotte comme les derniers ronflements des orgues dans une église" (p. 1226; a throat so deep and powerful that it echoed through the grotto like the last throbbing tones of a church organ). Her voice is not only powerful but harsh: "Elle jeta ce cri sauvage que les naturalistes comparent au bruit d'une scie" (p. 1226; She uttered that wild cry that naturalists compare to the grating of a saw). The soldier hears her leaping behind him, "jetant par intervalles ce cri de scie, plus effrayant encore que le bruit sourd de ces bonds" (p. 1228; periodically uttering that grating cry, even more frightening than the thud of her paws). A curious contrast comes into play here. A two-way communication system has been established. If the panther's cry announces her imminent arrival to the soldier, the soldier summons the panther by crying out to her. But while the panther communicates in strident tones ("jetant ... ce cri de scie"), the soldier addresses Mignonne "en voix de fausset" (p. 1228; in a falsetto voice). An element of sexual ambiguity is introduced by this chiasmus, which attributes a male vocal quality to the female and a female vocal quality to the male.

But even more striking is the insistent intrusion of the panther's tail into this text. The first description of the panther quite naturally includes a remark about her tail: "C'était une femelle. . . . La queue musculeuse était également blanche, mais terminée par des anneaux noirs" (p. 1224; It was a female. . . . Her muscular tail was also white, but marked by black rings at the tip). Hereafter hardly a scene with the panther goes by without succumbing to what is evidently a fascination commanded by this impressive tail. In response to the soldier's caresses, "la bête redressa voluptueusement sa queue" (p. 1226; the beast voluptuously raised her tail), a rather ambiguous metaphor of female sexual arousal. Rather curious, as well, to note its effect on the soldier, who had "l'ineffable bonheur de lui voir remuer la queue par un mouvement presque insensible" (p. 1227; the ineffable joy of seeing her almost imperceptibly move her tail). The sexual implications of the soldier's reaction are so clear that they must be veiled by the covering vagueness of a metaphorical fig-leaf (l'ineffable bonheur). Like everything else about the panther, her tail is an object of dread as well as seduction and elicits conflicting reactions in the soldier:

Mignonne ne grondait même plus quand il lui prenait la touffe par laquelle *sa redoutable queue* était terminée, pour en compter les anneaux noirs et blancs, *ornement gracieux,* qui brillait de loin au soleil comme des pierreries. [p. 1230; emphasis added]

[Mignonne no longer snarled when he took hold of the tuft at the tip of *her formidable tail,* to count the black and white rings, those *graceful ornaments* which shone in the sun like jewels.]

The compulsive return of the tail threatens danger. In the middle of a general description of the panther, narrative attention suddenly shifts to focus on the tail: "Elle avait trois pieds de hauteur et quatre pieds de longueur, sans y comprendre la queue. Cette arme puissante, ronde comme un gourdin, était haute de près de trois pieds" (p. 1227; She was three feet tall and four feet wide, without considering her tail. This powerful weapon, rounded like a cudgel, was nearly three feet tall). It is an arm, a weapon. When it does not burst abruptly into the text, it insinuates itself, using mechanisms of displacement and transformation. When, for example, the gleaming rings of the panther's tail undergo a metamorphosis, emerging as the magnetic eyes of a snake, the adjective *magnétique* faithfully retains an element of the tail's compulsive attraction:

La présence de la panthère, même endormie, lui faisait éprouver l'effet que les yeux magnétiques du serpent produisent, dit-on, sur le rossignol. Le courage du soldat finit par s'évanouir un moment devant ce danger. [p. 1225]

[The presence of the panther, even asleep, induced in him the feeling that a serpent's magnetic eyes are said to produce on a nightingale. After a while the soldier's courage began to fail before this danger.]

There is an uncanny metaphorical resemblance between the panther's tail, the felled tree, and the amputated limb. But while the tail is recurrently emphasized, the tree and the leg, as I discussed earlier, are largely suppressed. We can hypothesize that they are symbolically equivalent constituents of a repressed conflict; left in suspension, these two floating limbs eventually merge and are affixed to the panther's rump. The return of the tail represents a graft of repressed material onto the official form of the story.

It should be obvious by now that the tail is not Mignonne's

only weapon; it is in fact a metonymical abbreviation, for Mignonne herself and every facet of her physique and behavior signal violence. Her voice, as we have seen, is compared to a saw. Sharpness is again involved when the narrator speaks of "la rigidité de ces yeux métalliques" (p. 1225; the rigidity of those metallic eyes). The soldier's name for the panther, Mignonne, is a recognition of the character trait she has in common with his first mistress, "qu'il avait surnommée 'Mignonne' par antiphrase, parce qu'elle était d'une si atroce jalousie, que pendant tout le temps que dura leur passion, il eut à craindre le couteau dont elle l'avait toujours menacé" (p.1228;[23] whom he had ironically nicknamed 'Mignonne' because she was so atrociously jealous that for every minute of their passion he lived in fear of the knife with which she had always threatened him).

Apposed to the series of cutting images is another series of destructive metaphors, this one composed of images of devouring. It is not her phallic attributes alone which make the panther a fearsome being. Her terrifying buccal cavity has already been evoked: "l'épouvantable appareil de ses dents et sa langue fourchue, aussi dure qu'une râpe" (p. 1225). In fact, even before his first encounter with the panther, the soldier is filled with "la peur d'être dévoré pendant son sommeil" (p. 1223; fear of being devoured in his sleep). When he sees her for the first time, he takes note of her bloodstained muzzle, remarking to himself that she has eaten well, "sans s'inquiéter si le festin avait été composé de chair humaine" (p. 1224). Though it does not occur to the soldier to worry about whether the banquet included human flesh, it obviously does occur to the narrator. So the idea of being devoured is very quickly associated with Mignonne. The soldier soon watches her licking the blood from her paws and her muzzle (p. 1225) and he begins to wonder, "Mais quand elle aura faim?" (p. 1227; But when she becomes hungry?). His fears are diminished, although the textual portent is intensified, when he finds Mignonne with the remains of his horse: "Les deux tiers environ étaient dévorés" (p. 1227; Approximately two-thirds was devoured). Indeed, the final tragedy is a result of a misunderstanding stemming from the soldier's fears of being devoured: "Moi, croyant qu'elle voulait me dévorer, je lui plongeai mon

poignard dans le cou" (p. 1232; I, thinking that she would devour me, plunged my dagger into her neck).

The much-feared mutilation by severing or devouring suggests a castration threat. That such a threat is embodied by a
female with phallic attributes indicates, here as in *Sarrasine,* a
refusal to recognize female sexuality as such, that is, to accept
sexual difference. Consequently it is disavowed by endowing the
woman with a metaphorical phallus (the tail) and with phallic
attributes—among which are the role of lawmaker and the
power to punish. The representation of Mignonne in fact evokes
the image of a combined parent-figure common to childhood
fantasies, which often portray sexuality in sadistic terms.

We have observed in some detail the curious mélange of
eroticism and aggression ascribed to Mignonne; these ambiva-
lent impulses are no less characteristic of the soldier, who alternately admires her voluptuous body and plots her death by dagger, scimitar, and rifle. At times the erotic and destructive
tendencies coincide:

Il essaya de jouer avec les oreilles, de lui caresser le ventre et lui gratter
fortement la tête avec ses ongles. Et, s'apercevant de ses succès, il lui
chatouilla le crâne avec la pointe de son poignard, en épiant l'heure de
la tuer. [p. 1226]

[He tried to play with her ears, to caress her belly and to scratch her
head hard with his nails. Perceiving his success, he tickled the top of her
head with the point of his dagger, watching for an occasion to kill her.]

The dagger is the implement of both love and death.

In another instance which is remarkably prophetic of what
actually occurs at the end, fondling Mignonne, simultaneously
reaching for his dagger, the soldier "pensait encore à le plonger
dans le ventre de la trop confiante panthére; mais il craignait
d'être immédiatement étranglé dans la dernière convulsion qui
l'agiterait" (p. 1228; still considered plunging it into the belly of
the overconfident panther; but he feared that he might be
strangled immediately in the throes of a final convulsion). Because of the amorous context, the dreaded death throes are cu-

riously evocative of erotic spasms. The "dernière convulsion" is at the very least ambiguous; the more forcefully so when juxtaposed with the parallel scene of the denouement. We here witness the beginning of a scene of great intimacy between the soldier and Mignonne:

Le Provençal et la panthère se regardèrent l'un et l'autre d'un air intelligent, la coquette tressaillit quand elle sentit les ongles de son ami lui gratter le crâne, ses yeux brillèrent comme deux éclairs, puis elle les ferma fortement. [p. 1231]

[The Provençal soldier and the panther looked at each other with an air of understanding; the coquette quivered when she felt her friend's nails scratch her head; her eyes flashed like lightning, and then she shut them hard.]

A set of ellipsis points and a blank in the text suppress the sexual act which is nonetheless signaled. The narrator lets the soldier's words stand for the conclusion of this tale: "Je ne sais pas quel mal je lui ai fait, mais elle se retourna comme si elle eût été enragée; et, de ses dents aiguës, elle m'entama la cuisse, faiblement sans doute. Moi, croyant qu'elle voulait me dévorer, je lui plongeai mon poignard dans le cou" (p. 1232; translation above). In this chaotic mingling of eroticism and aggression, the two superimposed tendencies are ultimately indistinguishable. The soldier's love-play somehow does Mignonne violence; there is every reason to believe that her love-bite is responsible for maiming him. And the soldier's final act of plunging his dagger into Mignonne's neck dramatically assimilates murder and coitus. The dagger is both knife and phallus; the stabbing is simultaneously an act of violence and a re-enactment of the elided sexual penetration.

But this phallic victory is denied even as it is asserted. Mignonne sinks her teeth into the soldier's thigh—as if to devour him. He plunges the dagger into Mignonne. Assuming metaphorical equivalence, the dagger-leg-phallus enters her body . . . and disappears. Deprived of the phallus, bereft of the woman, the soldier is punished. Mignonne paradoxically embodies both the desired object of the transgression and the lawgiver who pun-

ishes it. Her structural resemblance to a combined parent-figure
is startling and invites closer attention. In more ways than one,
the soldier's fantastic Egyptian adventure is mysteriously bound
to his modest Provençal origins.

V

It was well said of a certain German book that "es lässt sich nicht
lesen"—it does not permit itself to be read. There are some secrets
which do not permit themselves to be told. Men die nightly in their
beds, wringing the hands of ghostly confessors, and looking them pit-
eously in the eyes—die with despair of heart and convulsion of throat,
on account of the hideousness of mysteries which will not *suffer themselves* to be revealed. Now and then, alas, the conscience of man takes
up a burthen so heavy in horror that it can be thrown down only into
the grave. And thus the essence of all crime is undivulged.

POE, "The Man of the Crowd"

One might reasonably assume that the soldier's desert passion
constitutes an extraordinary episode of his life. Given the radical
difference of this experience, it is unsettling to find its narration
punctuated by intrusions of past experience whose quotidian
quality does not prevent the conflation of the two. The text is
subject to a dual movement: the manifest exploration of the exotic and the unknown is doubled by a continuing effort to assimilate it to the familiar and the well-known. Lost in the desert, the
soldier is struck by the aspect of the palm trees: "Il regarda ces
arbres solitaires, et tressaillit! ils lui rappelèrent les fûts élégants
et couronnés de longues feuilles qui distinguent les colonnes sar-
rasines de la cathédrale d'Arles" (p. 1221; He looked at the solitary trees and started. They reminded him of the distinctive Sar-
acen columns of the cathedral at Arles, for these columns had
elegant shafts crowned with long leaves). Surveying the desert
sands and sky, the soldier dreams of France:

Il sentait avec délices les ruisseaux de Paris, il se rappelait les villes par
lesquelles il avait passé, les figures de ces camarades, et les plus légères
circonstances de sa vie. Enfin, son imagination méridionale lui fit bientôt entrevoir les cailloux de sa chère Provence dans les jeux de la chaleur
qui ondoyait au-dessus de la nappe étendue dans le désert. [p. 1222]

[With what delight he recalled the smell of the gutters of Paris! He remembered the cities he had passed through, the faces of his friends, the most trivial circumstances of his life. His southern imagination even allowed him to glimpse the stones of his beloved Provence in the heat waves which played above the outstretched desert sheet.]

The soldier thus passes his time engaged in a vacillation between opposing poles: "Il eut l'âme agitée par des contrastes. . . . C'était une vie pleine d'oppositions" (p. 1229; His soul was stirred by contrasts. . . . Life was full of oppositions). Even as his desert solitude reveals all its secrets to him, even as he discovers in the desert sunrise and sunset "des spectacles inconnus au monde" (p. 1229; sights unknown to the world), he is drawn back to the past: "Il passait des heures entières . . . à comparer sa vie passée à sa vie présente" (p. 1230; He spent hours . . . comparing his past to his present life).

The series of assimilated binary oppositions (which, we recall, also characterizes the description of the panther) is not limited to the soldier's story; it marks the entire text. Ultimately this narrative provides a record of collapsed polarities: past and present, foreign and familiar, savage and tame, unknown and known are antithetical categories which do not remain distinct.

The question "savage or tame?" which opens the tale and is in play throughout proves itself unresolvable, indeed, unaskable, when the antithesis savage/tame dissolves. At the beginning, the woman accompanying the narrator is aghast and uncomprehending before the paradox of a wild hyena performing as if tamed: "'Par quels moyens, dit-elle en continuant, peut-il avoir apprivoisé ses animaux?'" (p. 1219) ("By what means," she continued, "can he have tamed his animals?"). Later on, the soldier addresses the panther "dont la férocité s'était adoucie pour lui" (whose ferocious nature was now gentle for him), in spite of the conflicting testimony furnished by her bloodied muzzle, speaking to her "comme à un animal domestique" (p. 1229; as if to a house pet). His desire to "faire bon ménage avec la panthère" (p. 1227; live happily with the panther) and his glimpse of his horse's carcass, all but devoured by her, are juxtaposed; the domestic metaphor coincides with the savage tableau. The savage beast deemed by the soldier "si bien apprivoisée" (p. 1230; so well tamed) in the end attacks him; the civilized being who was his first mistress was no different. So there is a constant shifting between savage and tame, which ultimately effaces the polarity.

The troubling pattern of antithesis and synthesis beneath the surface of this text is particularly well described by a representative question which dominates the narrative frame: "known or unknown?" In the opening section, the woman considers the spectacle before her eyes dreadful, too bizarre to be believed, and smiles incredulously (p. 1219). The narrator, on the other hand, declares it to be "une chose naturelle" (p. 1219). He goes on to explain that he had a similar original reaction to such a spectacle: "une exclamation de surprise" (p. 1219). However, his skepticism toward what he at the time termed "this mystery" (p. 1220) was challenged (and eventually dispelled) by the soldier's knowing comment: "Connu!" (p. 1220; Well known!). So known and unknown are opposing elements of an unresolved conflict. Furthermore, the 1845 (Chlendowski) edition of the text divided it into nine chapters; Balzac's title for the first section—"Histoire naturelle d'une histoire surnaturelle"—reinforces the already reiterative use of the polarity.

The question "known or unknown?" receives an enigmatic answer in the closing section of the frame, as the two opposing terms of the polarity fuse. Where the narrator's written text breaks off, the following dialogue ensues:

"Eh bien, me dit-elle, j'ai lu votre plaidoyer en faveur des bêtes; mais comment deux personnes si bien faites pour se comprendre ont-elles fini? . . .—Ah! voilà . . . Elles ont fini comme finissent toutes les grandes passions, par un malentendu! [p. 1232]

["Well," she said to me, "I've read your defense of the beasts; but how did two people who understood each other so well end?"
    "Ah, well! . . . They ended in the way all great passions end; by a misunderstanding."]

The savage (bêtes) slides into the civilized (deux personnes); the very strange love affair is generalized and smoothly transferred to the realm of familiarity (Elles ont fini *comme finissent toutes les grandes passions* [emphasis added]). As the text comes to an end, the soldier's expression of what the affair meant to him closes the space between known and unknown: "Oh! cela ne se dit pas, jeune homme" (p. 1232; Oh! that cannot be told, young man). To the question "known or unknown?" the response is "known *and* unknown," as knowledge is hushed, made secret, expressed as suppression.

Such merging of originally antithetical categories was closely studied by Freud in his essay "The 'Uncanny.'" The principal tension (known/unknown) underlying *Une Passion* in fact comes terribly close to the contradiction which, according to Freud's etymological analysis, is responsible for the uncanny effect. That is, the term *unheimlich* (uncanny) develops from its opposite, *heimlich,* which, from a primary sense of "homelike," "belonging to the house," "tame," "familiar," comes to refer to something concealed, secret, withdrawn from the eyes of others—precisely the meaning usually ascribed to *unheimlich.*[24]

Now, a similar verbal pattern prevails in *Une Passion,* where we have seen the categories of familiar and unfamiliar, known and unknown, grow together and coincide. So it is not surprising that the psychic force to which Freud attributes the creation of the uncanny can also explain the assimilation of opposites in Balzac's text: "We can understand why linguistic usage has extended *das Heimliche* ["homely"] into its opposite, *das Unheimliche,* for this uncanny is in reality nothing new or alien, but something which is familiar and old-established in the mind and which has become alienated from it only through the process of repression . . . something which ought to have remained hidden but has come to light."[25]

Details of Balzac's tale bind past to present and mark the narrative matter as repressed material compulsively seeking to resurface. The panther provokes in the soldier a "souvenir de son jeune âge" comparable to the déjà-vu phenomenon, for the memory is spontaneous and uncontrolled: "Il songea *involontairement* à sa première maîtresse" (p. 1228 [emphasis added]; He *involuntarily* thought of his first mistress).

Certain stylistic elements symptomatize an ongoing process of textual repression. Foremost among these are the multiple ellipses, broken-off sentences, and circumlocutions, which hold in abeyance what should not be explicitly said. The text speaks, when it does, in spite of itself. Frequent scattered phrases suggest passivity; the characters submit to their reactions instead of reacting; they are, so to speak, communicated instead of actively communicating:

—Oh! s'écria-t-elle *en laissant errer* sur ses lèvres un sourire d'incrédu-lité. [p. 1219]
—J'avoue qu'*il m'est échappé*, comme à vous, une exclamation de sur-prise. [p. 1219]
—Eh! bien, reprit-il *en laissant échapper* un geste d'impatience . . . [p. 1232; emphasis added here and above].

["Oh!" she cried, *letting* an incredulous smile play on her lips.
"I confess that *I let* an exclamation of surprise *slip out*, as you did."
"Well, he replied, *letting* a gesture of impatience *escape him*. . . ."]

    The narration provides the sharpest reflection of the textual dilemma "to tell or not to tell?" and of its resolution to tell *and* not to tell. The narrator tells his story only when heavily per-suaded and expecting to be well rewarded: "elle me fit tant d'agaceries, tant de promesses, que je consentis" (p. 1220; she flirted so much, she made me so many promises, that I agreed). And when the pen refuses to continue, the voice proceeds—when urged—by indirection: "C'est horriblement difficile, mais vous comprendrez . . ." (p. 1232; It's horribly difficult, but you will understand . . ."). A similar reluctance characterizes the soldier's voice, the inner narration reported to us indirectly. A bottle of champagne prods him to volubility, but his tale ends in repres-sion, in that refusal to be spoken which acknowledges as it de-nies: "cela ne se dit pas" (p. 1232).
    If it is evident that *Une Passion* is to be read as a disguised reenactment of the repressed, the content of the repressed story is less evident and needs to be reconstructed by assembling the many clues we have been gathering. Given that this tale of man and beast is a revised version of a story about a man and a woman, and that the woman who insistently reappears in the text emerges unsummoned from a shadowy past, we might sur-mise that this stranger is only estranged and that this tale of the wild in fact masks a most familiar story.

At the close of the text, the soldier's voice enters as the narrator cites his evaluation of the desert:

—Eh bien, monsieur, reprit-il après un moment de silence, j'ai fait depuis la guerre en Allemagne, en Espagne, en Russie, en France; j'ai bien promené mon cadavre, je n'ai rien vu de semblable au désert. . . . Ah! c'est que cela est bien beau. [p. 1232]

["Well, sir," he continued after a moment's silence, "since then I've fought in Germany, Spain, Russia, and France; I've hauled my carcass around quite a bit, I've never seen anything like the desert. . . . Ah! It is so beautiful."]

When probed about the significance of the experience, the soldier's first response ("Cela ne se dit pas") is followed by: "D'ailleurs je ne regrette pas toujours mon bouquet de palmiers et ma panthère. . . . Dans le désert, voyez-vous, il y a tout, et il n'y a rien" (p. 1232; Besides, I do not always pine away for my bouquet of palm trees and my panther. . . . In the desert, you see, there is all, and there is nothing).

The desert is, then, a representation of the absolute ("tout et rien"), of a confinement or seclusion reminiscent of origins and ends. And the desert does in fact link the two rather explicitly; on the one hand, its essential constituent elements, the tree and the panther ("mon bouquet de palmiers et ma panthère") evoke, respectively, the soldier's hometown (the columns of the cathedral at Arles) and his first love, while on the other hand, "mon cadavre," the soldier's metaphorical reference to his post-desert self, marks the desert as a place of figurative death.

So, waiting for death in the Egyptian desert, the French soldier returns to his origins as he acts in his own personal passion play. He commits a fatal crime whose terrible cost he cannot at the time evaluate: he cuts down a tree which had previously sheltered him ("qui, la veille, lui [avait] servi de toit" [p. 1223]). Now this palm, at which he hacks away for an entire day, before effecting its fall, is no ordinary tree; it is "ce *roi* du désert" (p. 1223), one of a group of palms whose "têtes . . . *majestueuses*" (p. 1221) project a protective shadow, and which recall "les fûts . . . *couronnés* de longues feuilles" (p. 1221; [emphasis added here and above]; *this king* of the desert; *majestic* . . . heads; the shafts . . . *crowned* with long leaves) which marked the cathedral columns of his youth. The regal majesty ascribed to this tree formally recognizes the office of king which it holds in this story.

My suspicion that this tall tree-king, source of shelter and protection, is a paternal metaphor is confirmed by the foreboding sound of a phantom voice which delivers a message of disaster to the soldier as the tree-king is struck down. A reinforcing metaphor of inheritance binds tree-king to soldier in a relationship of father to son:

Comme un héritier qui ne s'apitoie pas longtemps sur la mort d'un parent, il dépouilla ce bel arbre des larges et hautes feuilles vertes qui en sont le poétique ornement, et s'en servit pour réparer la natte sur laquelle il allait se coucher. [p. 1223; emphasis added]

[*Like an heir who does not spend much time mourning a parent's death,* he stripped this fine tree of the tall, wide green leaves which are its poetic ornament and used them to repair the mat he was going to sleep on.]

After dethroning the paternal figure, the son strips and despoils him in an overdetermined gesture which incorporates implicit references to several different myths. The filial violation of the prohibition against nudity recalls that scene in Genesis in which Noah's son Ham acquiesces in his father's nakedness, while his two brothers make haste to cover the great patriarch. The large leaves described as the tree's "poetic ornament" suggest the fig leaf (and thus, the attainment of sexual knowledge), the emphasis here placed on stripping rather than donning. Finally, the appropriation of the father's spoils by the son is a Promethean gesture.[26] Balzac's condensation of these myths of filial revolt may be traced to a primal plot: the son desires the father's knowledge, wants to unveil the truth he is assumed to possess, and furthermore wants to take on this knowledge, deprive the father of his truth, his power, appropriate them for himself. Thus the soldier despoils the tree and absconds with the leaves to repair his sleeping mat; the crime is a Promethean theft of paternal power.

The plot becomes thicker still when some biographical information is apposed: Balzac's father, dead in an accident at the age of eighty-three (one and a half years before *Une Passion* appeared) had been convinced that "grâce à l'économie des forces vitales *(et à un régime à base de sève d'arbres)*, il ne mourrait que centenaire"[27] (thanks to economizing his vital forces [*and to following a diet whose staple was tree sap*], he would live to be a hundred). So that the association father-tree has more than one determinant. Viewed against the biographical backdrop, the narrative act of cutting down the tree—stopping the sap flow equivalent to the life source in his father's eyes—constitutes (figurative) parricide.

The panther is the second member of that original lost triad implied in the soldier's nostalgia for "mon bouquet de palmiers et ma panthère."[28] It should come as little surprise that the panther plays queen-mother to the palm's king-father. She is at various moments referred to as "reine des sables" (p. 1231); "reine solitaire" (p. 1227); "sultane du désert" (p. 1226); "sultane délaissée" (p. 1231); "courtisane impérieuse" (p. 1226; queen of the sands; solitary queen; sultana of the desert; forsaken sultana; imperious courtesan). Her attributes are as regal as her person: her lair is called "l'antre royal" (p. 1224; the royal lair) her robe has "un éclat impérial" (p. 1225; an imperial luster).

The jump from panther-queen to mother can be traced through the metaphoric patterns of the text. The metaphoric itinerary must be tracked from its starting point in a comparison (the soldier's) which explicitly equates the panther and the desert: "'Elle a une âme . . .' dit-il en étudiant la tranquillité de cette reine des sables, dorée comme eux, blanche comme eux, solitaire et brûlante comme eux . . ." (p. 1231) ("She has a soul . . ." he said as he considered the calm of this queen of the sands, golden like them, white like them, solitary and burning like them . . .). From this point of departure, the route then follows the desert's metaphoric traces, seeking to determine the qualities of the panther-queen by a transitive process.

As we proceed, we notice a rather troubling transformation of the desert. The epitome of aridity, it paradoxically becomes, by metaphor, its opposite: the ocean, the sea, figure of all things flowing and wet. The soldier surveys the desert which surrounds him: "Il voyait un océan sans bornes. . . . Il ne savait pas si c'était une mer de glaces ou des lacs unis comme un miroir" (p. 1221; He saw a boundless ocean. . . . He couldn't tell if it was a sea of mirrors or lakes smooth as glass). A bit further on, the sand is "agité par petites vagues menues" (p. 1222; shifting in small wavelike movements), and the horizon is bordered, "comme en mer, quand il fait beau, par une ligne de lumière" (p. 1222; as at sea, on a clear day, by a line of light). Towards the end of the text, the soldier studies "les effets de la lune sur l'océan des sables où le simoun produisait des vagues, des ondulations" (p. 1230; the effects of the moon on the ocean of sand, where the simoom produced waves and ripples). The aquatic metaphor is extended to the heat, "qui ondoyait au-dessus de la nappe étendue dans le désert" (p. 1222; which undulated above the outstretched desert sheet), and it becomes mirage when, inspired with longing for his past by his desert exile, the soldier "sentait avec délices les ruisseaux de Paris" (p. 1222). Like metaphor, mirage involves a play of presence and absence, the production of a perceptive illusion. Metaphor and mirage perform analogically in this text, for each presents a distorted image which in fact is a corrective for the decentering strategies we have uncovered. Their importance lies in the use made of a potential to convey occulted meaning to the surface of the text.

The metaphoric sea is, ultimately, the buried "source" of meaning in this narrative, as dramatically manifested by the soldier's discovery of a "source perdue dans les sables" (p. 1223; spring hidden in the sands), immediately following his "cruel mirage" (p. 1222). It is significantly also the evolutionary source of life, hypostatically one with the ontogenetic source of life, as is conveniently represented by the French homophony, *mer/mère*.

This coincidence becomes the leitmotif of *L'Enfant maudit*, an early novel in which Balzac develops the parallel sea/mother. The son, Etienne, passionately devoted to his mother, has an equally strong affinity for the sea, which, "semblable à un visage de femme, avait . . . une physionomie, des sourires, des idées, des caprices"[29] (like a woman's face, had . . . a countenance, smiles, ideas, caprices). The sea eventually becomes his mother's replacement, for after her death, "enfin, il avait épousé la mer, elle était sa confidente et son amie" (p. 914; he had married the sea, who had become his confidante and his beloved). An even stronger statement of equivalence is made when his mother is on her deathbed:

Pendant la fatale soirée où il allait voir sa mère pour la dernière fois, l'Océan fut agité par des mouvements qui lui parurent extraordinaires. C'était un remuement d'eaux qui montrait la mer travaillée intestinement; elle s'enflait par de grosses vagues qui venaient expirer avec des bruits lugubres et semblables aux hurlements des chiens en détresse. Etienne se surprit à se dire à lui-même: "Que me veut-elle? elle tressaille et se plaint comme une créature vivante! Ma mère m'a souvent raconté que l'Océan était en proie à d'horribles convulsions pendant la nuit où je suis né." [p. 909]

[During the fatal evening when he was to see his mother for the last time, the Ocean seemed extraordinarily restless to him. The waters stirred as if the sea were internally disturbed; it sent forth huge swells which died with mournful sounds like dogs howling in distress. Etienne found himself wondering: "What does it want of me? it shudders and moans like a live creature! My mother often told me that the Ocean was prey to horrible convulsions the night I was born."]

This external evidence confirms the panther's role as mother and clarifies the references to the soldier's "première maîtresse," who can now be traced to the very distant past and the most primal of mistresses.

But we cannot ignore the contrary-to-fact element of this exhumed story. The soldier is in a desert; while he has found a grotto and a spring, the wide expanse of water, the waves and the sea, are figments of sheer fantasy. Does the metaphoric network then collapse, pulling with it the figured mother? Or does the paradox of the absent presence itself become significant?

The very potency of the absence, which causes its emphatic (negative) intrusion into the story, supports the latter hypothesis. The force I have dubbed "negative presence" might more succinctly be named "desire," or, consistent with the metaphoric terminology of the text, "thirst." In *Le Lys dans la vallée*, Félix de Vandenesse equates thirst with erotic desire and the quenching of thirst with erotic satisfaction: "Non, je n'ai pas aimé, mais j'ai eu soif au milieu du désert"[30] (No, I have not loved, but I have been thirsty in the middle of the desert).

The analogy undergoes a further refinement in *L'Enfant maudit,* which develops an ideal of (maternal) love based largely on a never-ceasing flow of milk.[31] When Etienne is born, the *accoucheur* counsels his mother: "Le sein est le remède à toutes les maladies des enfants. . . . Du lait! du lait! S'il reste toujours sur votre sein, vous le sauverez" (pp. 890–91; The breast is the remedy for all childhood illnesses. . . . Milk! milk! If he is always at your breast, you will save him). When Etienne becomes a young man, his mother's love continues to be measured in metaphors of lavishly flowing milk:

Lorsque Etienne ne comprenait pas tout d'abord quelque démonstration, un texte ou un théorème, la pauvre mère, qui assistait aux leçons, semblait vouloir lui infuser la connaissance des choses, comme naguère, au moindre cri, elle lui versait des flots de lait. [p. 902]

[Whenever Etienne did not at first understand some proof, a text or a theorem, his poor mother, who was in attendance at his lessons, seemed to want to infuse knowledge into him as formerly, at the least cry, she would supply streams of milk.]

This ideal mother, who makes of her son "un simulacre d'amant" (p. 903; the likeness of a lover), is lover as well as nurturer to him. After the mother's death, Etienne soon feels "le besoin d'aimer, d'avoir une autre mère" (p. 912; the need to love, to have another mother). Erotic love and maternal love are inextricably bound, and thirst becomes a metaphor of ambiguous desire, sating thirst a metaphor of ambiguous fulfillment.[32] The desert, with its *mers fantômes,* is actually the image of a *mère négative,* a cold non-nurturing mother, and *Une Passion* is very much a fantasy, a wish fulfillment: the most literal of family romances.

Another connection assures the functioning of the metaphoric network. The aquatic qualities attributed to the desert are doubled by blade-like characteristics:[33] "Il voyait un océan sans bornes. Les sables noirâtres du désert s'étendaient à perte de vue dans toutes les directions, et ils étincelaient *comme une lame d'acier* frappée par une vive lumière" (p. 1221; emphasis added) (He saw a boundless ocean. The dark desert sands stretched out of view in all directions, and they glittered *like a steel blade* struck by bright light). The marinelike horizon is sealed "par une ligne de lumière *aussi déliée que le tranchant d'un sabre*" (p. 1222 [emphasis added]; by a line of light *as sharp as the edge of a sword*). The desert sharpness reflects the knife imagery proper to the panther-woman, and provides an additional element of internal corroboration for the desert/panther metaphor.

The story is complicated by the maiming metaphors, which impose a sobering quality on the family romance. These metaphors can best be understood as figures of severing—and severance—applied within an oedipal context. For *Une Passion* is Balzac's version of the Oedipus story, no more or less valid for deviating from the Sophoclean drama, no more or less significant for preceding Freud.[34] Having extricated its constituent parts, we can remove the seal of censorship ("cela ne se dit pas") from this story and make it emerge from the silence at the core of the text.

The story opens with the soldier, like Oedipus, wandering through the desert. Fearing marauding desert animals, he cuts down a tree, intending to use it as "une barrière à la porte de son hermitage" (p. 1223; a barrier to the entrance of his hermitage). Though he does succeed in felling the tree, he does not manage to cut it in pieces during the day (p. 1223). Now, it is precisely because the tree (the totemic father) fails to function as a barrier that the union of the soldier and the panther (mother) takes place; it is as if the soldier ambivalently seeks a paternal interdiction in the form of this (incest) barrier even as he defies the father and causes his authority, in the form of the tree, to topple. The father overthrown ("ce roi du désert tomba" [p. 1223]), disaster is predicted to the son by a voice which combines echoes of the Apollonian oracle and Hamlet's ghost: "Le bruit de sa chute . . . fut comme un gémissement poussé par la solitude; le soldat en frémit comme s'il eût entendu quelque voix lui prédire un malheur" (p. 1223).

The next stage of the saga juxtaposes two diachronic episodes of the classic Oedipus story: the trial of the Sphinx and the union with the queen-mother are condensed into the single (extended) adventure with the panther.[35] Like the Sphinx, the panther is a composite figure, comprising woman, feline beast, reptile, and bird. These fragmented elements are scattered through the text and must be read like a rebus. When he first glimpses the panther in the dark, the soldier wonders: "Etait-ce un lion, un tigre, ou un crocodile?" (p. 1223; Was it a lion, a tiger, or a crocodile?). He soon resolves this and recognizes the animal as a panther: "ce lion d'Egypte" (p. 1224; the lion of Egypt). The feminine element is introduced metaphorically, as we have observed at some length; the reptilian element, by the snakelike tail and the effect of the panther's presence, which is likened to that of "les yeux magnétiques du serpent" (p. 1225). The bird element enters the text surreptitiously with the panther's movement, for "elle bondit avec la légèreté des moineaux" (p. 1226; she leapt with a sparrow's ease).

While the panther is at first bewildering to the soldier (he measures her body "curieusement" [p. 1227]), she ultimately represents a kind of initiation experience, for he discovers the hitherto unknown and attains access to unnamed mysteries: "Cette compagnie permit au Provençal d'admirer les sublimes beautés du désert. . . . La solitude lui révéla tous ses secrets. . . . Il découvrit dans le lever et le coucher du soleil des spectacles inconnus au monde" (p. 1229; This company allowed the Provençal soldier to admire the sublime beauties of the desert. . . . Solitude revealed all its secrets to him. . . . He discovered in the desert sunrise and sunset sights unknown to the world). The riddle of the Sphinx is answered as the soldier tames the unknown (epitomized by the panther) and possesses it.

Knowledge and ignorance, sight and blindness, are at stake in this text and are put into question at every stage and on every narrative level. The father's truth is uncovered but unassimilated as the son goes on to commit his crime. The riddle of the Sphinx is posed (the panther-desert *is* this riddle) and answered ("Connu," says the soldier, and the double entendre is significant); it is nevertheless essentially unrevealed, suppressed ("cela ne se dit pas"), though alluded to at the very end, when God the Father is recognized and becomes the last word: "Le désert," says the soldier, "c'est Dieu sans les hommes" (p. 1232; The desert . . . is God without men).

At the time of the oracle's warning, however, the young *hé-*

ritier is unheeding; he goes on to despoil the fallen tree-father, and, though one might expect him to have "put on his knowledge with his power," he proceeds quite literally to make a bed for himself in the "antre royal," the royal lair, the panther's boudoir. This act prefigures the actual union of the denouement, which culminates in tragedy as the soldier, fearing the worst, (but too late) plunges his dagger into the panther even as he sexually penetrates her. This juxtaposition is quite complex. It recalls the deaths of the Sphinx and Jocasta, separate in the classical story but both brought about by Oedipus; it associates the incest and the punishment and the matricide, as if the chastised son had finally recognized the father's law (represented by the return of the dead father in the form of the mutilating combined parent) and, overcome with guilt, killed his partner in crime to annihilate the continued reminder of the transgression. The punishment is thus double: it is at once the maimed leg and the loss of love, severing and severance. The imposition of the paternal interdiction is itself the punishment, symbolically represented by physical maiming or castration. Freud's incisive statement that "the prohibition against an incestuous choice of object . . . is perhaps the most drastic mutilation which man's erotic life has in all time experienced"[36] nicely describes this narrative, which paradoxically, however, represents the mutilation as both a drastic loss and a long-desired recovery. For the severed tree (the dead father), having been tracked through the desert by the soldier, then temporarily transferred to the panther's rump, is finally found—and simultaneously lost—by the chastised soldier, who, according to talion law, gives "a limb for a limb" and discovers his oedipal identity as "amputé de la jambe droite" (p. 1219), that is, "wounded foot."

VI

La tragédie serait la représentation au compte de l'Autre du non-représentable aux yeux du sujet.

ANDRÉ GREEN, *Un Oeil en trop*

Like a stone thrown into the water, the monolithic story, cast into oblivion, appears to generate a series of concentric narrative reflections of diminishing intensity. At the center of the text, a silenced oedipal story, told by nobody, hushed by all. Encircling this core, three ringed narratives which retell that same story, the untold generative source which radiates so many concentric layers of protection. Around the silent core, the soldier's story, a virtual narrative which we hear of but never directly hear. Surrounding this story, the narrator's account of it, destined for the lady, mostly transmitted in writing, partly orally. Encircling (and including) these inner rings, the printed narrative called *Une Passion dans le désert*. The narrator who addresses an anonymous reader purportedly coincides with the character who is narrator of the soldier's tale, but the roles he plays as narrator of *Une Passion* and narrator/author of the embedded text diverge. The split is formally reflected by the presence of two titles in the narrative. The title which heads the text, and which refers to it in its entirety, *Une Passion dans le désert,* is soon followed by a second title which applies solely to the narrator's written account of the soldier's adventure: "Le lendemain elle reçut donc cet épisode d'une épopée qu'on pourrait intituler: Les Français en Egypte" (p. 1220; The next day, then, she received this episode of an epic that could be entitled "The French in Egypt").

The midtext switch from title to subtitle is curious and has several important consequences. If the narrator's written tale is excerpted from an epic bearing its own title, that title properly belongs to the excerpt as well; the inclusive title *Une Passion* is therefore not merely a reflection of the embedded story, for if that were so, the two titles would be identical. The combination story-plus-frame evidently is more than or different from story alone, and *Une Passion dans le désert* refers to something more or other than one soldier's erotic perversion in the Egyptian desert. So we need to examine just what goes on in the frame, asking how it is related to the desert passion.

A further complication arises from the fact that the internal title is an intertextual reference. That it is part of a literary work written by an extratextual author (an author potentially equivalent to Balzac, who planned but never completed a trilogy prospectively entitled *Les Français en Egypte*) signs it as an authentic text and endows it with an element of external literary substance which distinguishes it from the soldier's narrative and from the narrator's account addressed to the lady, even though all three narrative acts ultimately converge in one text. It is as if the different narrative layers were accentuated to hide their eventual collapse into oneness.[37]

Through a series of metaphors of representation, our attention is directed from the vague outer rim into the interior, always further inward toward the dark, absent center. The repressed resurfaces through a compromise which distances as it reveals, denies as it acknowledges. The desert adventure is presented as a text-within-a-text (but overflowing the internal textual bounds), the "real" story, but "only a story." A series of theatrical metaphors continues and reinforces the theme of representation, beginning with the very first line of the narrative: "Ce spectacle est effrayant!" (p. 1219; This show is appalling!). The scene is a menagerie show; the narrator and his friend are among the audience. Within this show is another menagerie show, for the narrator recalls the performance at which he met the soldier who related his tale. The embedded menagerie show leads into another theater metaphor, this one attributed to the soldier's perception of his experience: "Il vit sans s'en rendre compte une tragédie dans cette aventure, et résolut d'y jouer son rôle avec honneur jusqu'à la dernière scène" (p. 1225; Without realizing it, he saw a tragedy in this adventure, and resolved to play his role with honor until the very last scene). The "dernière scène," as we know, will coincide with the primal scene, the spectacle of the combined parent-figure, and the soldier will be both actor and spectator, playing his role of observer with the requisite fervor of desire and anxiety, retrospectively observing his part in a triangular drama.

But it is difficult to conceive how this soldier, intrepid as he might be, could resolve to play a role in a tragedy he saw without being aware of seeing (il vit sans s'en rendre compte). One can only attribute the perception of tragedy and the consequent role assignment to the narrator responsible for the theater metaphor. In the final analysis, he is the one who sees without realizing (like Oedipus, who answers the riddle but does not see that he himself is implicated) as he represents the soldier's drama in lieu of his own.

Every effort is made to distance the content of the soldier's story, to label it as *spectacle*—belonging to the spectacular, the extraordinary. But we have seen that such categories become meaningless in this text, where ordinary and extraordinary overlap and intermingle, where menageries bring the untamed secrets of the wild to the civilized streets—and boudoirs—of Paris, and where childhood memories intrude upon exotic perversions. The extraordinary immediately involves the ordinary, the Other brings into play the Self, and the actor, as Hamlet incompletely realized, implicates the spectator. The embedded story, metaphorically theatricalized, is a means of projecting into make-believe (and thus disavowing) something which is in fact all too real. Ernest Jones comments: "It is known that the occurrence of a dream within a dream (when one dreams that one is dreaming) is always found when analyzed to refer to a theme which the person wishes were 'only a dream,' i.e. not true. I would suggest that a similar meaning attaches to a 'play within a play,' as in *Hamlet*. So Hamlet (as nephew) can kill the King in his imagination since it is 'only a play' or 'only in play.'" [38]

In turn, I suggest that the soldier's adventure is a multi-embedded play, an alibi, a mediating story "framed" as the spectacular center of attention. I call it an alibi because it is in truth a pretext, a very assertive substitution for the suppressed text. It is the projection of a vague suppressed fear (fear of authoring, fear of desiring) emanating from the outermost ring and culminating in the reconstructed mythical core. The soldier is a passive instrument for the narrator of *Une Passion dans le désert*. While staged as an erotic drama, and simultaneously as a drama of suffering and loss, *Une Passion* turns out to be a veritable passion play: a drama of redemption which offers the soldier's martyrdom as a deferred replacement for the narrator's own.

Tantamount to a model of story-telling theory, this story tells us that the telling can be infinitely varied, but the story never changes. Like the virtual oedipal core of *Une Passion,* like the surrounding desert tale of a soldier, a panther, and a palm, adhering to the frame (though not quite contained by it) is a triangular tale of obstructed desire. The note of seduction which defines the soldier-panther rapport echoes in the narrator's relationship with his lady. The narrator's consent to draft the risqué story is obtained through his friend's provocative wiles: "Rentrée chez elle, elle me fit tant d'agaceries, tant de promesses, que je consentis. . . ." Like Mignonne, she is coy and coquettish, feigning a shock and an incomprehension laid on rather too heavily to be believed, and thereby intimidating her rather meek friend. That her ignorance is sham is evident from her consuming curiosity to hear every last detail of the affair; furthermore, the knowing comments she "inadvertently" drops indicate a worldliness and a comprehension which belie her professed naiveté.

Also like Mignonne, this woman is an imposing figure, so much so that the narrator resorts to *writing* the continuation of the story he has begun orally, as if to avoid direct contact which might cause embarrassment (probably more to the narrator than to the woman) and leave him *interdit,* unable to continue because at once speechless and *forbidden* to speak. So writing acts as a screen for the narrator's timidity, a mode of self-mastery which will grant his words an autonomy and an authority they would otherwise not attain.

But the status of this internal text is problematized. While it most immediately represents an effort to overcome what is apparently a rigid self-imposed censorship, the internal text is also defined by its structural conditions of being: its form and its existence as an act of communication. Written by the narrator for the lady, to whom it is sent, this text is a letter carrying a message from sender to addressee. The message is the soldier's tale appropriated by the narrator through the act of retelling it in the form of a personal letter. The letter, addressed to a woman in exchange for "tant de promesses," is a promise in return, an intimate message, a message of desire.

The lady is not at all naive when it comes to reading the soldier's tale; she is quite aware of the personal message hidden between the lines. Her response to the manuscript betrays her knowledge: "Eh bien, me dit-elle, j'ai lu votre plaidoyer en faveur des bêtes; mais comment *deux personnes* si bien faites pour se comprendre ont-elles fini? . . ." (emphasis added). As her tongue slips from "beast" to "person," it reveals her instant understanding of the allegorical nature of the desert story.

The authority of the narrator's text is ultimately undermined by its founding alibi. The soldier's tale brings the narrator's desire into play, acting as a screen which both conceals this desire and works it through its own mesh, where it settles almost imperceptibly.

Because the narrator's desire is *en jeu* (at play and at stake) in his edition of the text, the tale he writes influences his telling of it. The maiming at the end of the soldier's tale (of which we are informed later, orally) is reflected by the narrator's "maimed" text, abruptly interrupted, unfinished. The narrator relinquishes his authorship and his authority as if struck impotent; he is unable to continue, as if contaminated by the figurative castration at the end of the story.[39]

The contamination in fact spreads to the outermost narrative ring. *Une Passion* closes amid a general fading of voices which represents a rather chaotic loss of narrative control. One would expect some kind of imposed symmetry from an authoritative narrator, a return to the opening structure of the frame, a final representation of the (internal) narrator and the lady. There is none: the lady disappears, leaving no trace, as does the narrator-protagonist we assume to be her lover. As their story is interrupted, cut off, we are left with the words of the soldier, the most removed, least responsible narrator, *and he abdicates, making God the final authority:* "C'est Dieu sans les hommes." Writing turns out to be an attempted authoritative act which cannot be consummated;[40] the would-be usurper yields before a higher power, the son recognizes and accepts his subordination, effaces himself before God the Father.

As in *El Verdugo,* Balzac appears to be recuperating the dead father on an abstract level (here as divine authority). This most transcendent of forms, however, turns out to be empty, a hollow representation. I suggested earlier that the soldier's relinquishment of his narratorial role leaves God as ultimate authority. But the trouble with God in this text is that his authority is withdrawn. The closing remark which would vest the remnants of narrative authority in God is a contradiction in terms: "C'est Dieu sans les hommes." The concept of God, like that of father, like that of language, depends on paradigmatic contrast, on definition by contradistinction.[41] "God without men" is a god with no posterity, a father without children; the proposition is self-nullifying.

The totalizing formula which ends the text takes the word of God as if to assure closure, but the word is emptied of closural power by the context. For the word of God *denotes* law, absolute command and prohibition; but as it is used here to describe the soldier's passion it *connotes* the infinity of desire and the limitlessness of transgression. The name of God as used to express a moment of erotic transport conflates the (antithetical) concepts of law and desire. If the father, generally speaking, is "celui dont la présence limite le rapport illimité de la mère à l'enfant,"[42] (he whose presence limits the limitless relationship between the mother and the child), and if the father's name is used, as it is here, to define an incestuous infinity, then the meaning of this name has been evacuated.

Since God as supreme father is the fundamental signifier, the signifying keystone, the source of names and purveyor of difference—"*celui qui sépare*"[43] (*he who separates*)—if the name of God then becomes an empty signifier, the concept of difference and the possibility of representation in language begin to be undermined. The anonymity which pervades the text is the most obvious token of this loss of distinctions. Neither the soldier nor the narrator-protagonist nor the lady is named; Mignonne is the only appellation given, and this is a displacement, a nickname borrowed from the past.

A more substantial manifestation of the signifying disorder is the repeated merging of polarities, most notably the sexual crossovers we have observed. The soldier's description of the desert well summarizes the underlying paradigmatic confusion: "Dans le désert, voyez-vous, il y a tout, et il n'y a rien." The desert, symbol of the absolute, is this everything that is equivalent to a nothing because it is raw totality marked by no structure, no differentiation. "Dieu sans les hommes" means the abolition of difference or creation denied, representation negated.

Although the structural elements of the family romance are present, their organizing potential is weakened; they are jumbled, patched together in an uneven, nonlinear representation. The informational inconsistencies, syntactic ruptures, and slippage of voices combine to produce a narrative stutter which dominates the presentation of this text and invites questions about the overt emphasis on representation. Such questions begin to surface in the Vautrin trilogy, where they come into play on a more conscious level, causing more flagrant thematic repercussions and narrative disruptions. As I discuss these novels, I want to suggest that the increasingly crisis-fraught status they accord to representation can be read as an elaboration of the problematized structure of *Une Passion dans le désert*.

PART II

REVISIONS

CHAPTER THREE

Mirrors and Fatherhood
Le Père Goriot

He had recalled: "Copulation and mirrors are abominable." The text of the encyclopedia said: "For one of those gnostics, the visible universe was an illusion or (more precisely) a sophism. Mirrors and fatherhood are abominable because they multiply and disseminate that universe."

JORGE LUIS BORGES, *"Tlön, Uqbar, Orbis Tertius"*

 N a short story called "Tlön, Uqbar, Orbis Tertius," Borges takes us from the account of an intellectual discussion bearing on narrative illusion to a digest of the history and geography, the philosophic, linguistic, and literary systems of a country named Uqbar and a planet called Tlön. The information presented, based on data which is detailed and comprehensive, orderly and coherent, is culled from various published sources (for the most part encyclopedias) whose status as reference works (and implicitly, referential works) is used to mask the fact that *they have no referents*.

For we learn that a secret society of experts drawn from diverse disciplines undertook the vast project of inventing at first a country, and then, more ambitiously, a world. The only explicit motivation for this Promethean enterprise is attributed to the group's patron, a millionaire named Ezra Buckley who, though an atheist, "wanted to demonstrate to [the] nonexistent God that mortal man was capable of conceiving a world."[1]

The first trace of the society's work is a "reference" (the

term is, of course, put in question) to Uqbar which is appended to one set of an encyclopedia "fallaciously called *The Anglo-American Cyclopaedia . . .* a literal but delinquent reprint of the *Encyclopaedia Britannica of 1902*" (p. 3). Later, the group was to publish forty volumes of *The First Encyclopedia of Tlön,* an undertaking which would provide the foundation for a subsequent, more detailed edition written in one of the languages of Tlön. This "revision of an illusory world" was called Orbis Tertius (p. 15).

As the preceding quotations suggest, the self-appointed gods responsible for creating Tlön and Uqbar (and more immediately, the texts which "represent" them) dealt in a kind of trickery consisting of presenting reprint upon reprint, revision upon revision, copy upon copy, as if to assure the veracity of the origin, the reality of the referent, through a play of mirrors which one senses could proceed indefinitely.

Borges engages in a similar strategy as he creates his text. Allusions to textual reeditions, translations and adaptations, linguistic repetitions and reformulations abound. Most notable is the discussion which opens the narrative: "a vast polemic concerning the composition of a novel in the first person, whose narrator would omit or disfigure the facts and indulge in various contradictions which would permit a few readers—very few readers—to perceive an atrocious or banal reality" (p. 3). Placed at the beginning, almost in epigraph, this commentary highlights the text and suggests a generic definition of narrative as illusion.

The narrator relates that while he and his friend conversed, "The mirror spied upon us. We discovered . . . that mirrors have something monstrous about them" (p. 3). Thus we are reminded that we are not witnessing the narrator's meeting with his friend, but instead a reflection of it, a mediated version, which, by virtue of the re-presentational factor, contains an element of excess, of monstrosity.

And indeed, the concern with narrative deception reflected by the tale and its telling returns to the teller in an Escher-like arabesque which blurs the line between copy and origin, narrative and narrative act. A postscript to the story reports the following: "I reproduce the preceding article just as it appeared in the *Anthology of Fantastic Literature*" (p. 14). The text which we read as original (that is, as an original representation, and therefore already a copy) is in fact secondary (if not tertiary), a reprinted article, a copy of a copy. As the status of the text is disturbed, the narrative voice, dislocated, comes to sound inauthentic, recorded; and, most unsettling, our status as readers is displaced. Evacuated from our position as primary readers of a short story and replaced by an anonymous audience, we have lost our origin. We, too, have become ghostly copies, readerly representations.

Borges's text reveals the specious relationship between life and art. Encyclopedias, by convention the most referential, the most mimetic of texts, are shown to be solipsistic, representing a reality which exists only insofar as the text creates it. But more significantly, the final twist effected by the postscript establishes the Tlön and Uqbar narratives as only hyperbolic versions of Borges's story—and indeed, of every text.

The end of the story tells of the real world being invaded and usurped by the highly organized, cogent fiction of Tlön: "How could one do other than submit to Tlön, to the minute and vast evidence of an orderly planet? . . . Enchanted by its rigor, humanity forgets over and again that it is a rigor of chess masters, not of angels" (pp. 17–18). Tlön illustrates one of fiction's imperatives, a potential danger inherent in any representational mode, for, as Borges muses elsewhere, "If art is perfect, then the world is superfluous."[2]

Although this story speaks to all mimetic enterprises, its implications for Balzacian narrative are overwhelming. The forty-volume *First Encyclopedia of Tlön*—"the vastest undertaking ever carried out by man" (p. 15)—strikingly recalls *La Comédie humaine*. Buckley's megalomaniacal attempt to vie with God by conceiving a world reminds us of Balzac's oft-quoted resolve to "faire concurrence à l'Etat-Civil." Furthermore, Buckley's project, read within the framework of Borges's story, qualifies Balzac's statement, points to its central ambiguity, and, we shall find, to Balzac's fundamental ambivalence. While generally accepted as an expression of mimetic intent, Balzac's "faire concurrence" also suggests a truly Promethean effort to bypass the real world, to generate a cosmos which is not representative but *other*.

These reflections on "Tlön, Uqbar, Orbis Tertius" form an especially pertinent backdrop as we move on to a study of what are usually perceived as Balzac's realist novels, for Borges consciously—indeed, craftily—manipulates representational questions only nascent in Balzacian realism. As we turn now to *Le Père Goriot,* and later to *Illusions perdues* and *Splendeurs et misères des courtisanes,* I will not attempt an integral analysis of the novels, but will examine them as the continuation of an issue—hyperbolically illustrated by Borges's story—which began to emerge in *El Verdugo* and *Une Passion dans le désert*: the related calling into question of narrative, language, and procreation.

I

C'est avec cet ouvrage [*Le Père Goriot*] que le romancier devient le maître incontesté du réalisme, le peintre de Paris et du grand monde.

ROSE FORTASSIER, Introduction to *Le Père Goriot*

Les romans les plus "réalistes" sont encore une "invention du vrai" qui prend tout son sens profond dans un mythe et s'organise selon les symboles de ce mythe.

ALBERT BÉGUIN, *Balzac visionnaire*

Le Père Goriot is often viewed as a point of rupture in the course of Balzac's literary production, the inauguration of a new aesthetic which radically breaks with the visionary aspects of the earlier works, in particular the *contes fantastiques*. Certainly this appraisal is justified. The form of the novels is different: they are longer, set in sharply defined, detailed time and space, peopled with a myriad of assorted characters whose separate intrigues, interactions, and interwoven plot threads cannot but alter the concentrated, monomaniacal tendency of earlier works.

While this formal evolution is significant, it is in itself not essential. The changing form is indicative of a deep-rooted narrative anxiety—a characteristic of the early works as well—now reshaped through more sophisticated techniques of self-protection and disguise made possible by the novelist's developing stylistic flexibility.

Both of the short stories we have looked at manifest a severe narrative discomfort most apparent in an interference between the teller and the tale. The story implicates—taints—the storyteller to such an extent that we may consider the frame as a device conceived to distance, to safeguard, the storyteller. Balzac's preface to *Le Lys dans la vallée* provides a flagrant confirmation of this fear of contamination by fiction and suggests that it is ultimately a projected anxiety about self-exposure, about laying bare fiction's source. He writes:

Le "moi" n'est pas sans danger pour l'auteur. . . . Beaucoup de personnes se donnent encore aujourd'hui le ridicule de rendre un écrivain complice des sentiments qu'il attribue à ses personnages; et s'il emploie le "je," presque toutes sont tentées de le confondre avec le narrateur. *Le Lys dans la vallée* étant l'ouvrage le plus considérable de ceux où l'auteur a pris le "moi" pour se diriger à travers les sinuosités d'une histoire plus ou moins vraie, il croit nécessaire de déclarer ici qu'il ne s'est nulle part mis en scène. *Il a sur la promiscuité des sentiments personnels et des sentiments fictifs une opinion sévère et des principes arrêtés. Selon lui, le trafic honteux de la prostitution est mille fois moins infâme que ne l'est la vente avec annonces de certaines émotions qui ne nous appartiennent jamais en entier.*[3]

[The first person is not without danger for the author. . . . Many people are still foolish enough to make a writer the accomplice of the sentiments he attributes to his characters; and if he says "I," almost all are tempted to confuse him with the narrator. Since *Le Lys dans la vallée* is the longest work in which the author has adopted the first person to wind his way through a story which is more or less true, he deems it necessary to declare here that he has nowhere represented himself. *He has fixed principles and severe opinions about the promiscuity of personal and fictional sentiments. As he sees it, the shameful trade of prostitution is a thousand times less abject than the publicized sale of certain emotions which never belong to us entirely.*]

Writing thus envisaged as a potential crime of sexual excess becomes an endless battle to preserve the writer's purity, to stave off an unnamed condemnation here vaguely expressed as his own "opinion sévère et . . . principes arrêtés." In this light we can begin to understand the motivation for fragmenting the vision, for peopling a world with a multitude of available carriers for it.

In much the same way as the escaped convict Jacques Collin eventually covers his back and shoulders with multiple scars to hide the tell-tale letters which reveal his fatal identity, Balzac assiduously deforms the marks of the fantastic tales which lie beneath the surface of the "realist" novels. But the text of the novels, like the scarred tissue on Collin's back, is a palimpsest which can be made to disclose traces of the ineffaceable original writing. What then surfaces on the putative clean slate of these novels is neither a biographical nor a social referentiality (though elements of both are scattered through the narrative), but an origin which is itself a fiction, the representation of a desired existence which functions as a corrective to a deficient reality.

In *El Verdugo* we discovered a vicarious oedipal drama played out through the protagonist's identification with the youngest son of a Spanish nobleman, whereby he dismisses his despised petit-bourgeois background and envisions himself promoted to the ranks of the aristocracy. In *Une Passion dans le désert*, through an interposed foreign adventure story, we read a longed-for union with an imaginary past: a conquest dependent upon its own degradation as a means, and upon loss as an end. Alternative versions of a family romance, these stories are compromise solutions to the oedipal dilemma which is spun out in fiction because it can neither safely nor satisfactorily be resolved in life.

But I do not want to exaggerate the homology between child and writer. The novelist creates, in writing, a narrative infinitely more complex than the unwritten one invented by the child. And the maturing novelist's version is yet more intricate than the story told by the neophyte writer. What is most interesting about Balzac's disposition of the family romance is less the fact that different texts can be reduced time and again to a particular configuration of the same story than that the same story is told so many times in different ways. As we pass from the contes to the novels, we already know what story is being told. We will therefore be more concerned with exploring *how* it is retold, tracing its continuity and evolution through the network of symbols which intermittently shrouds and reveals it.

II

Cette vie de Paris est un combat perpétuel.

BALZAC, *Le Père Goriot*

La femme a un duel avec l'homme.

BALZAC, *Letter to Mme. Hanska*

Foedora, vous la rencontrerez. Elle était hier aux Bouffons, elle ira ce soir à l'Opéra, elle est partout, c'est, si vous voulez, la Société.

BALZAC, *La Peau de chagrin*

The second part of *La Peau de chagrin* is devoted to the protagonist's attempted conquest of the countess Foedora, "la femme sans coeur." Cold, unresponsive, she fulfills Raphael's worst fears when "au théâtre une scène attendrissante la trouvait froide et rieuse"[4] (at the theater a moving scene found her cold and gleeful). She is a huntress: "Foedora n'avait pas lâché sa proie" (p. 201; Foedora had not let go of her prey). She is a predatory animal: "Si j'avais voulu faire un pas de plus au-delà de cette câlinerie fraternelle, j'eusse senti les griffes de la chatte" (p. 187; If I had wished to go one step beyond this chaste fondling, I would have felt the cat's claws).

So extreme is Foedora's indifference that it renders her sexuality ambiguous: "Je croyais voir ce monstre qui, tantôt officier, dompte un cheval fougueux, tantôt jeune fille, se met à sa toilette et désespère ses amants, amant, désespère une vierge douce et modeste" (p. 179; I thought I saw before me the monster who, as an officer, breaks in a spirited horse; then, as a young girl, dresses up and devastates her admirers; and then, as a lover, drives an innocent young girl to despair).

Raphael's attraction to this unobtainable, hermaphroditic creature ultimately casts doubt on his own sexual constitution, a doubt elucidated by the following statement of his erotic doctrine:

Je ne conçois pas l'amour dans la misère. . . . Certes, je me suis cent fois trouvé ridicule d'aimer quelques aunes de blonde, du velours, de fines batistes, les tours de force d'un coiffeur, des bougies, un carrosse, un titre, d'héraldiques couronnes peintes par des vitriers ou fabriquées par un orfèvre, *enfin tout ce qu'il y a de factice et de moins femme dans la femme;* je me suis moqué de moi, je me suis raisonné, tout a été vain. . . . En France heureusement pour moi, nous sommes depuis vingt ans sans reine, j'eusse aimé la reine! [pp. 142–43; emphasis added]

[I cannot conceive of love amidst penury. . . . To be sure, many times I have laughed at myself for loving a few meters of lace, velvet, or fine cambric, a coiffeur's creations, candles, a carriage, a title, heraldic coronets painted on glass or crafted by a goldsmith—*all that is most artificial and least womanly in a woman;* I have mocked myself, I have tried to be reasonable, but all in vain. . . . In France, fortunately for me, we have not had a queen for twenty years; I would have loved the queen!]

Raphael's love for what artificially supplements a woman, for that part of her which is "least womanly," is remarkably fetishistic and is reminiscent of the soldier's fascination with the panther's masculine attributes in *Une Passion.* Indeed, the equation of a title, nobility, the accoutrements of luxury and fashion with fetishistic presences is transparently formulated here, but is far from unique; such traits consistently define the ideal love object for Balzac's male characters.

Foedora is an archetype, a model of the Parisian woman here described in similar terms:

La Parisienne dont toute la beauté gît dans une grâce indescriptible, vaine de sa toilette et de son esprit, *armée de sa toute-puissante faiblesse, souple et dure, sirène sans coeur* et sans passion . . . ne manquait pas. [p. 110; emphasis added]

[The Parisienne, whose beauty resides in an indescribable grace, who is vain about her appearance and her wit, *who is armed with an allpowerful weakness, supple and hard, a siren without heart* and without passion . . . was not missing.]

The oxymoronic all-powerful weakness which arms her connotes a lack which becomes a supplement, and, reinforced by the adjectival antithesis supple and hard, again evokes the hermaph-rodite.

First an individual and then the Parisienne, Foedora is, in the epilogue of *La Peau de chagrin*, transformed into an allegory: "Foedora . . . c'est, si vous voulez, la Société" (p. 294). The sud-den announcement of her metamorphosis suggests a last-minute disavowal of otherwise compromising material, and as such, provides a valuable clue to the novels of society.

The site of a transformation, *La Peau de chagrin* stands like a literary cocoon between the contes and the novels. Immersed in visionary patterns, it is anchored in quotidian detail and his-torical fact. Similarly, it may be read as both (either) a phan-tasmic portrait of a woman and (or) the symbolic representation of a social reality. The allegorical element is at best ambiguous. Much like the panther/woman analogy in *Une Passion*, it works both ways; it is unclear which is the concrete, which the abstract term.

If we can read Foedora as society, it becomes increasingly apparent, as we delve into the societal novels, that we should also read society as Foedora. When, in *Illusions perdues*, David Séchard gives Lucien dispensation to forsake his humble origins and begin his upward climb in pursuit of his aristocratic dream, he uses a sexual metaphor as he advises him: "Profite de ta vir-ginité sociale"[5] (Take advantage of your social virginity). And in *Le Père Goriot*, a disillusioned Rastignac paints the social sphere as a bejeweled (and implicitly feminine) horror as he counsels his friend Bianchon: "Quelque mal que l'on te dise du monde, crois-le! il n'y a pas de Juvénal qui puisse en peindre l'horreur couverte d'or et de pierreries"[6] (Whatever evil you hear about the world, believe it! No Juvenal could paint the horror covered over with gold and gems).

The journalist Lousteau presents a revealing parable of so-cial climbing:

Toujours la même ardeur précipite chaque année, de la province ici, un nombre égal, pour ne pas dire croissant, d'ambitions imberbes qui s'é-lancent la tête haute, le coeur altier, à l'assaut de la Mode, cette espèce de princesse Tourandocte des *Mille et un jours* pour qui chacun veut être le prince Calaf! Mais aucun ne devine l'énigme. [*I.P.*, p. 346]

[Every year the same fervor propels them from the provinces to Paris, in equal if not increasing number: these beardless young men, ambition incarnate, rush forward with high head and haughty heart, to conquer Fashion, the Princess Turandot of the *Thousand and One Days,* for whom everyone would be Prince Calaf! But no one can guess the riddle.]

Now, Turandot was a Chinese princess who agreed to marry the man who could answer her questions; all other suitors were beheaded. Calaf alone emerged victorious.[7] Social custom, then, is a Sphinx-like figure who punishes by death the youths who attempt her conquest.

Once we understand how the analogy operates, it is only a small step further to read Rastignac's well-known challenge to society as the acceptance of an endless struggle with a cold and ruthless womankind. At the end of *Le Père Goriot,* as he looks down upon Paris, dominating the city from the heights of Père-Lachaise, he sees it "tortueusement couché" (like a reclining woman), ablaze with lights. We are reminded of Victor's opening stance in *El Verdugo,* when he overlooks a brilliant vista lit by the stars, the gleaming sea, and the illuminated castle, all metonymically suffused with the glow of Clara's name. Here, too, a woman is the hidden visual object, the veiled object of desire. Avidly fixing upon "ce beau monde dans lequel il avait voulu pénétrer" (this bright world he had wanted to penetrate), Rastignac "lança sur cette ruche bourdonnant un regard qui semblait par avance en pomper le miel, et dit ces mots grandioses: 'A nous deux maintenant!'" (*P.G.,* p. 290; cast upon this humming hive a glance which seemed to pump its honey in anticipation, and spoke these grandiose words; "It's a fight to the death now!"). Since his first challenging gesture to society will of course be to go dine with Delphine de Nucingen, "society" must be read as the rather figurative object of Rastignac's challenge. The sexual nature of his glance which probes, indeed pumps the "society" he had longed to penetrate, is unmistakable. And as Rastignac's duel with society becomes a more intimate tussle, we are forced to reevaluate the entire social framework of the novel.

While Balzac's attitudes toward a society formed in Foedora's image consistently echo his disposition toward women, his depiction of this society is more explicitly dominated by another metaphor. From *Le Père Goriot* to *Illusions perdues* through *Splendeurs et misères des courtisanes,* Paris is repeatedly described as an ocean. As the floundering Rastignac attempts to stay afloat in society, we are told that:

A l'exécution, ses déterminations devaient donc être frappées de ces hésitations qui saisissent les jeunes gens quand ils se trouvent en pleine mer, sans savoir ni de quel côté diriger leurs forces, ni sous quel angle enfler leurs voiles. [*P.G.,* p. 75]

[The execution of his resolve was inevitably marked by the hesitation that overcomes young men when they find themselves at sea knowing neither in what direction to steer their energies nor at what angle to set their sails.]

The social sphere is no less foreboding for Lucien, and gives rise to a similar image: "cette affreuse mer parisienne" (*I.P.,* p. 324; this terrible Parisian sea).

In *El Verdugo,* the sparkling ocean was one of several figurative replacements for Clara, and was the site of the British incursion which led to Clara's loss. As such it was a figure of desire and its dire consequences. The metaphoric network of *Une Passion* linked ocean and wave imagery to the panther-woman through the mediating terms of erotic thirst and the quenching of desire. It is therefore not surprising to find that the ocean metaphor as applied to society is similarly motivated. When the metaphoric tissue is closely examined, it is evident that society becomes an ocean through the mediation of a woman. The metaphor is introduced at the beginning of *Le Père Goriot* in an exposition which articulates Parisian society, sexuality, and writing, the three terms essential to an understanding of the Vautrin trilogy:

Paris est un véritable océan. Jetez-y la sonde, vous n'en connaîtrez jamais la profondeur. Parcourez-le, décrivez-le: quelque soin que vous mettiez à le parcourir, à le décrire; quelque nombreux et intéressés que soient les explorateurs de cette mer, il s'y rencontrera toujours un lieu vierge, un antre inconnu, des fleurs, des perles, des monstres, quelque chose d'inouï, oublié par les plongeurs littéraires. [*P.G.*, p. 59]

[Paris is a veritable ocean. You may try to plumb it, but you will never reach its bottom. Sail over it, describe it; but no matter how carefully you survey it and describe it, no matter how numerous and avid the explorers of this sea, there will always remain a virgin space, an unknown lair, flowers, pearls, and monsters unheard of, forgotten by literary divers.]

The female paradigm is immediately apparent: "un lieu vierge, un antre inconnu" (we remember the panther's lair), "des fleurs, des perles" (Asie speaking to Nucingen later refers to Esther as "ta perle"[8]), "des monstres" (such is the term often used to refer to hermaphrodites, phallic women, and creatures whose sex is uncertain), "quelque chose d'inouï, oublié. . . ." These treasures forgotten in the depths of the ocean recall Facino Cane's buried gold, and their retrieval bears similar sexual connotations, which are doubled by references to writing. Those who have explored this sea, plunged into it, dived for treasure, are implicitly writers: "les plongeurs littéraires." The invitation to explore this ocean is expressed in a tripartite formula which relates penetration ("jetez-y la sonde"), navigation ("parcourez-le"), and writing ("décrivez-le").

In another instance, the metaphor passes by way of a metonymy as "Nucingen trouva son ange plongé dans cet océan de réflexions, de résolutions, sur lequel flottent les esprits femelles, et d'où ils sortent par des mots incompréhensibles pour ceux qui n'y ont pas navigué de conserve" (*S.M.*, p. 598; Nucingen found his angel deep in that ocean of reflections and resolutions upon which the female mind floats, and from which it emerges amid words incomprehensible to those who are not of the convoy).

Upon abandoning his studies in favor of his ambitions, Rastignac finds himself with "quinze mois de loisirs pour naviguer sur l'Océan de Paris, pour s'y livrer à la traite des femmes, ou y pêcher la fortune" (*P.G.*, p. 122; fifteen months of free time to sail on the Ocean of Paris, to traffic in women, or to fish for his fortune). The two propositions given as alternatives are in fact equivalents. The economic undertone of Rastignac's traffic in women is clear, since the fortune for which he fishes is to take the form of a series of potential benefactresses. The erotic-economic confusion is augmented by the ambiguous expression "la traite des femmes." Most patently modeled on "la traite des Noirs" (the slave trade), it also recalls "la traite des vaches" (the milking of cows). This second nuance is illuminated by a curious passage which appears two pages earlier. There, Rastignac writes to his mother: "'Ma chère mère, vois si tu n'as pas une troisième mamelle à t'ouvrir pour moi. Je suis dans une situation à faire promptement fortune. J'ai besoin de douze cents francs, et il me les faut à tout prix'" (*P.G.*, p. 120; My dear mother, see if you have a third breast that will flow for me. I am in a position to make my fortune quickly. I need two hundred francs, and I must have them at all costs"). That Rastignac's pecuniary demands are expressed by an attempt to "milk his mother dry," and that he extends this purpose to women in general, is startling but hardly unprecedented. My discussion of *Une Passion* and periph-erally of *L'Enfant maudit* showed that the ever-flowing breast and, (by extension) other flowing substances work as recurrent vehicles for maternal-erotic love and satisfaction in the Balzacian text.[9] The schema is modified here by the addition of the eco-nomic theme. But more significantly, the economic theme is mod-ified—in fact absorbed—by the erotic schema, and invites a reappraisal of the fortune-seeking motif.

The ocean is a Protean metaphor in the Vautrin cycle, fluc-tuating in accordance with the protagonists' growing disillusion-ment with society and disenchantment with women. From a vast body of water signifying an infinite, indomitable unknown, it becomes a swamp, a mud-heap, a mire. Finally made aware of Delphine's selfishness, Rastignac "voyait le monde comme un océan de boue dans lequel un homme se plongeait jusqu'au cou, s'il y trempait le pied" (*P.G.*, p. 262; saw the world like an ocean of mud in which a man sunk up to his neck if he dipped a foot"). He has a similar reaction upon learning about Anastasie's abuse of her father: "—Mais, dit Eugène avec un air de dégoût, votre Paris est donc un bourbier" (*P.G.*, p. 89; "But," said Eugène with an air of disgust, "This Paris of yours is a quagmire").

The metaphor is based in a neutral referentiality; the description of nineteenth-century Paris situated "dans cette illustre vallée . . . de ruisseaux noirs de boue" (*P.G.*, pp. 49–50; in this illustrious valley . . . of mud-covered gutters) is not without veracity. A long digression in *Splendeurs et misères des courtisanes* thrusts a bit of historical authentication upon us:

Les deux puissantes murailles de l'arcade Saint-Jean étaient revêtues à six pieds de hauteur d'un manteau de boue permanent produit par les éclaboussures du ruisseau; car les passants n'avaient alors, pour se garantir du passage incessant des voitures et de ce qu'on appelait les coups de pied de charrette, que des bornes depuis longtemps éventrées par les moyeux des roues. Plus d'une fois la charrette d'un carrier avait broyé là des gens inattentifs. Tel fut Paris pendant longtemps et dans beaucoup de quartiers. [*S.M.*, p. 705]

[The two massive walls of the Saint-Jean Arcade were covered six feet high with a permanent coating of mud produced by splashes from the gutter. For in order to protect themselves from the constant passing of carriages and what were called cart-kicks, the passers-by in those days had only a series of posts that had long since been smashed by wheel hubs. More than once some quarryman's cart had crushed inattentive people there. Such was Paris for many years, in many quarters.]

Such is the material which fortifies the realist arsenal; such, too, the stuff which disarms it, when the metaphor is read contextually. No amount of realist doctrine can explain the hyperbolic extension of the image from a realist detail to a frenzied excoriation of women.[10]

For it is when the metaphor becomes most negatively charged that it most explicitly refers to women. In *Splendeurs et misères des courtisanes*, placed under the aegis of Vautrin/Herrera, a paroxysm of hatred is discharged in the form of an oozing morass, a sea of slime which seeps through the entire text as if safely emanating from the person of Herrera; it is liberated but contained. Herrera's denunciation of women borrows the mud image more often than any other. He warns Lucien about Esther: "Quand je t'ouvre les salons du faubourg Saint-Germain, je te défends de te vautrer dans les ruisseaux" (*S.M.*, p. 477; When I open the doors to the salons of the Faubourg Saint-Germain for you, I forbid you to wallow in the gutters). He later reminds him:

"Si je n'avais pas pris les rênes de ta passion, où en serais-tu aujourd'hui? Tu aurais roulé avec la Torpille dans la fange des misères d'où je t'ai tiré" (*S.M.*, p. 479; If I had not seized the reins of your passion, where would you be today? You would have rolled with the Torpedo back into the mire of misfortune from which I pulled you). We read here the triple equation of Esther, the impure woman, and the mud of Paris. As Herrera continues, speaking of the concern felt by Lucien's friends, he equates Lucien with divine light (as his name suggests) and Esther with mire: "Sachez-le, ma fille: une personne aimée de Lucien a des droits à leur respect, comme un vrai chrétien adore la fange où, par hasard, rayonne la lumière divine" (*S.M.*, p. 458; Know this, my daughter: a person loved by Lucien has a right to their respect, as a true Christian adores the mire in which, by chance, divine light shines). And speaking of his faithful female lackey, Herrera comments: "Europe sort de la boue et a peur d'y rentrer" (*S.M.*, p. 486; Europe rose from a mud-heap and is afraid of returning there).

A close look at the text reveals that these images entrenched in the mire of misogyny are in fact not confined to Herrera; they are spoken by the narrator's voice as well. Thus, for example, the following allegory:

On prit des carpes à un étang bourbeux pour les mettre dans un bassin de marbre et dans de belles eaux claires, afin de satisfaire un désir de Mme de Maintenon qui les nourrissait des bribes de la table royale. Les carpes dépérissaient.... "Elles sont comme moi, répliqua cette reine inédite, elles regrettent leurs vases obscures." Ce mot est toute l'histoire d'Esther. [*S.M.*, p. 468]

[Carps were taken from a muddy pond and placed in a marble basin, in clear, clean water, to satisfy a caprice of Madame de Maintenon, who nourished them with royal table scraps. The carps wasted away.... "They are like me," remarked this singular queen, "they miss their obscure mud-puddle." This comment contains Esther's entire story.]

Such leaks from Herrera's voice into the general narrative stream are not infrequent; they remind us that Herrera is but a conduit, that is, a *porte-parole,* for a more extensive discourse about women.

Two different approaches to society have led to identical end-points: by following Foedora's traces, and via the sea, we have arrived at a common conclusion which is the origin of the novels of society. As Balzac's representation of social mores co-incides with his depiction of female characteristics, social climbing turns out to be a sublimated form of erotic conquest.

Thus when Lucien begins to frequent Mme. de Bargeton's salon, a sexual allusion is used to express his upward mobility: "Lucien mordit à la pomme du luxe aristocratique et de la gloire" (*I.P.*, p. 174; Lucien bit into the apple of glory and aristocratic luxury). The analogy is then articulated: "Il aimait, et voulait s'élever, double désir bien naturel chez les jeunes gens qui ont un coeur à satisfaire et l'indigence à combattre" (*I.P.*, p. 175; He was in love and wanted to rise, a dual desire which is natural in young people who have a heart to satisfy and poverty to combat).

Rastignac's introduction into society is disclosed as a sexual entry through metaphors of the body and of penetration:

"Mettre le pied au faubourg Saint-Germain chez la vicomtesse de Beau-séant, le genou dans la Chaussée d'Antin chez la comtesse de Restaud! plonger d'un regard dans les salons de Paris en enfilade, et se croire assez joli garçon pour y trouver aide et protection dans un coeur de femme! [*P.G.*, p. 78]

[To get a foot in the door of the Faubourg Saint-Germain, at the home of the Vicomtesse de Beauséant, and then a knee in the Chaussée d'Antin, at the home of the Comtesse de Restaud! To plunge into the salons of Paris with a glance that sweeps through them, confident that you are handsome enough to procure help and protection in a woman's heart!]

The dead metaphor ("mettre le pied") is revived by the parallel construction using "genou," and the progression from one to the other creates an erotic innuendo.

Thus these novels are *Bildungsromane* which represent a double education: they speak at once of a social and a sexual initiation. The fantasied rebirth to socially elevated parents is evoked as an inversion of regular birth; as Eugène de Rastignac and Lucien de Rubempré plunge into the Parisian ocean, they are reborn in a fabulously sexualized version of the usual process.

Much as the *El Verdugo* narrator invented the aristocratic Léganès as Victor Marchand's surrogate family, and in *Une Passion,* as the French soldier of humble background recreated his origins in the form of a king father and a queen-of-the-desert mother, Eugène and Lucien exalt their beginnings as they reenvision them. Mme. de Beauséant, Eugène's first protectress, is "l'une des reines de la mode à Paris" (*P.G.,* p. 76; one of the queens of Paris fashion), and Lucien's benefactress, Mme. de Bargeton, is repeatedly described as "la reine," or "la souveraine d'Angoulême." Each of these women (and their successors as well) is described as a mother to her protégé, and dispenses maternal care to him.

But the fantasy is often revealed in the novels by an increasing effort to distinguish narrator from characters. The split frequently results in multiple perspectives, as in the following excerpt, where conflicting information complicates the pattern of the idealization:

La passion d'un poète devient alors un grand poème où souvent les proportions humaines sont dépassées. Le poète ne met-il pas alors sa maîtresse beaucoup plus haut que les femmes ne veulent etre logées? Il change, comme le sublime chevalier de la Manche, une fille des champs en princesse. Il use pour lui-même de la baguette avec laquelle il touche toute chose pour la faire merveilleuse, et il grandit ainsi les voluptés par l'adorable monde de l'idéal. . . . Lucien en était là. Sa nature poétique, nécessairement extrême en tout, en bien comme en mal, avait deviné l'ange dans la fille . . . il la voyait toujours blanche, ailée, pure et mystérieuse. [*S.M.,* pp. 475–76]

[A poet's passion becomes a great poem in which human proportions are often left behind. Doesn't the poet place his mistress much higher than women want to be kept? Like the sublime knight of La Mancha, he changes a country girl into a princess. He thus uses for himself the magic wand with which he transforms all things, and he adds to sensual pleasures the delightful sphere of the ideal. . . . This was the point Lucien had reached. His poetic nature, necessarily extreme in everything, in good as in evil, had divined the angel in the prostitute . . . he saw her always white, winged, pure, and mysterious.]

Lucien-as-poet exalts his lowly mistress much as he seeks to reinstate his mother to a more elevated status. The narrator-as-poet, however, reminds us that the angel is a woman of the streets, and the princess a common prostitute.

Thus the dream of exaltation is lined with the stuff of degradation. Almost systematically, as a formerly closed, much desired social sphere becomes accessible, as the conquest of a desired woman becomes a reality, disillusionment sets in (whether on the character's or the narrator's level). Then the social milieu is revealed to be corrupt, the woman, defiled: the ocean turns to mud. The attained ideal is denied only to be retained on an abstract level. It is as if the ideal object can be preserved only through such a compromise process: the vision of the ideal remains, while degradation is the price of conquest.

This frantic effort to preserve a gradually eroding ideal haunts the text of *Le Père Goriot*. My reading of the novel traces a desperate attempt to cling to the structure of the family romance as a guarantor of family stability, a sanction of desire's fulfillment through fantasy, and an affirmation of the ordering power of narrative language—despite increasing evidence of failure on all three counts.

III

Things fall apart; the centre cannot hold;
Mere anarchy is loosed upon the world.

YEATS, "The Second Coming"

When we confront *Le Père Goriot* as title with the peripeties of the novel's plot, a curious paradox develops. The title seems to designate a definite focal point, but as the novel progresses, we become aware that its focus continually shifts among three characters: Goriot himself, the incarnation of biological paternity, Vautrin, the figure of artificial creation, in whom the charge of paternal power appears to be vested, and Eugène de Rastignac, the son who sets himself the task of appropriating the advantages of paternal status in the form of social power, wealth, and privileged access to women.

At the beginning of the novel, it becomes apparent that Ras-

tignac's departure from the family estate coincides with a repudiation of his provincial origins and an attempt to recreate himself, to forge a new, more exalted birthright. The following
passage is indicative of his self-imposed disinheritance:

> Ses illusions d'enfance, ses idées de province avaient disparu. Son intel-
> ligence modifiée, son ambition exaltée lui firent voir juste au milieu du
> manoir paternel, au sein de la famille. . . . La comparaison qu'il fut
> forcé d'établir entre ses soeurs, qui lui semblaient si belles dans son
> enfance, et les femmes de Paris, qui lui avaient realisé le type d'une
> beauté rêvée, l'avenir incertain de cette nombreuse famille qui reposait
> sur lui, . . . enfin une foule de circonstances inutiles à consigner ici dé-
> cuplèrent son désir de parvenir et lui donnèrent soif des distinctions.
> [P.G., pp. 74–75]

> [His childhood illusions, his provincial ideas, had disappeared. His new
> understanding, his exalted ambition, forced him to look clearly at his
> family in the paternal manor. . . . The comparison he had to make be-
> tween his sisters, who had seemed so beautiful in his childhood, and
> the women of Paris, who incarnated the beauty of his dreams, as well
> as the uncertain future of a large family which depended on him, and,
> more generally, a multitude of circumstances unnecessary to record
> here, multiplied his desire to succeed and made him eager to distinguish
> himself.]

Whence a second paradox. Rastignac's very determined
march to social success is launched from an absent (because effaced) point of origin. He is introduced as a man without anchor,
cut adrift, unfixed. His personal meanderings recall the novel's
drifting course, and suggest that the two paradoxes are in fact
one. For as he navigates Paris in search of a mooring, he reflects
and gives form to the novel's quest for a lost or displaced center.

The three points which vie for a position of centrality in the
novel are in fact variations on a theme. When we privilege Goriot's plot or Vautrin's (the two are separate but parallel), we read
the novel as the story of a man's search for a scion who can affirm
his paternity. When we follow Rastignac's plot, we read the same
story from an inverted perspective: the search for an acceptable
father upon whom and against whom filial ambitions can be
modeled. Although the three plot lines are ultimately inter-

twined, we are directed to read from Rastignac's perspective—a perspective which is alternately influenced and threatened by the other two. When Rastignac is presented, we are told:

Sans ses observations curieuses et l'adresse avec laquelle il sut se produire dans les salons de Paris, ce récit n'eût pas été coloré des tons vrais qu'il devra sans doute à son esprit sagace et à son désir de pénétrer les mystères d'une situation épouvantable aussi soigneusement cachée par ceux qui l'avaient créée que par celui qui la subissait. [*P.G.*, p. 56]

[Without his observant curiosity and the skill with which he managed to gain access to the salons of Paris, this story would not have been colored by the tones of truth which it doubtless owes to his sagacity and his desire to penetrate the mysteries of an appalling situation which was as carefully hidden by the victim as by those responsible for it.]

As Rastignac is identified with a narrative presence, the narrative is presented as the discovery of hidden mysteries. Thus the narrator is implicitly a detective, and Rastignac's ubiquitous role as the Maison Vauquer's resident sleuth will repeatedly assign him a narrative role in the novel.

The mysteries to be probed revolve around two men: Vautrin, for it is very quickly apparent that "il y avait au fond de sa vie un mystère soigneusement enfoui" (*P.G.*, p. 62; there was some mystery carefully buried in his life)—and Goriot, of whom Rastignac comments: "sa vie me paraît être trop mystérieuse pour ne pas valoir la peine d'être étudiée" (*P.G.*, p. 94; His life seems too mysterious not to be worth investigating).

Moreover, a closer look at the nature of the enigmas which arouse Rastignac's curiosity reveals that his detective work is specifically concerned with unearthing sexual secrets. The prurient nature of his curiosity is obvious as we watch him, like a young Oedipus anxious to unravel the enigma of his birth, like a small child seeking the primal mystery, become voyeur and eavesdropper, peeking in keyholes, hiding in dark corridors and adjoining rooms to behold or listen in on private interchanges. Rastignac's interest in Goriot is more precisely a desire to uncover the identity of the two young women who surreptitiously visit him, to perceive the scenes played out behind closed doors. Thus he spies on Anastasie, as on her sister Delphine, in order to "savoir quelles étaient ses relations avec le père Goriot" (*P.G.*, p. 100; find out the nature of her relations with Père Goriot).

Like a child in the process of acquiring sexual knowledge, Rastignac casts himself as hero in narratives of his own invention: "Cette femme . . . lui semblait tout un mystère. Il voulait pénétrer ce mystère, espérant ainsi pouvoir régner en souverain sur cette femme si éminemment parisienne" (*P.G.*, p. 100; This woman . . . was a complete mystery to him. He wanted to penetrate the mystery, hoping in this way to gain sovereign power over this eminently Parisian woman).

Rastignac's investigation of Vautrin is less defined.[11] The Vautrin enigma is never explicitly formulated in *Le Père Goriot*, only referred to through a series of largely literary allusions. On one occasion Rastignac has the impression that Vautrin has "la profondeur immobile d'un sphinx qui sait, voit tout et ne dit rien" (*P.G.*, p. 133; the unmoving depths of a sphinx who knows all, sees all, but says nothing). At another point he is referred to as the "terrible sphinx de la Maison Vauquer" (*P.G.*, p. 151). The sphinx, as my reading of *Une Passion* suggests, works as the figure of the hermaphrodite, the emblem of problematized sexuality. Homosexuality is thereby subtly attributed to Vautrin and is again implied through another literary allusion. Vautrin offers to make Rastignac his heir, and continues:

Voyez le père Goriot: ses deux filles sont pour lui tout l'univers, elles sont le fil avec lequel il se dirige dans la création. Eh bien, pour moi qui ai bien creusé la vie, il n'existe qu'un seul sentiment réel, une amitié d'homme à homme. Pierre et Jaffier, voilà ma passion. Je sais *Venise sauvée* par coeur. [*P.G.*, p. 186]

[Look at Père Goriot: his two daughters are the whole universe for him, they are the thread by which he finds his way around creation. Well, as for me, after having thoroughly probed life, there is only one genuine sentiment: a friendship between men. Pierre and Jaffier, that is my passion. I know *Venice Preserved* by heart.]

Vautrin's discourse here sets up an analogy which equates Goriot and his offspring with himself and Rastignac as potential heir. Thus he posits a father-son bond which is reiterated throughout the novel. But the reference to a male friendship, qualified as a "passion" and reinforced by the literary illustration, renders Vautrin's idealized paternity ambiguous, suggesting that it is a euphemism for an erotic bond.

Having posed riddles of a textual nature about Vautrin's secret, the narrator appropriately reveals Vautrin's identity through a text: the identifying letters on the escaped convict's shoulder. Rastignac's investigation, then, is closely associated with the literary enterprise; his sexual inquiries are simultaneously textual exercises.

As Rastignac plays detective/narrator, however, he meets with some competition from Vautrin, who often is able to "guess" what the fledgling detective has taken great pains to discover and frequently reverses the rules of the game, spying upon spy: "Il lui semblait [à Rastignac] que ce singulier personnage pénétrait ses passions et lisait dans son coeur, tandis que chez lui tout était . . . bien clos" (*P.G.*, p. 133; It seemed to him [Rastignac] that this singular character was penetrating his innermost feelings and reading his soul, while his [Vautrin's] own secrets were tightly kept). Vautrin is characterized by "un certain regard profond et plein de résolution" (*P.G.*, p. 61) rather perturbing for the self-styled investigator, especially at those moments when Vautrin casts toward him "un de ces regards par lesquels cet homme semblait s'initier aux secrets les plus cachés du coeur" (*P.G.*, p. 118; one of those glances with which this man seemed to initiate himself into the soul's best-hidden secrets).

When the intense stare is attributed to Balzac's characters, it is, as we have remarked, a sign of both sexual and literary activity. Victorine is sensitive to the penetrating quality of Vautrin's gaze: "Je ne voudrais pas être vue ainsi par cet homme, il a des expressions qui salissent l'âme, et des regards qui gênent une femme comme si on lui enlevait sa robe"(*P.G.*, pp. 205–06;[12] I don't want to be seen like this by that man; he has ways of looking at you that sully the soul and make you feel as if you were being undressed). And when Rastignac temporarily surrenders to Vautrin, he becomes passive; he loses his desire to probe as if vanquished before the (staring) contest even begins: "Dans son for intérieur, il s'était abandonné complètement à Vautrin, *sans vouloir sonder* ni les motifs de l'amitié que lui portait cet homme extraordinaire, ni l'avenir d'une semblable union" (*P.G.*,

p. 194 [emphasis added][13] In his innermost being, he had already completely surrendered to Vautrin, *without seeking to probe* either the motives for this extraordinary man's friendship for him, or the future of such a union).

The stakes in this staring contest are high, for ultimately Vautrin and Rastignac are playing for narrative domination. The tell-tale stare which marks Vautrin as a literary figure apposes his activity to Rastignac's. Vautrin tells him: "Je suis un grand poète. Mes poésies, je ne les écris pas: elles consistent en actions et en sentiments" (*P.G.*, p. 141; I am a great poet. But I don't write my poems: they consist of actions and feelings). The poetic production Vautrin has in mind is to take the form of a southern plantation in the United States, a grandiose patriarchal fantasy in which the misogynist will immaculately sire a swarm of children overnight in the guise of two hundred slaves: "Des nègres, voyez-vous? c'est des enfants tout venus dont on fait ce qu'on veut" (*P.G.*, p. 141; Slaves, you see, are ready-made children; you do as you like with them). The plantation fantasy is to be created through an embedded plot which features Rastignac's marriage to the would-be heiress, Victorine Taillefer; Vautrin, as Machiavellian marriage broker (for the brother, as official heir, must first be dispensed with) will understandably receive a cut of the dowry as just reward and commission. Rastignac is to play a role not unlike that of the plantation slaves: obedient son to "papa Vautrin" (*P.G.*, p. 137), created character in the author's drama. Vautrin anticipates this creative rapport before the fact, as he tells Rastignac: "Je vous connais comme si je vous avait [sic] fait" (*P.G.*, p. 135; I know you as if I had made you).

Meanwhile, however, another rivalry implicitly pits Vautrin against Goriot. For Goriot, too, has a plot to impose on Eugène and, through him, on the novel, in the form of a biological creation: his daughter, Delphine de Nucingen. Goriot's scenario has two explicit motifs (and at least as many buried themes, as we will later discover). Like a hidden god or an omnipotent narrator, he wants to append Rastignac to his daughter's life, and so revise her story: "Eh bien, Delphinette, Ninette, Dedel! n'ai-je pas eu raison de te dire: 'Il y a un joli appartement rue d'Artois, meublons-le pour lui!' Tu ne voulais pas. Ah! c'est moi qui suis l'auteur de ta joie, comme je suis l'auteur de tes jours" (*P.G.*, p.

228; Well, Delphinette, Ninette, Dedel! Wasn't I right to tell you: "there's a charming apartment on the Rue d'Artois, let's furnish it for him!" You didn't want to. Ah! I am the author of your joy, just as I am the author of your days). In addition, Rastignac is to be appropriated as a son ideally destined to fulfill Goriot's paternity and to rectify his daughters' failure to do so. In a moment of pity for the old man and passion for his daughter, Rastignac vows: "j'aurai soin de lui comme d'un père, je lui donnerai mille jouissances" (*P.G.*, p. 215; I will care for him as if he were my father, I will give him a thousand pleasures).

While Rastignac, faced with the choice of a father, vacillates between Vautrin and the Victorine plot, Goriot and the Delphine plot, the shape of the novel hangs in the balance. As Rastignac must fill the vacant paternal position, so the novel must choose a plot and make it stick, or remain directionless.

But Rastignac's search for the right version of paternity, like the novelist's aesthetic quest, is doomed to failure. While a choice is imperative, Balzac's novels (which time and again reenact the same creative dilemma) continually express dissatisfaction with either alternative. Natural paternity, epitomized by Goriot, is depicted as paternal annihilation, a constant diminution of the father's force. In the mythical story, Cronos defeats (castrates) his father, but is in turn dethroned by his own son, Zeus. Goriot's story is no different. On his deathbed, he cautions Rastignac: "Ah! mon ami, ne vous mariez pas, n'ayez pas d'enfants! Vous leur donnez la vie, ils vous donnent la mort" (*P.G.*, p. 273; Oh, my friend, do not marry, do not have children. You give them life, they give you death). And the mythical pattern is invoked in full when Goriot later declares: "Leurs enfants me vengeront" (*P.G.*, p. 277; Their children will avenge me).

The father is struck through his children even when they are not direct agents of his punishment. In *Splendeurs et misères* when Peyrade (that other emblem of devoted paternity) is undone through the abduction and rape of his daughter, his friend Corentin cries: "Oh! ai-je eu raison de ne pas avoir de famille. . . . Un enfant! c'est, ma parole d'honneur, comme le dit je ne sais quel philosophe, un otage qu'on donne au malheur!" (*S.M.*, p. 679; Oh! Wasn't I right not to have a family. . . . A

child! A child, I swear it, is—as some philosopher said—a hos-
tage that you give to misfortune!).

As we continue on to *Illusions perdues* and *Splendeurs et
misères,* it will become apparent that the theme of biological
creation is doubled by an aesthetic theory which holds that the
origin (the vision) is inevitably destroyed through its representation, its incarnation in writing, much as the world in human
terms is invaded and usurped by Borges's Tlön, a narrative construct.

The alternative, of course, is Vautrin's artificial paternity, in
which no organic bond attaches father to son, creator to creation, vision to text. Such a version of creation, paradoxically
founded in sterility, is very similar to Baudelaire's artificial ideal,
and is admirably summarized by Sartre's remarks on that poet:

Ce qu'il ne peut souffrir dans la paternité, c'est cette continuité de vie
entre le géniteur et les descendants qui fait que le premier, compromis
par les derniers, continue à vivre en eux d'une vie obscure et humiliée.
Cette éternité biologique lui semble insupportable: l'homme rare em-
porte dans la tombe le secret de sa fabrication; il se veut totalement
stérile, c'est la seul façon dont il puisse se donner du prix.[14]

What he cannot bear about paternity is the continuity of life between
progenitor and descendents which makes it necessary for the former,
compromised by the latter, to continue to live through them a humbled,
mediocre life. This biological immortality is unbearable to him. The
exceptional man carries the secret of his creation to the grave; he wants
to be completely sterile, for this is the only way to assure his own
worth.]

Taken to its extreme, fully adhered to, this refusal can ensure the
integrity of the origin and the originator; the vision can remain
intact.[15]

Vautrin's avoidance of women, his Lancelot-like purity, endows him with a similar strength of ten. In *Splendeurs et misères*
he revels:

Oh! combien de force acquiert un homme quand il s'est soustrait,
comme moi, à cette tyrannie d'enfant, à ces probités renversées par la

passion, à ces méchancetés candides, à ces ruses de Sauvage! La femme, avec son génie de bourreau, ses talents pour la torture, est et sera toujours la perte de l'homme. [*S.M.*, p. 934]

[Oh! What strength a man acquires when, like me, he escapes that childish tyranny, that probity overcome by passion, that candid malice, that primitive guile! Woman, with her executioner's genius and her talent for torture, is and will always be the ruin of man.]

At times, however, his principled sterility is put in question by an accompanying hint of nostalgia for the women he does not desire, the children he does not sire. The rather lyrical revelation of his patriarchal plantation dream, peopled by two hundred "children," complicates the resolutely invulnerable character and threatens the sanctity of the vision. In *Splendeurs et misères,* his attachment to virile young men is presented as a compromise, a vicarious indulgence in rejected pleasures: "Trompe-la-Mort dînait chez les Grandlieu, se glissait dans le boudoir des grandes dames, aimait Esther par procuration. Enfin il voyait en Lucien un Jacques Collin beau, jeune, noble" (*S.M.*, p. 813; Trompe-la-Mort dined with the Grandlieus, slipped into the boudoirs of great ladies, loved Esther vicariously; for he saw Lucien as a young, handsome, noble Jacques Collin). Vautrin's artificial fatherhood is in the end no more fulfilling (and scarcely less dangerous) than its natural counterpart.

As backdrop to these two flawed paternal alternatives, the novel stages a series of minor paternal dramas, as if to compensate, by quantity and diversity, for the absence of a satisfactory father figure and the lack of a stable narrative center. The scene is set with the novel's opening description of the Maison Vauquer, for the living room walls are covered in "un papier verni représentant les principales scènes de *Télémaque*" (*P.G.*, p. 53; a varnished paper depicting the principal scenes from *Télémaque*)—Fénelon's version of the archetypal son in quest of a father.

Threaded through the novel is the secondary drama of a young girl disinherited by her millionaire father. Victorine Taillefer's story is in fact an inversion of Goriot's; she, as daughter, is humble, patient, and forgiving before the father who scorns her, as is Goriot before his unresponsive daughters. Goriot seems to sense the ironic reversal, for he is deeply touched by Victorine as if by his mirror image: "Le vieillard oubliait de manger pour contempler la pauvre jeune fille, dans les traits de laquelle éclatait une douleur vraie, la douleur de l'enfant méconnu qui aime son père" (*P.G.*, p. 94; The old man forgot to eat as he studied the poor girl, whose features were deeply marked by sorrow— the sorrow of an unrecognized child who loves her father").

Through Mlle. Michonneau's story, we glimpse yet another variation on paternity, in the form of a drama of inheritance. This *pensionnaire* purportedly took care of an ailing gentleman abandoned by his children; his will makes her the beneficiary of a life income which is periodically disputed by the heirs (*P.G.*, p. 58).

And finally, there is Rastignac's own "prehistory": the story of his real father's paternal experience, which precedes and overlaps his Paris rebirth. We can reconstruct its broad outline through Rastignac's exchange of letters with his mother and sisters. The passage which paraphrases the letters to his sisters is densely studded with ill-concealed implications of forbidden relations and fantasized crimes, and merits careful examination:

Il écrivit à chacune de ses soeurs en leur demandant leurs économies; et, *pour les leur arracher sans qu'elles parlassent en famille* du sacrifice qu'elles ne manqueraient pas de lui faire avec bonheur, il intéressa leur délicatesse *en attaquant les cordes de l'honneur* qui sont si bien tendues et résonnent si fort dans de jeunes coeurs. Quand il eut écrit ces lettres, *il éprouva néanmoins une trépidation involontaire: il palpitait, il tressaillait.* Ce jeune ambitieux connaissait *la noblesse immaculée* de ces âmes ensevelies dans la solitude, il savait *quelles peines* il causerait à ses deux soeurs, et aussi quelles seraient leurs joies; *avec quel plaisir elles s'entretiendraient en secret de ce frère bien-aimé,* au fond du clos. *Sa conscience se dressa lumineuse,* et les lui montra *comptant en secret leur petit trésor:* il les vit, déployant le génie malicieux des jeunes filles *pour lui envoyer incognito cet argent, essayant une première tromperie* pour être sublimes. "Le coeur d'une soeur est *un diamant de pureté,* un abîme de tendresse!" se dit-il. *Il avait honte d'avoir écrit.* Combien seraient puissants leurs voeux, *combien pur* serait l'élan de leurs âmes vers le ciel! Avec *quelles voluptés* ne se sacrifieraient-elles pas? [*P.G.*, p. 121; emphasis added]

[He wrote to each of his sisters, asking for their savings, and, *in order to extract the money from them without their discussing at home* the sacrifice they would gladly make for him, he appealed to their delicacy by *aiming for the cords of honor* that are so tightly strung and vibrate so loudly in young hearts. Yet when he had finished writing the letters, *he could not help feeling some trepidation: he quivered and trembled.* This ambitious young man knew *the immaculate nobility* of those souls buried in solitude; he knew *how much pain* he would cause his two sisters, and also how much joy: *he knew how much pleasure they would draw from talking about this beloved brother in secret,* in some far corner of the orchard. *His conscience rose like a beacon,* and shone on a vision of his sisters *secretly counting their small treasure;* he pictured them, ingeniously devising some girlish scheme *in order to send him this money incognito, experimenting with their first deception* in order to reach the sublime. "A sister's heart is *a diamond of purity,* it holds such depths of tenderness!" he said to himself. *He was ashamed of his letters.* How fervent their hopes for him would be, how pure the surge of their prayers! What exquisite pleasure sacrifice would bring them!]

Rastignac's request for money is represented as a violation of his sisters' purity. We note the emphasis on their pure hearts, their immaculate souls, which are to be corrupted by the brother's demand for money. This demand is in effect an assault, for it is described in a vocabulary of violence and inflicted pain ("arracher," "attaquant," "peines"). Requesting a gift of money becomes a metaphor for soliciting sexual favors, as Eugène pictures the pleasure and sensual delights ("quel plaisir," "quelles voluptés") his sisters' presents will bring to them. There is a kind of suppressed excitement in the involuntary tremors he feels: "trépidation," "palpiter," "tressaillir" are ambiguous terms, signs of strong emotion but also of erotic arousal. We glean a perverse pleasure in the shame he feels as he imagines the sisters discussing him secretly, stealthily counting their little treasure, experimenting with their first act of deception. This "première tromperie" can also be read in stronger terms, as a first infidelity. For the forbidden favor requested of these sisters is a crime against the father. The need for secrecy is insisted upon as Rastignac twice pictures their activities carried on "en secret," and thinks of them sending the money to him "incognito." Furthermore, the entreaty not to speak of the transaction before the family is a

euphemistic way of asking them not to tell the father, for Rastignac has already written to his mother with a demand for funds,
and has included his aunt in the entreaty. This leaves only his
father uninformed. And indeed, when his mother responds, she
instructs him: "Fais un bon emploi de cet argent, je ne pourrais,
quand il s'agirait de te sauver la vie, trouver une seconde fois une
somme si considérable *sans que ton père en fût instruit, ce qui
troublerait l'harmonie de notre ménage"* (P.G., p. 126; [empha-
sis added]; Use this money well; I could not—even if it were a
question of saving your life—come up with such a large sum
again without your father finding out, and that would trouble
our relationship").

Thus the plea for money is an act of lawlessness: the pecuniary theft figuratively replaces Rastignac's arrogation of forbidden sexual rights. When the money is actually delivered, its sexual value becomes manifest:

A l'instant où l'argent se glisse dans la poche d'un étudiant, il se dresse
en lui-même une colonne fantastique sur laquelle il s'appuie. Il marche
mieux qu'auparavant, il se sent un point d'appui pour son levier. . . . il
désire à tort et à travers. . . . Enfin, l'oiseau naguère sans ailes a retrouvé
son envergure. . . . "Ah! si les femmes de Paris savaient! se disait Rastignac . . . elles viendraient se faire aimer ici." [P.G., p. 131)

[At the very instant a student feels money slip into his pocket, a fantastic column springs up for his support. He carries himself better than he
previously did, he now has a power base. . . . his desires run wild. . . .
The fledgling bird has found his wings. . . . "Ah! if the women of Paris
knew!" Rastignac told himself. . . "they would come here to be loved."]

And so Rastignac appropriates the father's power as, transgress-
ing his law, he receives the money.[16] The symbolic equivalence of
financial and sexual potency is underscored by a transaction between Vautrin and Rastignac. Once again solvent, the student
makes haste to pay back some money lent him by Vautrin. The
"sphinx en perruque" thereupon exclaims: "On dirait que vous
avez peur de me devoir quelque chose? . . . en plongeant un regard divinateur dans l'âme du jeune homme" (P.G., p. 133;
Could it be that you are afraid of being in my debt?" . . . as he

cast a divining glance into the young man's heart). Rastignac's instinctive reluctance to be Vautrin's debtor translates his refusal to be sexually bound to him.

When all is said and done, Rastignac's repudiated father returns from the provincial shadows to which he has been banished as history repeats prehistory and the primordial pattern reduplicates itself. Both the Victorine and the Delphine plot manifest a fundamental repetition of the Rastignac family plot. Each of the scenarios features the father as victim of Rastignac's thievery. In Taillefer's case, the pecuniary theft is the more important one, since Victorine has been repudiated; in Goriot's case, the sexual and financial embezzlements are given equal emphasis, for as we shall see, a good deal of jealousy—and considerable financial deprivation—accompany Goriot's gift of his daughter to Rastignac.

There is, however, one important innovation in the Delphine and Victorine plots. Whereas Rastignac's epistolary seduction was quite clearly a transgression of the father's law, his access to Delphine and Victorine paradoxically devolves from the father. Despite a certain amount of jealousy, Goriot gives his daughter to Rastignac, indeed entreats him to take her. And Vautrin, as self-appointed guardian of Victorine's hand, bestows it upon the prospective suitor. Here we begin to confront the gaping chaos that the novel desperately seeks to order. For both prospective fathers—Goriot and Vautrin—ultimately abdicate their position, relinquish their authority to say no; whence an unregulated circulation of women, an uncontrolled flow of money, a mad proliferation of familial and social relations. As we begin to look at the perturbed relationships which arise in a frenzied attempt to supplement the missing core, we enter into a truly Yeatsian turmoil.

Blood relations and carnal relations intertwine, fuse, and reduplicate themselves, producing a human labyrinth. Vautrin's offer of paternity is doubled by an erotic invitation, and Goriot's paternity is no less ambiguous. The force of his fatherly passion can in fact only be understood through all that is ulterior to it. His attitudes toward his daughters, consistently compared to those of a lover, are startlingly summarized by the exclamation he utters on his deathbed: "Mes filles, c'était mon vice à moi;

elles étaient mes maîtresses, enfin tout!" (*P.G.*, p. 275; My daughters were my vice; they were my mistresses; they were everything to me!). This incestuous fervor is explained by an erotic transference. Widowed after seven years of blissful marriage, "Il reporta ses affections trompées par la mort sur ses deux filles . . . il voulut rester veuf" (*P.G.*, p. 124; He transferred his affections, which death had cheated, to his two daughters . . . he wished to remain a widower).

Now, if Goriot's daughters are as mistresses to him, and if Rastignac is his surrogate son, then Rastignac's relations with Delphine are triply defined: she is lover, sister, and mother to him.[17] As she unveils the luxurious apartment she has furnished for him with Goriot's money, she poses as fairy godmother: "Enfant! vous êtes à l'entrée de la vie. . . . vous trouvez une barrière insurmontable pour beaucoup de gens, une main de femme vous l'ouvre" (*P.G.*, p. 229; Child! You are at life's threshold. . . . you find a barrier which would be insurmountable for many others, and a woman's hand opens it for you). The maternal-erotic pattern established by Rastignac's rapport with his "real-life" family again follows the oedipal schema with Delphine and Goriot. A passive but sustained rivalry develops between Goriot and the student. Rastignac sets out to dine with Delphine, and her father contemplates him "avec une sorte d'envie" (*P.G.*, p. 168). The apartment designed to be a trysting-place for Rastignac and Delphine begins to look very much like the site of a ménage à trois in a scene in which Delphine is almost simultaneously caressed by Rastignac and Goriot; Rastignac repeatedly feels "des mouvements de jalousie" (*P.G.*, p. 232). And at an earlier point in the novel (when he is still pursuing Delphine's sister Anastasie), Rastignac expresses all the horror of the child who believes his mother, his idol, is being sullied by his father's monstrous contact: "Jamais on ne me fera croire, s'écria l'étudiant, que la belle comtesse de Restaud appartienne au père Goriot" (*P.G.*, p. 87; "Never will I believe," cried the student, "that the beautiful Comtesse de Restaud belongs to Père Goriot"). He accordingly disqualifies his rival as he ponders "le mystère des liaisons criminelles de *ce vieux rat sans queue* et de cette belle femme" (*P.G.*, p. 103 [emphasis added]; the secret of the criminal ties between *this old rat with no tail* and that beautiful woman).

But the relationship between Goriot and Rastignac is still more complex. Identical in their passion for Delphine, united more often than divided by it, the two are doubles creating a joint role. Goriot writes the script; Rastignac acts it out. After furnishing the trysting-place, Goriot informs Rastignac: "Je me suis mis dans tout cela jusqu'au cou. Mais, voyez-vous, il y avait à moi bien de l'égoisme" (*P.G.*, p. 197; I have been in on these plans up to my neck. But you see, it was in my own interests to be). Rastignac is the agent through whom Goriot realizes his desire, vicariously possesses his daughter:

Le père Goriot se voyait un peu plus près de sa fille Delphine, il s'en voyait mieux reçu, si Eugène devenait cher à la baronne. . . . Mme de Nucingen, à laquelle mille fois par jour il souhaitait le bonheur, n'avait pas connu les douceurs de l'amour. Certes, Eugène était, pour se servir de son expression, un des jeunes gens les plus gentils qu'il eût jamais vus, et il semblait pressentir qu'il lui donnerait tous les plaisirs dont elle avait été privé. Le bonhomme se prit donc pour son voisin d'une amitié qui alla croissant. [*P.G.*, p. 162]

[Père Goriot thought he might be brought closer to his daughter Del-phine, he thought he might be better received, if the Baroness became fond of Eugène. . . . Madame de Nucingen—whose happiness he longed for a thousand times each day—had never known the pleasures of love. Eugène certainly was—to use his expression—one of the nicest young men he had ever met, and he seemed to sense that he would give her all the pleasures she had never known. Thus the old man felt a growing friendship for his neighbor.]

The rapport which binds Delphine to Goriot through Rastignac's mediation is thus a variation of Vautrin's projected bond with Rastignac through the interposition of Victorine. The ostensible difference is Rastignac's position in the respective relationships; in one, he is the indirect object, or the means, in the other, the direct object, or the end. However, a closer look at the nature of Goriot's affection for the student reveals that the distinction is superficial. Goriot's passion for his daughter knows no bounds, ignores differentiation, and by extension envelops her lover. Go-riot tells Rastignac as much when he rhapsodically plans their ménage à trois: "Je serai là. Vous me parlerez d'elle tous les soirs. . . . Si j'étais malade, ça me mettrait du baume dans le coeur de vous écouter revenir, vous remuer, aller. *Il y aura tant de ma fille en vous!*" (*P.G.*, p. 197; [emphasis added]; I'll be there. You will tell me all about her every evening. . . . If I were sick, it would ease my pain to hear you coming and going, moving about. *There will be so much of my daughter in you!*).

As Rastignac becomes the secondary object of the father's overflowing passion, he turns out to play both son and lover to Goriot. The traditional amorous triangle is complicated here by Goriot's bilateral passion: "Il était en tiers dans ces jeunes émotions et ne paraissait pas le moins heureux. Il aimait déjà Rastignac et pour sa fille et pour lui-même" (*P.G.*, pp. 198–99; He was the third person in this couple, but didn't appear the least happy of the three. He already loved Rastignac both for his daughter and for himself). We repeatedly witness his effusive displays of physical affection for Rastignac: "Laissez-moi vous embrasser. (Et il serra l'étudiant dans ses bras.)" (*P.G.*, p. 199; "Let me embrace you." [And he clasped the student in his arms]). And: "Le père Goriot saisit la main de l'étudiant et la lui serra. Il aurait voulu la baiser" (*P.G.*, p. 212; Père Goriot took the student's hand and squeezed it. He would have liked to kiss it).

Thus, throughout the explicitly delineated relationships which structure *Le Père Goriot*, we trace the more important, the more heavily charged network of relations which we perceive as virtual lines of force, a welter of tangled threads which superimpose paternity, conjugality, incest, and homosexuality. This mass of overlaid lines ill disguises the fact that the origin from which they all emanate, the center which should properly impose an order on the chaos and command a cessation of the mad proliferation of relationships, is a lack, a gaping abyss.

The simultaneous failure of paternity and of language which we read between the crisscrossed lines suggests that the quest for an absent father which structures *Le Père Goriot* is inseparable from the search for an ineffable meaning, an irretrievable significance which must be created if it does not exist. Thus Balzac's language repeatedly names the sublimity it is unable to express, poses the father it is unable to find:

Le père Goriot était sublime. . . . Souvent l'être le plus stupide arrive, sous l'effort de la passion, à la plus haute éloquence dans l'idée, si ce n'est dans le langage. . . . Il y avait en ce moment dans la voix, dans le geste de ce bonhomme, la puissance communicative qui signale le grand acteur. [*P.G.*, p. 161]

[Père Goriot was sublime. . . . Often the dullest creature, under the sway of passion, reaches the heights of eloquence in thought, if not in language. . . . At this moment the old man's voice and gesture contained the expressive power that marks a great actor.]

Whence, too the multiplication of comparisons which are essentially tautologies, piled-up repetitions of other representations:

Pour bien peindre la physionomie de ce Christ de la Paternité, il faudrait aller chercher des comparaisons dans les images que les princes de la palette ont inventées pour peindre la passion soufferte au bénéfice des mondes par le Sauveur des hommes. [*P.G.*, p. 231]

[In order to depict the features of this Christ of Paternity, one would have to compare it to the images invented by those princes of the palette who painted the passion suffered for the benefit of humanity by the Savior of men.]

Roland Barthes characterizes such instances of redundancy where meaning is excessively named as "une sorte de babil sémantique . . . marqué par la peur obsessionnelle de manquer la communication du sens"[18] (a kind of semantic babble. . . . marked by the obsessive fear of failing to communicate meaning). The signifying disturbance is symptomatic of the paternal quest, for the ideal father would both organize the disarray of relations and order the semiotic anarchy.

In the absence of a language powerful enough to create such a father, Balzac turns to figures of excess and paradox. He overwrites in order to underwrite, to guarantee the inviolability of paternity and the indestructible presence of meaning. But more is inevitably less, as the excess denotes its motivating deficiency. Thus, for example, the epithet intended to designate Goriot's absolute paternity, "ce Christ de la Paternité," supplements the fa-

ther, qualifies him as the archetypal son, and in so doing under-
mines his overdetermined fatherhood.

This confusion of father and child comes to a dizzying peak
atop Goriot's deathbed. The dying man raves:

Les pères devraient vivre autant que leurs enfants. Mon Dieu, comme
ton monde est mal arrangé! Et tu as un fils cependant, à ce qu'on nous
dit. Tu devrais nous empêcher de souffrir dans nos enfants. Mes chers
anges. . . . Venez, venez vous plaindre ici! Mon coeur est grand, il peut
tout recevoir. Oui, vous avez beau le percer, les lambeaux feront encore
des coeurs de père. Je voudrais prendre vos peines, souffrir pour vous.
[*P.G.,* p. 248]

[Fathers should live as long as their children. My God, how poorly your
world is arranged! And yet, you have a son, according to what we are
told. You should prevent us from suffering through our children. My
beloved angels. . . . Come, come tell me your troubles. My heart is large
enough to hold them all. Even if you were to break it, each broken bit
would make a new father's heart. How I'd like to bear your troubles,
suffer in your place.]

Goriot begins by rather drolly analogizing his parental problems
with God's. By virtue of the fact that God has a son, he should
be in a position to understand, and hence remedy, the anguish
children visit upon their fathers. By the end of the passage, however, Goriot has identified himself with the son, casting himself
in the role of martyr, implicit brother to his suffering children.
But Goriot as son is simultaneously, eternally, father. A grotesque
image of irrepressible procreation foresees the stigmatized shreds
of his martyr's heart spontaneously generating father's hearts.[19]

Thus Goriot's paternal status is weakened, repudiated, in
the very effort to affirm it. The novel's title reflects this, denigrating "Goriot père" as "le père Goriot." A powerless father figure
ruled by his children, he is a *deus abdicatus,* a would-be god who
has relinquished his authority. The hierarch removed, the hierarchy crumbles; meaning must now be sought in accumulation
and excess rather than in distinction and order. Goriot heaps
relation upon relation in a paroxysmal striving toward a totalizing substitute:

"Mais, c'est mon fils, notre enfant, ton frère, ton sauveur," criait le père Goriot. "Embrasse-le donc, Nasie! Tiens, moi je l'embrasse," reprit-il en serrant Eugène avec une sorte de fureur. "Oh! mon enfant! je serai plus qu'un père pour toi, je veux être une famille. Je voudrais être Dieu, je te jetterais l'univers aux pieds. Mais, baise-le donc, Nasie? ce n'est pas un homme, mais un ange." [*P.G.*, p. 252]

["But he is my son, our child, your brother, your savior," cried Père Goriot. "Embrace him, Nasie! Wait, I will embrace him myself," he continued, clasping Eugène to him in his frenzy. "Oh, my child! I will be more than a father for you, I want to be an entire family. Could I but be God, I would fling the very universe at your feet. Will you not kiss him, Nasie? This is no man, but an angel."]

As family structure and relations crumble, there is a furious over-coding, as if to compensate. Goriot wants to make of Rastignac all relations, all sexes and none (ce n'est pas un homme, mais un ange), much as Vautrin does. Sexual and relational distinctions are blurred in the frenzied accretion of superimposed connections which recalls the artist Frenhofer's failed masterpiece: "des couleurs confusément amassées et contenues par une multitude de lignes bizarres. . . . ce chaos de couleurs, de tons, de nuances indécises, espèce de brouillard sans forme"[20] (colors confusedly piled up and contained by a multitude of bizarre lines. . . . this chaos of colors, tones, unclear nuances, like an amorphous fog).

Goriot's familial dream meets with much the same fate as Frenhofer's artistic vision. And Balzac's totalizing quest fares no differently. In both cases, the medium (relations, painting, language) is nullified in the service of transcendent ends. The signifying process is interrupted; we are told that a transcendent signified exists, but it is detached from any signifier, and we have no way to reach it. The novel dramatically represents this semiotic breakdown in its final scene. As Goriot is being buried, attended only by Rastignac and the servant Christophe, we are told of the last-minute approach of "deux voitures armoriées, mais vides, celle du comte de Restaud et celle du baron de Nucingen" (*P.G.*, p. 290; two emblazoned, but empty, carriages, one belonging to the Comte de Restaud and the other to the Baron de Nucingen"). These two emblazoned carriages, vehicles of an absent meaning, are empty signifiers; the family crests they bear

refer to a disrupted signifying relation, a signified which is detached, *elsewhere*.

With Goriot's death and burial, the title and the final page—
our first and last points of contact with the novel—are placed in
ironic symmetry. Our reading experience is enclosed and defined
by the two framing fathers of the text: the title's *Père Goriot* and
the closing *Père-Lachaise* cemetery. The trajectory that takes us
from one father's name to its echo in the other's retains the name
of the Father but subjects it to a transformation in meaning: we
pass from a figure of generation to one of death. By the time
Goriot is entombed at the novel's end, the two fathers have
merged: one paternal "plot" has absorbed the other. Balzac's
title for the novel's last chapter, "La Mort du père," might then
be understood as a retrospective title for the novel—a title which
amends the paternal centrality of *Le Père Goriot* and which refers as much to the symbolic effacement of paternity as to Goriot's own death.

Goriot's failure is not Balzac's. The rupture of signification
within the narrative does not result in the decomposition of the
text, because the text succeeds in representing this rupture. The
novel ends on an upbeat; as Rastignac surveys Paris from the
heights of Père-Lachaise, he, as figure of the narrator, has
achieved mastery. He has come to dominate Paris, women, and
the novel. He has avoided both Vautrin's attitude of revolt
against society (which is, by extension, an undervaluation of
women, procreation, and representation) and Goriot's attitude
of obedience (an overvaluation of women, procreation, and representation). His poise, however, is precarious, as is Balzac's victory over the threat of textual disintegration. The breakdown of
signification figured in the text is absorbed, because the tremen-
dous destructive energy it releases is thematized, that is, bound
in representation. But the threat remains, and each novel reveals
the renewed struggle of a novelist caught between Scylla and
Charybdis, between Vautrin and Goriot, between a representation sacrificed to preserve a vision, and a vision compromised to
achieve a representation.

CHAPTER FOUR

Madmen and Visions, Sages and Codes
Illusions perdues, Splendeurs et misères des courtisanes

Un fou est un homme qui voit un abîme et y tombe. Le savant l'entend tomber, prend sa toise, mesure la distance, fait un escalier, descend, remonte, et se frotte les mains, après avoir dit à l'univers:

"Cet abîme a dix-huit cent deux pieds de profondeur, la température du fond est de deux degrés plus chaude que celle de notre atmosphère." Puis il vit en famille. Le fou reste dans sa loge. Dieu seul sait qui du fou, qui du savant a été le plus près du vrai.

BALZAC, *Théorie de la démarche*

alzac's writings consistently posit two alternative paradigms for comprehending the world. On the one hand, there is the paradigm which we may place under the rubric "science," which comprises sight, observation, calculation, codification and representation, realism, and materialism; on the other, "poetry," which envelops second sight or vision, intuition, pure thought and mysticism, and spiritualism—all that is ineffable, inarticulate, absolute, and whose extreme derivative is madness. The narrator of *Facino Cane* (often considered to be the writer's manifesto) identifies these two paradigms as the dual components of writing: "Chez moi *l'observation* était déjà devenue *intuitive,* elle pénétrait l'âme sans négliger le corps." [1]

Among the theoretical texts, there is an essay called *Théorie de la démarche* which develops and elucidates this dualistic concept of writing. The parable of the *fou* and the *savant,* cited in epigraph above, associates madness with isolation, muteness, and celibacy, while relating science to community, communication, and family. Balzac here caricatures the scientist and the visionary; the scientist or sage is the assiduous, meticulous scholar, the realist fastidious to a fault, while the madman is the visionary fallen away from reality, lost in his mystic revery. Clearly neither one of these two prototypes is sufficient, but together they epitomize the necessary constituents of a successful literary endeavor:

Ici, je serai toujours entre la toise du savant et le vertige du fou. Je dois en prévenir loyalement celui qui veut me lire; il faut de l'intrépidité pour rester entre ces deux asymptotes. Cette *Théorie* ne pouvait être faite que par un homme assez osé pour côtoyer la folie sans crainte et la science sans peur.[2]

[Here I shall remain between the scientist's measurements and the madman's vertigo. I should, in good faith, warn my reader: remaining between these two asymptotes calls for boldness. This *Théorie* could be developed only by a man daring enough to skirt madness without fright and science without fear.]

Balzac proceeds to explain the literary process in terms which are strikingly sexual. The vision which gives rise to the *Théorie* is untouched territory, unexplored by science: "Elle est quasi-vierge. J'espère pouvoir démontrer la raison coefficiente de cette précieuse virginité scientifique" (*T.D.*, p. 259; It is quasi-virginal. I hope to be able to explain the precious virginal state of this science, find its causal factor.) The vision or idea is consistently described in feminizing terms, as in the following instance: "l'idée malicieuse, luxuriante, luxueuse, belle comme une femme magnifiquement belle" (*T.D.*, pp. 264–65; the malicious, lush, luxurious idea, as beautiful as a magnificently beautiful woman).

But the vision is not enough: "L'écrivain, chargé de répandre les lumières qui brillent sur les hauts lieux, doit donner à son oeuvre *un corps littéraire* (*T.D.*, p. 277 [emphasis added]; The writer, whose task is to shed light on the ideal, must give *literary body* to his work). The ideal must be incorporated, incarnated, given a formal representation. Whence the writer's next step: "Je résolus de constater simplement les effets produits en dehors de l'homme par ses mouvements, de quelque nature qu'ils fussent, de les noter, de les classer; puis, l'analyse achevée, de rechercher les lois du beau idéal . . . et d'en rediger un code" (*T.D.*, p. 274; I resolved simply to observe the external effects of man's movements, whatever their nature, to note them down, to classify them; then, the analysis completed, to seek the laws of the ideal, and codify them). At this point the need for remaining "between the two asymptotes"—science and madness—becomes imperative. The ideal must be incarnated without being reduced in the process. The writer must merge with the visionary: "Être un grand écrivain et un grand observateur . . . tel est le problème; problème insoluble" (*T.D.*, p. 277; To be a great writer and a great observer . . . that is the problem, the insoluble problem). The problem is insoluble because its optimal resolution, for Balzac, can never be more than a compromise. When the ideal is articulated, when the transcendent signified is recuperated by the signifier, it is no longer transcendent, and it is no longer ideal. When the signifier most completely translates the signified, it replaces it, reduces it to language, and so abolishes it, thereby challenging the very possibility of representation.

This impasse, Balzac's creative nemesis, recurs in numerous texts. *Massimilla Doni,* a story of impossible love, eloquently allegorizes the inherent impossibility of representation. This text recounts a tale of madness, a derangement affecting the protagonist, Emilio, who is unable to integrate spiritual love and carnal love. While his physical passion for the courtesan Clara Tinti is repeatedly satiated, his idealized love for the duchess Massimilla Doni remains a mystic ecstasy which cannot be consummated. We are told that Emilio "amenait . . . sa jeune amie au bord de ce que toutes les femmes nomment l'*abîme,* et se voyait obligé de cueillir les fleurs qui le bordent, sans pouvoir faire autre chose que les effeuiller en contenant dans son coeur une rage qu'il n'osait exprimer"[3] (led . . . his young friend to the edge of what all women call *the abyss,* and found himself obliged to gather the flowers growing along the edges, unable to do more than pull off the petals, as he contained within him a rage he dared not express). In the specific context, the abyss quite clearly functions as the metaphorical locus of sexual penetration (in positive terms, the site of a conception; in negative terms, of a fall). As the locus of impregnation, it in turn becomes a metaphor for the formulation of an idea, the verbal incarnation of an abstraction.[4] Thus when Emilio's friend Vendramin counsels him on the folly of transcending "la sphère où s'enfantent les oeuvres plastiques par les procédés de l'imitation" (the representational sphere) in order to accede to the spiritual realm of abstraction, Emilio responds: "Tu viens d'expliquer mon amour pour la Massimilla" (p. 585; You have just explained my love for Massimilla).

Because Emilio's madness is due to a split between erotic and spiritual love, his cure will depend upon integrating the two. The doctor who undertakes Emilio's therapy therefore advises Massimilla to take the courtesan's place, to take on a courtesan's passion, to deceive Emilio so that, believing he is making love to the courtesan Clara Tinti, he will unwittingly consummate his hitherto spiritual relationship with Massimilla.

We are forewarned that the outcome of such a cure cannot be entirely positive. Vendramin pontificates: "Raphaël seul a réuni la Forme et l'Idée. Tu veux être Raphaël en amour; mais on ne crée pas le hasard. Raphaël est un raccroc du Père éternel qui a fait la Forme et l'Idée ennemies, autrement rien ne vivrait.... Nous devons être ou sur la terre ou dans le ciel" (p. 601; Only Raphael successfully united Form and Idea. You want to be the Raphael of love, but chance is not created. Raphael is an accident of the Eternal Father, who made Form and Idea antagonistic; otherwise nothing would live.... We have to be either on earth or in heaven). And Vendramin turns out to be Balzac's spokesman. The novel comes to a rather sardonic close: "Comment dire le dénouement de cette aventure, car il est horriblement bourgeois. Un mot suffira pour les adorateurs de l'idéal. La duchesse était grosse" (p. 619; How can the dénouement of this adventure be told, for it is terribly bourgeois? A word will be enough for the worshippers of the ideal. The duchess was pregnant). Massimilla's pregnancy is the most manifest sign possible of an incarnation. But this incarnation is problematic; if it marks a cure (both textual and sexual), it also signals a loss. For the ideal is sacrificed when love becomes attainable, when the father is represented in the child; the vision is destroyed when the signified no longer transcends the signifier.[5]

The alternative, of course, is Louis Lambert, the madman who falls into the abyss and, unlike the scientist, neither measures it, codifies its laws, or expresses what he has seen there; unlike the cured Emilio, he does not fecundate it. The narrator relates Louis's affinity for mysticism: *Abyssus abyssum,* me disait-il. *Notre esprit est un abîme qui se plaît dans les abîmes. . . . Cette prédilection lui fut fatale.*"[6] (*"Abyssus abyssum,"* he told me. "The mind is an abyss that likes being in abysses." . . . This predilection was fatal for him). Fatal because the fall into the abyss is a fall into abstraction, into an unverbalized ideal. Louis's madness comprises a double dissociation: the separation of body and spirit, and the rupture of word and thought. Indeed, on the eve of his marriage, Louis attempts to castrate himself, fearing that carnal knowledge will annihilate ideal knowledge: "Peut-être a-t-il vu dans les plaisirs de son mariage un obstacle à la perfection de ses sens intérieurs et à son vol à travers les Mondes Spirituels"[7] (Perhaps he viewed the pleasures of his marriage as an obstacle to the refinement of his inner senses and his flight through the Realm of the Spirit). While his castration attempt is foiled, he falls into a cataleptic state, thus metaphorically accomplishing the act he did not realize. He becomes aphasic, speaking only in fragments, unable to represent his thought verbally.

The analogy here suggested between linguistic disturbance, or aphasia, and sexual impotence, or castration, underlies many of Balzac's narrative patterns; I will have occasion to explore it in greater detail in relation to *Illusions perdues* and *Splendeurs et misères.* My passage through these two texts will be guided by a dialectic of fecundity and sterility, incarnation and disincarnation, representation and ideality, expression and expressive blockage.

I

The artist is Icarus looking for safe ground.

GEORGE STEINER, *The Death of Tragedy*

The first panel of the triptych known as *Illusions perdues* is called *Les Deux Poètes.* The title refers to David Séchard and Lucien de Rubempré (né Chardon) and at first glance appears to involve a misnomer, for if Lucien is a poet by vocation, temperament, and physique, David is a scientist, an inventor. But the two in fact have a common origin; they are like Siamese twins whose vital functions are shared:

Quoique destiné aux spéculations les plus élevées des sciences naturelles, Lucien se portait avec ardeur vers la gloire littéraire; tandis que David, que son génie méditatif prédisposait à la poésie, inclinait par goût vers les sciences exactes. Cette interposition des rôles engendra comme une fraternité spirituelle. [*I.P.*, p. 142]

[Although he had been destined for the highest speculations of natural science, Lucien ardently aspired to literary glory, while David, whose contemplative talents predisposed him to poetry, preferred the exact sciences. This interchange of roles engendered a kind of spiritual fraternity between them.]

Like Siamese twins severed after birth, Lucien and David go different routes, but the complementarity of their divergent paths bespeaks the initial fusion. While Lucien is endowed with an ethereal nature, a penchant towards abstraction manifested by "le sourire des anges tristes" (*I.P.*, p. 145; the smile of sorrowing angels), David is characterized by a nature "qui se dégoûtait facilement des jouissances tout idéales en y portant les clartés de l'analyse" (*I.P.*, p. 145; which easily lost interest in imagined pleasures once they had been seen in the clear light of analysis). We once again find the two facets of writing, split here into two personae who together present an integral personification of the writer.

David, the printer who invents a new process for producing paper, "embrassait . . . la Presse . . . dans ses conséquences matérielles" (*I.P.*, p. 560; committed himself to . . . the material aspects . . . of the Press). He figures the concrete, applied side of writing, while Lucien, author of a novel and a collection of sonnets, embodies its visionary aspect.[8] Together "les deux poètes" mirror the production of the text in which they appear.

It is precisely because they do not remain together, giving the vision a material form, that the drama of *Illusions perdues* unfolds. Their separation opens a gap between signified and signifier which the rest of the novel, and its continuation in *Splendeurs et misères*, strains to close. David will replace his lost half by Eve, Lucien's sister, and go on to experience the trials of the scientist seeking the right formula. Once he has succeeded, the inventor devotes himself to study and to entomology—to a work of classification and codification. He retires to the countryside with his wife and three children. Like the savant of the parable, "puis il vit en famille."

Lucien's destiny is different. David is replaced by Herrera, and, accessorily, by a series of women who always divide Lucien's world into two irreconcilable paradigms, significantly labeled in literary terms:

"Quel dommage, se dit-il, de trouver sa femme *en deux volumes!* d'un côté, *la poésie,* la volupté, l'amour, le dévouement, la beauté, la gentillesse. . . . De l'autre, la noblesse du nom, la race, les honneurs, le rang, *la science* du monde! . . . Et aucun moyen de les réunir en une seule personne!" [*S.M.,* p. 518; emphasis added]

["What a shame," he said to himself, "to find the woman you want *in two volumes!* In one, *poetry,* sensuality, love, devotion, beauty, kindness. . . . In the other, an aristocratic name, breeding, honor, social rank, worldly *science!* . . . And no possibility of uniting them in a single person!"]

Condemned to unproductiveness by his hermaphroditic nature—he is "une jeune fille déguisée" (*I.P.,* p. 145; a girl in disguise), endowed with one of those "natures à demi féminines" (*I.P.,* p. 551; half-feminine natures)—he will produce no offspring, and eventually give up writing, content to dream, never more to incarnate the vision.

While David stands for production and reproduction, Lucien figures destruction and sterility. His homosexuality is apposed to David's heterosexuality, and he becomes in every respect David's inverted counterpart. The metaphors of textual and sexual production and destruction come together in a remarkable juxtaposition of two incidents at the close of the novel. Lucien leaves David at the point where the latter has discovered, by chewing raw vegetal matter, how to produce paper. He finds Herrera, who hails him and seduces him with the anecdote of a man who fetishistically destroyed paper by chewing it. This man, secretary to the Baron de Goertz, is analogous to Lucien, who is invited to be Herrera's secretary. Herrera's words to Lucien equate his own situation with the baron's:

Je me trouve dans la situation où fut le baron de Goertz . . . qui arriva
sans secrétaire dans une petite ville en allant en Suède, comme moi je
vais à Paris. Le baron rencontra le fils d'un orfèvre, remarquable par
une beauté qui ne pouvait certes pas valoir la vôtre. . . . Le baron de
Goertz trouve à ce jeune homme de l'intelligence, comme moi je vous
trouve de la poésie au front; il le prend dans sa voiture, comme moi je
vais vous prendre dans la mienne; et, de cet enfant condamné à brunir
des couverts et à fabriquer des bijoux dans une petite ville de province
comme Angoulême, il fait son favori, comme vous serez le mien. Arrivé
à Stockholm, il installe son secrétaire et l'accable de travaux. Le jeune
secrétaire passe les nuits à écrire; et, comme tous les grands travailleurs,
il contracte une habitude, il se met à mâcher du papier. . . . Notre beau
jeune homme commence par du papier blanc, mais il s'y accoutume et
passe aux papiers écrits qu'il trouve plus savoureux. On ne fumait pas
encore comme aujourd'hui. Enfin le petit secrétaire en arrive, de saveur
en saveur, à mâchonner des parchemins et à les manger. . . . Mais . . .
prenez un cigare, et fumez-la en attendant notre calèche. [*I.P.,* pp.
692–93]

[I find myself in the same situation as the Baron de Goertz . . . who
arrived without a secretary in a small town on his way to Sweden, as I
am on my way to Paris. The baron met a goldsmith's son, remarkably
handsome, although certainly less so than you. . . . The Baron de
Goertz found this young man intelligent, as I find you poetic; he took
him in his carriage, as I am going to take you in mine; and this young-
ster fated to burnish tableware and craft jewelry in a small provincial
town like Angoulême became his protégé, as you will be mine. When
he got to Stockholm, he settled his secretary in and overwhelmed him
with work. The young secretary spent his nights writing, and, like all
hard workers, he developed a habit, he began to chew paper. Our fine
young man began with blank paper, but he got bored with it and went
on to written sheets, which he found more tasty. People didn't smoke
then as they do today. Finally, after moving from taste to taste, he ended
up chewing documents, and eating them. . . . But . . . have a cigar,
smoke it while we are waiting for our carriage.]

It is not surprising that Proust was to praise the allusive quality
of this seduction scene,[9] for its eloquence is understated. Lucien's
identity with the young paper chewer is firmly established by
means of the proffered cigar: if, as the passage suggests, the Baron's secretary took to chewing paper because smoking was not
yet the custom, we may inversely assume that the cigar, for Lu-

cien, is a more socially acceptable—but analogous—chewing material. The cigar, however, is only a mediating device that links Lucien to the more condensed (and certainly more subtle) paper metaphor. Lucien's entire story is in a sense contained in one metaphoric wad of chewed paper substituted for another: the seduction by Herrera, the sexual inversion, the textual obliteration which succeeds David's production of a textual surface.

Moreover, everything written—and obliterated—on this piece of paper has already happened, and will happen again. Lucien's life is a series of repetitions which vary in detail but not in foundation. Each new love object is, as we shall see, a replay of every preceding attachment. There is wisdom in the naïveté which prompts him later to ask d'Arthez: "Mais, Daniel, est-ce que l'amour n'est pas partout semblable à lui-même?" (*I.P.*, p. 421; But, Daniel, isn't love the same everywhere?). His suicide manqué by the banks of the Charente is only postponed. Like the fou of the parable, Lucien is "un homme qui voit un abîme et y tombe." [10] He is to end his life "précipité dans les abîmes du suicide" (*S.M.*, p. 789; plunged in the abysses of suicide). Like the fou, too, in essence Lucien "reste dans sa loge"—or in any case returns there. For when he is incarcerated, in *Splendeurs et misères*, "Lucien, en entrant dans sa cellule, trouva . . . la fidèle image de la première chambre qu'il avait occupée à Paris, à l'hô-tel Cluny" (*S.M.*, p. 716; Lucien, upon entering his cell, found . . . the faithful image of the first room he had occupied in Paris, at the Hôtel Cluny). The cell-like room which was to be the hothouse for his visions reappears (and is retrospectively eluci-dated) as the prison-house of vision, the sterile, reflexive self-enclosure finally assumed in suicide, the irrevocable delivery of the self to the self.

But between the first cell and the last there is that long, circuitous detour which forms the substance of two novels. It is important that Lucien does not drown himself in the waters of the Charente, even if his ultimate fate is not very different, be-cause the interim reveals a textual Eros, or life-preservative in-stinct, which exists in conflict with the character's Thanatos, or conservative instinct, and resists a premature death, even though it would have the same shape at either point in time. [11]

We remember that Balzac refuses to choose between the

madman—the visionary in the service of meditation, introspection, an ineffable signified which is ultimately a figure of death, and the scientist—the sage in the service of form, reproduction, and a signifying process which is metaphorically tantamount to life: "Dieu seul sait qui du fou, qui du savant a été le plus près du vrai" (T.D., p. 265). We recall, too, Vendramin's remark that "the Eternal Father . . . made Form and Idea antagonistic; otherwise nothing would live." Like so many of Balzac's apparently facile aphorisms, this contains an astute observation on psychic and semiotic processes. Balzac is in fact alluding to the struggle between life and death instincts, formal and ideal tendencies, which inevitably gives victory to death and the ideal (the ineffable), but which yields life and narrative as happy by-products. If life is the hiatus between non-being and death, the signifier is perhaps that gap between semiotic emptiness and the ineffable which makes meaning possible.

And so Balzac writes and rewrites Lucien's story, much as we read and reread a novel for a second, a third, or a fourth time: because what matters is not death or the ending, but the circuitous route that takes us there, the patterns that are formed along the way. And so for much the same reasons we shall trace Lucien's story through its many repetitions (often disguised or distorted), setting up a "case history" designed to restore Lucien's partially obliterated text to legibility and meaning.

II

Those who neglect the plane of representation and close themselves in the realm of pure significations are struck dumb. One cannot begin by placing oneself within the domain of full signification and hope also to speak.

PETER BROOKS, *The Melodramatic Imagination*

Like so many Balzacian heroes, Lucien comes into the world ill-favored by birth and fortune, endowed with a powerful determination to redress his wrongs, and a resolute desire to restage his beginnings. Born Chardon, son of a petit-bourgeois father and a native aristocrat mother, Lucien inherits only the name when his father dies. This bitter legacy is a constant reminder of his humble origin, an obstacle to his grandiose ambition—a literal thorn in his flesh.

Appropriately, the poet's family romance will be spelled out in letters, played out on an onomastic level. As Lucien begins to frequent the provincial aristocracy, he feels the pricks of shame each time he passes the shop whose sign, in yellow letters on a green background, reads:

Pharmacie de POSTEL, successeur de CHARDON.
Le nom de son père, écrit ainsi dans un lieu par où passaient toutes les voitures, lui blessait la vue. [*I.P.*, p. 178]

[POSTEL Pharmacy, formerly CHARDON]
[His father's name, displayed for all the passing carriages to see, was an eyesore to him.]

It is not surprising that Lucien, raised by his mother and sister, shaped by an undiluted feminine influence (reflected by his physique and temperament, constantly described in terms of effeminacy) should believe that he, like his mother, "si grande dame dans son abaissement" (*I.P.*, p. 177; a noblewoman despite her humbled state), is debased, degraded by the lingering patronymic sting; not surprising, then, that he is susceptible to his aristocratic patroness's advice to "répudier audacieusement son père en prenant le noble nom de Rubempré" (*I.P.*, p. 173; boldly repudiate his father by taking the noble name of Rubempré). This name, his mother's name, is to open the doors of provincial society, later the salons of Parisian aristocracy, to the low-born poet, functioning much as Mme. de Beauséant's name for Rastignac, as "un fil d'Ariane" (*P.G.*, p. 117; an Ariadne's thread) in the social labryinth.

Thus Lucien is to be his mother's child, sired by no man if not by himself; he is readily persuaded by Mme. de Bargeton, his patroness, that men of genius are entitled, indeed, obligated, to be self-centered: "Le génie ne relevait que de lui-même; il était seul juge de ses moyens, car lui seul connaissait la fin: il devait donc se mettre au-dessus des lois" (*I.P.*, p. 174; Genius was responsible only to itself; it was sole judge of its means, because it alone knew what the ends were to be; it therefore had to be beyond the law).

These early signs of a narcissistic personality appear to be directly associated with the familial situation which dominated Lucien's youth. Raised, in the absence of a paternal figure, as the adored object of two self-sacrificing women who vest in this cherished child all their hopes, dreams, and affections, his route toward self-adoration is well-paved. Indeed, his first erotic attachment to another person (upon which all the others are to be modeled) is fundamentally still auto-erotic, since the sister he desires is defined by her self-abnegation, her devotion to him. Lucien loves in a mirror, then, through this early incestuous bond, and nothing changes later, as he repeatedly contemplates his own image in the series of reflective surfaces his admiring lovers willingly constitute for him.

Lucien and Eve are in fact mirror images of each other; the man, Lucien, marked by numerous signs of femininity,[12] the woman, Eve, by "les symptômes d'un caractère viril" (*I.P.*, p. 179). As in the Platonic myth of the androgyne, they together form a third sex, an ideal being which, when severed, will yield two incomplete creatures condemned to remember (fatally, for one of the two) a lost integrity: "Lorsque l'union des âmes a été parfaite comme elle le fut au début de la vie entre Eve et Lucien, toute atteinte à ce beau idéal du sentiment est mortelle" (*I.P.*, p. 648; When the union of souls was as perfect as it was in the early lives of Eve and Lucien, any blow to this emotional ideal is mortal).

Thus when Eve writes to her brother "Je te voulais auprès de toi quelque femme dévouée, une seconde moi-même" (*I.P.*, p. 324; I was hoping you would have some devoted woman—my double—at your side), she wishes him, quite logically, what he would wish himself: not only a second Eve, a projection of herself, but, by extension, a second self, his own reflection. Lucien in fact fulfills his sister's aspirations for him, in form if not in substance, for the women he loves form a chain of copies made in Eve's semantic image. Seduced by Mme. de Bargeton's aristocratic charms, Lucien "mordit à la pomme du luxe aristocratique et de la gloire." Seduced by the actress Coralie, Lucien devours "les fruits délicieux que lui avait tendus l'Eve des coulisses" (*I.P.*, p. 418; the delicious fruits that had been offered him by the Eve of the stage). His well-born Parisian conquests (Mme. de Sérizy,

Mme. de Maufrigneuse, Clotilde de Grandlieu), compromised by their ardent letters, are "trois filles d'Eve enveloppées par le serpent de la correspondance" (*S.M.*, p. 883; three daughters of Eve encircled by the serpent of correspondence). The otherwise banal Edenic metaphors are revitalized and rerouted through the eponymic mediation of the poet's sister, Eve, to whom they ultimately refer.

The sister, however, plays a maternal-erotic role in the relationship. Her own child is to be named "Lucien," as if to realize symbolically the desired maternal relationship to her brother (as if, also, to imagine him the father of a child bearing his name). And when Eve is completely disillusioned with her brother, her milk for the little Lucien dries up, as a sign of her withheld love and a confirmation of the identity of the two Luciens.

The incestuous pattern of the Lucien-Eve relationship recurs in other bonds. When Lucien moves away from his sister's maternal embrace, he is enveloped by Mme. de Bargeton, "une bienfaitrice qui allait s'occuper de lui maternellement" (*I.P.*, p. 169;[13] a benefactress who would take care of him like a mother). Mme. de Bargeton is replaced by another maternal figure, the actress Coralie, whose seductive allure is marked by "le soin et l'amour d'une mère pour un petit enfant" (*I.P.*, p. 409; the loving care of a mother for a little child). If the maternal element is considerably reduced, if not absent, in Esther, it is only because Vautrin-Herrera has entered the scene and usurped the role.

Following the pattern established by Eve, Lucien's subsequent amorous involvements supply him with the necessary dose of amour-propre. Particularly striking is the egotism generated by Lousteau's observation to Lucien that Coralie is "mad" about him: "—Bah? . . . pauvre fille! dit Lucien dont toutes les vanités furent caressées par ces paroles et qui se sentit le coeur gonflé d'amour-propre" (*I.P.*, p. 389;[14] "Oh, poor girl!" said Lucien, whose vanity was flattered by these words, which made his heart swell with pride).

If we are to understand Lucien's susceptibility to Herrera, it is imperative that we recognize his homosexuality as gradually emergent, inherent in his earliest attachments, latent in his narcissistic relational patterns. It is crucial, therefore, that we carefully define Lucien's rapport with David, because while manifestly narcissistic, it is already virtually homosexual, a kind of psychic bridge linking two sexual dispositions.

Here, as in *Le Père Goriot,* we should not be duped by the superficial pattern of relations imposed upon Lucien, David, and Eve, but should recognize, with Proust, that "sous l'action apparente et extérieure du drame, circulent de mystérieuses lois de la chair et du sentiment";[15] (beneath the manifest external action of the drama flow mysterious laws of the flesh and the heart). I spoke earlier of David and Lucien as initial Siamese twins, later to be split, and mentioned that David would "replace his lost half by Eve"—without, however, entering into the innuendos of this substitution. The apparently blissful courtship and marriage can only be comprehended as the rather scandalous compromise it is when read in the shadow of the persistent original bonds between David and Lucien on the one hand, and Eve and Lucien on the other.

David's relationship with Lucien precedes his rapport with Eve; this temporal priority dominates the affective mode as well. David's attraction to Lucien is eminently erotic; he is "vivement séduit par le brillant de l'esprit de Lucien" (*I.P.,* p. 146; seduced by Lucien's dazzling mind). Also, David provides the reflective surface which qualifies all of Lucien's partners: "L'un des deux aimait avec idolâtrie, et c'était David. Aussi Lucien commandait-il en femme qui se sait aimée. David obéissait avec plaisir" (*I.P.,* p. 146; One of the two loved with idolatry, and that was David. Therefore Lucien was in command like a woman who knows she is loved. David was glad to obey). Sexual paradigms are here disrupted, as they consistently are when Lucien is referred to. Moreover, David complies with the maternal role originated by his predecessors, copied by all of their successors: "David outra la foi que la mère et la soeur de Lucien avaient en son génie, il le gâta comme une mère gâte son enfant" (*I.P.,* p. 142; David surpassed the faith Lucien's mother and sister had in his genius; he spoiled him like a mother spoils her child). It will never be otherwise with Lucien's paramours; he will always love, in male as in female admirers, his own maternal image (his image of his mother or his mother's image of himself) embodied in another.[16] Lucien loves, like Narcissus, another who is not other, a second self. In words which curiously prefigure the terms of Herrera's pact, David tells Lucien: "Sois heureux, je jouirai de tes succès, tu seras un second moi-même. Oui, ma pensée me permettra de vivre de ta vie" (*I.P.*, p. 184; Be happy, and I will take pleasure in your success; you will be my double. Yes, my imagination will allow me to live through you!).

When David and Eve come together, each seeking in the other that part of the self lost when severed from Lucien, what results beneath the explicit marriage is the virtual union of Lucien with Lucien. Their love for each other initiates in their love for Lucien, and inevitably returns to this first object. David's attraction to Eve is described in terms which give evident priority to his relations with Lucien: "L'amitié de ces deux jeunes gens [David et Lucien] devint en peu de jours une de ces passions qui ne naissent qu'au sortir de l'adolescence. David entrevit bientôt la belle Eve, et s'en éprit" (*I.P.*, p. 142; The friendship between these two young men [David and Lucien] became within a few days one of those passions that are only born at the end of adolescence. David soon caught sight of the beautiful Eve and fell in love with her). Similarly, David's appeal for Eve is mediated by Lucien: "La plus grande séduction de l'imprimeur était son fanatisme pour Lucien: il avait deviné le meilleur moyen de plaire à Eve" (*I.P.*, p. 180; The printer's greatest appeal was his fanatic attachment to Lucien: he could not have discovered a better means of attracting Eve).

Thus Lucien, primitive love object for both Eve and David, is to remain the sublimated object of their love for each other. David courts Eve in the name of Lucien, and Eve accepts his advances in the same name. When Eve proposes to David: "Il fait beau, voulez-vous aller nous promener le long de la Charente? nous causerons de Lucien" (*I.P.*, p. 186; It is a beautiful evening; would you like to take a walk along the Charente? We will talk about Lucien), Lucien is both pretext and subtext, the former acting as a kind of screen for the latter. In much the same vein, Eve is to receive the most ambiguous marriage proposal ever uttered by would-be suitor: "Eve! Eve! . . . je voudrais être le frère de Lucien. Vous seule pouvez me donner ce titre, qui lui permettrait de tout accepter de moi. . . . Chère Eve, épousez-moi par amour pour Lucien." (*I.P.*, pp. 214–15; Eve! Eve! . . . I want to be Lucien's brother. You alone can give me this title, which would permit him to accept everything from me. . . . Dear Eve, marry me for love of Lucien). Pretext and subtext are again entangled in this passage, another one of those cases (similar to the inverted metaphor whereby a woman is represented as a literal beast) where the letter is flagrantly displayed in order to be most successfully hidden. David and Eve's union is based on a contractual agreement concerning a third party object who is thereby entitled to "tout accepter." Ratification takes place retroactively, after the terms of the contract have been effected. When David has decided to sacrifice all his savings to Lucien's ambition, thereby consigning Eve and himself to penury, we witness "le plus ardent baiser que deux fiancés aient jamais échangé" (*I.P.*, p. 254; the most ardent kiss that two fiancés have ever exchanged), the uncharacteristic ardor marking a grotesquely excessive element in the ceremony of assent: the interposition of Lucien.

But we must pause now to reflect upon this most recent manifestation of a triadic configuration, which, at the present point of this study, begins to elicit a series of echolike responses from texts we have dealt with earlier. Beneath the overt fraternal, conjugal, and comradely relations of Lucien, Eve, and David, we have disengaged occulted patterns of incest, hermaphroditism, and homosexuality, and correlatively, implied disruptions of sexual and familial paradigms. In retrospect, we note that the patterns underlying the Goriot-Delphine-Rastignac configuration are decidedly similar, and that the Vautrin-Victorine-Rastignac triad differs only by the negated bond between Vautrin and Victorine. When we look back upon *El Verdugo,* we recall the Juanito-Clara-Victor group, with its latent patterns of incest and doubling (which textual superimposition would identify as virtual homosexuality, though not yet present in the text). The virile female panther of *Une Passion* and the trio formed when the soldier is added to this male-female being is yet another case in point. This already considerable list should be extended to include Sarrasine plus the male-female Zambinella, and the triad composed of de Marsay, Paquita, and Mariquita in *La Fille aux yeux d'or.* Our list can be summarized by the archetypal hermaphrodite, Séraphîta-Séraphîtus, alternately accompanied by Wilfred and Minna.[17]

While these configurations vary in the relative emphasis placed on incest and homosexuality and in degree of explicitness, they share a common focus on either a composite or integral hermaphroditic figure representative of the union of difference, or ultimately, sameness. It is significant that incest and homosexuality so often appear together in the Balzacian text, frequently mediated by hermaphroditism, because they belong to the same paradigm of identity and elimination of difference. The equivalence of the three terms devolves from Plato's myth of the androgyne; we remarked upon the Platonic derivation of the incestual couple formed by Eve and Lucien, originally bound in perfect union, and we note another Platonic allusion when homosexuals are dubbed "le troisième sexe" (S.M., p. 840).[18]

When the myth is appropriated by Balzac, and narcissism is appended to the other three figures of sameness, it is pressed into narrative service to express thematically that which the text strives toward, structurally and linguistically, but can never attain while retaining its textual status, its status as tissue of meaning: a lost unity, a vision remembered or dreamed, an absolute which is by definition detached, disengaged, and hence necessarily extraverbal. It can only be figured in the ways we have seen, threatening havoc, bringing it perilously close at times, but never actually wreaking it—and it can be tautologically paraphrased. It is the "Dieu sans les hommes" of Une Passion; it is the irretrievable loss paraphrastically expressed by Mariquita when she faces Paquita's mutilated corpse: "Adieu . . . rien ne console d'avoir perdu ce qui nous a paru être l'infini"[19] ("Adieu . . . nothing can console when we have lost what was infinity to us"). It is also those typically Balzacian moments when the narrator gives in to what Martin Kanes dubs "linguistic despair"[20] and resorts to tautological formulae such as "words cannot express . . ." and "only an artist's brush could paint. . . ." At these moments when the absolute, the "unloosed" begins to infiltrate the text, there *is* a formal threat, because anything detached or unloosed is properly alinguistic, adrift in incommunicability, aphasic.

As we return to Lucien's history, we will continue to trace the proliferation of figures of sameness in the text, following them to a crisis point at which the text recognizes and assumes the abolition of difference it has created. Wrenched from its course, radically decentered and temporarily stalled, the narrative will then resume under a new ideology.

III

Aussi, peut-être un jour le sens inverse de l'ET VERBUM CARO FACTUM EST, sera-t-il le résumé d'un nouvel évangile qui dira: ET LA CHAIR SE FERA LE VERBE, ELLE DEVIENDRA LA PAROLE DE DIEU.

BALZAC, *Louis Lambert*

Between the time of Lucien's implied erotic rapport with David and the moment of his seduction by Herrera, when his homosexuality becomes more or less overt, there is a period of latency during which he is successively involved with Mme. de Bargeton and Coralie. During this interim period, however, a slowly rising structure of allusions skillfully and thoroughly prepares the groundwork for the encounter with Herrera.

David is of course Herrera's most obvious forerunner.[21] But the fervent bonds of friendship which at least temporarily unite Lucien with Daniel d'Arthez and the other members of the *Cénacle* repeat that fraternal pattern of "amitié amoureuse."[22] We note in particular Lucien's haste to reimburse the loan made him by his friends, and the responding words of Fulgence, an almost exact echo of Vautrin's incisive comment to Rastignac when the latter returned his money and thereby implicitly refused his sexual advances: "On dirait que tu as peur de nous devoir quelque chose" (*I.P.*, p. 324; One might say that you are afraid of being in our debt).

For the most part, though, Lucien's bisexuality is played out metaphorically, sublimated in his journalistic adventures. We have at various moments glimpsed the sexual connotations that writing has for Balzac;[23] correlatively, a certain form of sexuality is alluded to through journalism, that specialized branch of writing. From the beginning, Lucien is endowed with "un esprit entreprenant, mais mobile" (*I.P.*, p. 146; an enterprising but fickle spirit); he is undefined, of indeterminate morality: "Ainsi était fait Lucien, il allait du mal au bien, du bien au mal avec une égale facilité" (*I.P.*, p. 178; That is how Lucien was: he went from evil to good, from good to evil with the same ease). Lucien's moral hermaphroditism finds an appropriate vocational outlet in journalism.

At the beginning of his journalistic career Lucien is a pronounced liberal, but when more profitable circumstances beckon (the false promise of a royal decree that would restore his mother's name and aristocratic status to him), he easily swings over to the royalists. As a critic, political and financial imperatives call upon him to praise a book or play he knows to be execrable, and conversely, to pan a literary or theatrical production worthy of encomium. He soon learns to answer such calls with little compunction.[24] His mad fluctuation from one end of the political and critical spectrums to the other can be explained by Balzac's theory of expenditure:

Ce qui nous use le plus, ce sont nos convictions. Ayez des opinions, ne les défendez pas, gardez-les; mais des convictions! grand Dieu! quelle effroyable débauche! Une conviction politique ou littéraire est une maîtresse qui finit par vous tuer avec l'épée ou avec la langue. [*T.D.*, p. 294]

[What wears us out the most are our convictions. Have opinions, if you like, don't defend them, keep them to yourself. But convictions! Good God! What an appalling debauchery! A political or literary conviction is a mistress who ends up killing you with the sword or the tongue.]

This theory, which dominates all of Balzac's writings, holds that the more one expends one's vital forces (and the sexual implications are manifest), the more quickly one's life is spent.[25] In the above citation (as in Lucien's story) the fear of an existential commitment betrays, through the metaphor of the homicidal mistress, an anxiety about sexual depletion, a castration anxiety. The way Lucien comports himself as a journalist ultimately corroborates his resemblance to the madman in the parable of the fou and the savant, for he is incapable of incarnating a vision, incapable of bringing an opinion to fruition in a conviction. In the narrator's terms, he is "plein de négligence et souhaitant l'ordre, un de ces génies *incomplets* qui ont *quelque puissance pour désirer* . . . mais qui n'ont *aucune force pour exécuter"* (*S.M.*, p. 473 [emphasis added]; full of negligence though craving order; one of those *incomplete* geniuses who have *a certain power of desire* . . . but *no power of execution*).

Lucien's incomplete potency is projected in his choice of female love objects, for the women he frequents are courtesans and prostitutes.[26] Since the nineteenth century commonly held prostitutes to be sterile,[27] Lucien's choice is a compromise which avoids the problem (literary as well as obviously biological) of conception and incarnation. Moreover, the descriptions which render these courtesans are decidedly hermaphroditic, relying quite frequently on wild animal similes, which here, as in *Une Passion,* translate sexual ambiguity. Esther, significantly nicknamed "la Torpille," appears to have all the force Lucien lacks: "Esther se dressa comme une bête fauve" (*S.M.*, p. 515; Esther rose like a wild creature). She becomes for Lucien "ce qu'est le gibier pour le chasseur" (*S.M.*, p. 475; what the game is for the hunter). Like Lucien, "*Les filles sont des êtres essentiellement mobiles.* . . . Elles sont, sous ce rapport, au-dessous de l'animal" (*S.M.*, p. 458 [emphasis added]; *Prostitutes are essentially fickle creatures.* . . . They are, in this regard, more lowly than animals). Given the dual characteristics of Lucien's women, made in his image, the maternal Herrera is only another step in a logical progression.

Lucien is overtaken by Herrera at the moment when, rejected by his mother, sister, and David, he is irrevocably (so it seems) delivered over to himself, denied the Other as reflected self-image. Suicide, the ultimate reflexive act, appears to him as the only possible replacement. He chooses a manner of death remarkably consistent with his personality and the blows it has been dealt: death by water, a negative birth, a return to the original perfect union he was never fully able to retrieve in life. Even the site of Lucien's death is dictated by self-image and negative self-image; an "amour-propre posthume" decides against indiscriminately casting himself into the Charente as too public a death, for Lucien is adamantly determined "de ne pas être vu dans l'horrible état où sont les noyés quand ils reviennent à fleur d'eau" (*I.P.*, p. 689; not to be seen in that horrible state drowned bodies are in when they return to the surface of the water). Instead he chooses an out-of-the-way pool, "une de ces nappes rondes . . . dont l'excessive profondeur est accusée par la tranquillité de la surface. L'eau n'est plus ni verte, ni bleue, ni claire, ni jaune; *elle est comme un miroir d'acier poli*" (*I.P.*, p. 689 [emphasis added]; one of those round pools . . . whose great depth is marked by the surface calm. The water is neither green, nor blue, nor clear, nor yellow; it is like a polished steel mirror). As Lucien approaches this pool, contemplating his final self-contemplation, Herrera stops him with a promise to serve as vital reflective surface: "Je me ferai vous!" (*I.P.*, p. 703; I will be your double!) "Je dirai: 'Ce beau jeune homme, c'est moi'" (*I.P.*, p. 708; I will say: "This handsome young man is me")—thereby obviating the plunge into the fatal mirror.[28]

Like the fisherman in so many hero myths, Herrera saves Lucien, who is then reborn to a new set of parents: "Je vous ai pêché, je vous ai rendu la vie, et vous m'appartenez comme la créature est au créateur," Herrera tells him (*I.P.*, p. 703; I have fished you out, I have given your life back to you, and you belong to me as the creature belongs to his creator). But the archetypal pattern is twisted by the fact that Herrera embodies both parents; he promises to love Lucien "comme un père aime son enfant" (*I.P.*, p. 708; as a father loves his child), and demands that Lucien obey him "comme un enfant obéit à sa mère" (*I.P.*, p. 703; as a child obeys his mother).

The entire scene is accomplished in a language which is masterfully subtle and elegantly indirect; the allusions are multiplied, however, to a point which leaves no room for misunderstanding what is not being stated. The reader, like Lucien, is seduced, led away from a language which proceeds by direction, to (and by) an inverted discourse which leaves meaning *sous-entendu*, soliciting the reader's complicity to restore it to the surface. Thus, for example, the following inversion metaphor: "Lucien se trouvait dans la situation de ce pêcheur de je ne sais quel conte arabe, qui, voulant se noyer en plein Océan, tombe au milieu de contrées sous-marines et y devient roi" (*I.P.*, p. 694; Lucien was like the fisherman in that Arabian tale who tries to drown himself in the middle of the Ocean, but instead falls into an underwater land and becomes king). Because the ocean has been such a pervasive symbol of a world ruled by femininity and heterosexual activity, the evocation of an underwater realm—an underworld—is a deft reverse image which requires no explanation. Lucien's *prise de conscience* is just as tacitly rendered, as he indicates Rastignac's birthplace to Herrera:

"Voici, dit-il, d'où est parti le jeune Rastignac. . . . Il est devenu, comme je vous le disais, l'amant de Mme de Nucingen, la femme du fameux banquier. *Moi, je me suis laissé aller à la poésie; lui, plus habile, a donné dans le positif.*" [*I.P.*, p. 695; emphasis added]

["This," he said, "is where young Rastignac set out from. . . . He became, as I was telling you, the lover of Mme. de Nucingen, the famous banker's wife. *I let myself be carried away by poetry; he was wiser, and chose a more positive direction.*"]

So begins the alliance which is to end by realizing the interrupted disaster that initiated it. The inevitability of this return of a postponed end is made clear by the fact that the homosexual episode marks a continuation, and not a revision, of Lucien's narcissism. Herrera lives a vicarious existence through Lucien, fully creating the fused being which remained nostalgic and virtual in the Lucien-David rapport: "Aucun sacrifice ne coûtait d'ailleurs à cet homme étrange, dès qu'il s'agissait de son second lui-même. Au milieu de sa force, il était si faible contre les fantaisies de sa créature qu'il avait fini par lui confier ses secrets" (*S.M.*, p. 502; No sacrifice was too costly for this strange man, as soon as it involved his second self. Despite his force, he was so weak when it came to his creature's whims that he ended by confiding in him). Like Wilde's Dorian Gray, Lucien is involved with women, but in a purely carnal sense; only Herrera provides a spiritual relationship, a communion of souls.

Lucien and Herrera live a symbiotic existence, each completing the other, each constituting a completed (hermaphroditic) being for the other. Lucien represents, for Herrera, "une femme manquée" (*S.M.*, p. 898); "efféminé par tes caprices, tu es viril par ton esprit," says Herrera (*S.M.*, p. 477; your caprices are effeminate, but you have a virile mind). And Lucien will have, in his patron Herrera, "une mère dont le dévouement est absolu" (*S.M.*, p. 477; an absolutely devoted mother). Even the paternity metaphorically ascribed to Herrera is sexually ambiguous:

Trompe-la-Mort avait réalisé la superstition allemande du DOUBLE par un phénomène de paternité morale *que concevront les femmes qui, dans leur vie, ont aimé véritablement, qui ont senti leur âme passée dans celle de l'homme aimé, qui ont vécu de sa vie.* [*S.M.*, p. 813; emphasis added]

[Trompe-la-Mort had realized the German superstition of the DOUBLE by a phenomenon of intellectual paternity *that will be comprehensible to women who have truly loved in their lives, who have felt their soul pass into that of the man they love, who have lived through him.*]

Herrera as double mediates between narcissism and homosexuality, participating in both domains. Balzac's representation of this double figure is extremely complex, due to an overdetermination which makes Herrera at once Lucien's mirror image, his mother, and his father. By identifying with Herrera as mother, Lucien can *be* the mother, love other men as he was once loved; by identifying with Herrera as father, he can *have* the mother, the woman whom the father has access to.

This happily overdetermined configuration dramatically collapses when Lucien denounces Herrera to the police. His unintentional denunciation is provoked by the judge's reference to Herrera's self-imputed paternity, the mere suggestion of which inspires such horror in Lucien that he unwittingly informs on his patron: "Lui! mon père! . . . oh! monsieur! . . . il a dit cela!" (*S.M.*, p. 772; He! my father! . . . Oh! sir! . . . he said that!) And after a moment's pause, during which his revulsion builds, it overflows: "un Jacques Collin mon père! . . . Oh! ma pauvre mère . . ." (*S.M.*, p. 773; a man like Jacques Collin my father! . . . Oh! My poor mother . . .). Thus Lucien repudiates his father (in Herrera's guise) for a second time, and for much the same reasons as the first, unable to bear the thought of his mother being sullied, obsessed with the idea of her degradation. We might in fact read the Herrera story as a hyperbolic fantasy which repeats Lucien's (unwritten) involvement with his real father, a dramatic replay which allows a virtual relationship to be expressed.[29]

Once Lucien has betrayed Herrera, his own death is inevitable. "Je vous ai trahi. Cette ingratitude involontaire me tue," he writes Herrera (*S.M.*, p. 789; I have betrayed you. This unintentional ingratitude calls for my death). Lucien believes that he has killed Herrera, committed a second parricide (the first symbolized by his rejection of the patronym): "J'ai disposé de vous sottement.... Votre fils spirituel, celui que vous aviez adopté, s'est rangé du côté de ceux qui veulent vous assassiner à tout prix," he writes (*S.M.,* p. 789; I have ruined you for no good reason.... Your spiritual son, whom you adopted, has sided with those who want to kill you at all costs). In a sense this indirect murder is already suicide, for, in "killing" Herrera, Lucien shatters his own image in the mirror. Deprived of Herrera as reflective surface, Lucien reverts to a narcissistic self-duplication as he prepares his suicide. "Je me retrouve ce que j'étais au bord de la Charente," he writes (*S.M.,* p. 790; I am once again what I was on the banks of the Charente). This time, the self-contemplation originally figured by the glasslike surface of the water is represented by a hallucinatory replication of his image. As Lucien in his prison cell climbs to the abutment from which he will hang himself, he surveys the Palais de Justice from above and enters a dreamlike trance in which a second sight juxtaposes two ages inhabited by two selves: "Il était deux Lucien, un Lucien poète en promenade dans le Moyen Âge, sous les arcades et sous les tourelles de saint Louis, et un Lucien apprêtant son suicide" (*S.M.,* p. 794; There were two Luciens, a Lucien as poet transported to the Middle Ages, under the arches and turrets of Saint Louis, and a Lucien planning his suicide).

So Lucien folds in upon himself for the final time, uniting in death with the original object for which all the others were evanescent replacements. We can review his life as one in which Thanatos persistently dominated Eros, forever renewing the drive to return to the beginning, to recuperate a longed-for origin in sameness. The original unity so resolutely staged in figures of narcissism, incest, and homosexuality—and so patently irretrievable on this side of death—is finally realized through death, as Lucien *and the text* effectively achieve the elimination of difference. At this point, however, the text has no more reason for being; all chaos breaks loose as the underlying structure of difference collapses and sexual, narrative, and linguistic systems come to a foundering halt. Lucien's accession to identity is replicated on the narrative-linguistic level by a tautological reproduction of the death note to Herrera.[30] The novel thus turns back, turns in upon itself, and temporarily ceases to advance, as if in requiem, as if in reflection of Lucien's death—it, too, struck in the mirror.

Lucien's suicide also completes his identity with Herrera, for the two characters fuse and are interchanged. In the moment before his death, Lucien takes on Herrera's metallic qualities: "Il devint, en un moment rapide comme un éclair, ce qu'était Jacques Collin, un homme de bronze" (*S.M.*, p. 776; In a flash, he became what Jacques Collin was: a man of bronze). When informed of his protégé's death, Herrera, on the other hand, "était devenu faible comme un enfant" (*S.M.*, p. 821; had become as weak as a child).

With the news of the catastrophe, sexual differentiation, already gravely undermined, is annihilated, as the previously frequent inversion metaphors increase exponentially. "Ce coup est pour moi bien plus que la mort, mais vous ne pouvez pas savoir ce que je dis. . . . Vous n'êtes pères, si vous l'êtes, que d'une manière; . . . je suis mère, aussi!" cries Herrera (*S.M.*, p. 817; This blow is worse than death for me, but you cannot understand what I am saying. . . . You are simply fathers—if in fact you are fathers—but I am a mother as well!) And, "Après avoir couvé Lucien par un regard de mère à qui l'on arrache le corps de son fils, Jacques Collin s'affaissa sur lui-même" (*S.M.*, p. 821;[31] After staring at Lucien with the longing of a mother who sees her son's body turn away from her, Jacques Collins crumpled to the ground).

The collapse of difference which problematizes the possibility of sense-making and consequently changes the shape of the novel is dramatically completed in the fusion of antitheses which marks Herrera's vigil beside the lifeless body, during which he keeps Lucien's cold hand tightly clasped:

On ne connaît pas d'homme qui puisse garder pendant dix minutes un morceau de glace en le serrant avec force dans le creux de sa main. La froideur se communique aux sources de la vie avec une rapidité mortelle. Mais l'effet de ce froid terrible et agissant comme un poison est à peine comparable à celui que produit sur l'âme la main raide et glacée d'un mort tenue ainsi, serrée ainsi. La Mort parle alors à la Vie, elle dit

des secrets noirs et qui tuent bien des sentiments; car, en fait de sentiment, changer, n'est-ce pas mourir? [*S.M.*, p. 818]

[There is no man known who can hold a piece of ice for ten minutes,
grasping it tightly in his palm. The chill is communicated to the sources
of life with fatal speed. But the effect of such terrible, deadly cold is
hardly comparable to that produced in the soul by the stiff, frozen hand
of a dead man thus held, thus grasped. Then Death speaks to Life, it
tells dark secrets that destroy many feelings; for, where feelings are concerned, doesn't change imply death?]

There is an element of grotesque intimacy in these two clasped
hands bridging life and death, coldness and warmth, femininity
and masculinity, a certain excess which shocks, because it represents the transgression of antithesis, the disturbance of paradigms, the merging of polarities.[32] The consequences will be
serious, for the advent of sameness marks the death of representation. With Lucien's death, Herrera becomes a metaphor of literary sterility. Self-appointed god sanctioned by his creation, he
was author of his creature's destiny: "Je suis l'auteur, tu seras le
drame," he had decreed (*S.M.*, p. 504; I am the author, you will
be the drama). Lucien was his opus, his text: "Il se faisait repré-
senter dans la vie sociale par ce poète" (*S.M.*, p. 502;[33] He was
represented in social life by this poet). Deserted by his creation,
deprived of his text, Herrera is an unrepresented author, symbol
of the simultaneous failure of language, fecundity, and narrative.
He is the desert elusively described as "Dieu sans les hommes"
in *Une Passion*. The personification of this childless god, he resembles "ces fievreux animaux du désert" (*S.M.*, p. 789; those
feverish animals of the desert)—the panther, the hermaphrodite,
the reunion of opposites; he is, in short, the desert of meaning.

For the abolition of difference inaugurates a reign of chaos,
the possibility of unregulated substitution, infinite changeability.
Because representation is dependent upon the organized replacement of one term by another (different) term, when all terms are
equivalent, there can no longer be any meaningful replacement.
Herrera-Collin, escaped convict, is reincarnated as Chief of the
Secret Police. Nucingen, society's financier, and Jacques Collin,
banker to the underworld, amount to the same thing, for Nucingen is "un monstre . . . qui a été Jacques Collin légalement et

dans le monde des écus" (*S.M.*, p. 923; a monster . . . who was a lawful Jacques Collin in the world of finance). Prostitutes and noblewomen are essentially interchangeable, for while Esther's correspondence transfigures, exalts her, Mmes. de Sérizy and de Maufrigneuse are degraded through their self-incriminating letters:

Les filles publiques en écrivant font du style et de beaux sentiments, eh bien! les grandes dames, qui font du style et de grands sentiments toute la journée, écrivent comme les filles agissent. Les philosophes trouveront la raison de ce chassé-croisé. [*S.M.*, p. 902]

[When streetwalkers write they express themselves with flair and fine feelings. Well—society women, who display their flair and fine feelings all day long, write the way streetwalkers act. No doubt philosophers will find a reason for this turnabout.]

Linguistic categories dissolve as well. There is a proliferation of disparate codes: the various invented languages used by Asie and Herrera, the prison slang, the Italian-based language in which Calvi and Herrera communicate, Nucingen's kitchen French. Amidst this linguistic scramble, there is no authentic language, no authoritative code. Letters and testaments are forged, and their inauthenticity goes undetected. Letters cause hierarchies to topple: duchesses become streetwalkers when they write, and the letters they receive are preserved as the precious archives of their degradation. Thus the duchesse de Maufrigneuse conserves Lucien's lurid correspondence "comme certains vieillards ont des gravures obscènes, à cause des éloges hyperboliques donnés à ce qu'elle avait de moins duchesse en elle" (*S.M.*, p. 877; much as some old men keep obscene prints, because of the hyperbolic praise given to what was least duchesslike in her). As language leads to one scandal after another, it begins to become apparent that *the scandal is language.*

In its etymological sense, scandal means "snare" (Greek *skándalon*); the scandal of words staged in *Splendeurs et misères* must be traced back to the linguistic snare in which Lucien is caught in *Illusions perdues.* The account of Lucien's stint as journalist furnishes a very concentrated exposition of a career in language: his imbroglios with the press constitute his struggle with the unreliability of language, and his growing awareness of journalistic perfidy and deceit coincides with an increasingly eroded conception of language as a vehicle of truth.

Lucien is at first aghast at the demands made on him by his journalist confrères to prostitute his critical judgment in the interest of political and professional rivalries. His inherent faith in an intrinsic correspondence of sign to referent is consistently undercut by a series of theatrical metaphors which compare the sign (and newspaper reviews) to hollow representations radically severed from any founding reality. Thus the actress Coralie advises him:

Fais de la critique . . . amuse-toi! Est-ce que je ne suis pas ce soir en Andalouse, demain ne me mettrai-je pas en bohémienne, un autre jour en homme? Fais comme moi, donne-leur des grimaces pour leur argent, et vivons heureux. [*I.P.*, p. 461]

[Go ahead and write reviews . . . have fun! Am I not to be dressed as an Andalusian tonight, tomorrow as a bohemian, and some other day as a man? Do as I do: give them different masks for their money, and let's live happily.]

The painful process of awakening from the dream of semiotic plenitude to the harsh light of semiotic vacuity is figured by the curtain's rise at the end of a theatrical performance:

Pour Lucien, ces deux heures passées au théâtre furent comme un rêve. . . . Le rideau se leva. . . . A la féerie de la scène, au spectacle des loges pleines de jolies femmes, aux étourdissantes lumières, à la splendide magie des décorations et des costumes neufs succédaient le froid, l'horreur, l'obscurité, le vide. Ce fut hideux. [*I.P.*, p. 391]

[For Lucien, the two hours spent at the theater were like a dream. . . . The curtain rose. . . . After the enchantment of the stage, the boxes full of pretty women, and the dazzling lights, after the splendid magic of the decorations and the new costumes, came the chill, the horror, the darkness, and the emptiness. It was hideous.]

The apprentice journalist's faith in verbal truth is seriously challenged in the course of his exposure to the critical techniques reigning in the newspaper world: he learns that reviews are written without cutting the pages of the books reviewed, that it is common procedure, when compiling a newspaper, to insert a "canard," defined as "un fait qui a l'air d'être vrai, mais qu'on invente pour relever les Faits-Paris quand ils sont pâles" (*I.P.*, p. 437; a story that appears to be true, but that is invented to spice up the Paris news when it is dull) and that it is also not unusual for a journalist to write an article diametrically reversing a position he has taken in an article published the preceding day. Lucien's initiation into this last technique, the art of palinode, reveals his fundamental conception of language as a transparent medium. When he is originally called upon to write a review denigrating Nathan's book (Nathan here falling indirect victim to an attack on the book's publisher) Lucien naively exclaims: "Mais que peut-on dire contre ce livre? il est beau" (*I.P.*, p. 442; But what can be said against this book? It's a fine book). Once instructed in the art of literary subterfuge by his colleague Lousteau, Lucien writes the unfavorable review, only to be asked to refute it in a subsequent article, in order to propitiate Nathan. At this point, however, Lucien, swayed by the authority of his unwilled words, has come to believe in his negative review; he now protests: "Mais je ne vois rien à dire en faveur du livre" (*I.P.*, p. 457; But I can't think of a thing to say in favor of the book).

Lucien is trapped by the language he persistently views as transparent because it is in fact opaque, an obstacle rather than a window to truth. His ultimate failure in journalism (as in language) is rooted in his inability to assimilate the message his colleagues repeatedly attempt to impress upon him, concerning the essentially reified nature of words: "Tout journal est . . . une boutique où l'on vend au public des paroles de la couleur dont il les veut" (*I.P.*, p. 404; Every newspaper is . . . a shop which sells the public truths of whatever shade it desires) he is told, and: "Nous sommes des marchands de phrases, et nous vivons de notre commerce" (*I.P.*, p. 458; We are vendors of phrases, and we make our living this way).

Nowhere is Lucien's linguistic naiveté more sharply and more comprehensively rendered than in the saga of his matronym. His trust that a purportedly forthcoming royal ordinance will sanction the appropriation of his mother's name, de Rubempré, and thereby set his tottering world aright, changing his fortune and reconciling his severely degraded public image with his more exalted self-image, constitutes a dramatic *mise en abyme* of his linguistic illusions. For not only does Lucien believe in the promises extended by his self-created enemies to intercede on his behalf before the king (though these "promises" are correctly read by everyone but Lucien as cruel jokes); he also believes implicitly that an aristocratic name is a transparent signifier capable of realizing aristocratic ambition and privilege.[34] Finally, he assumes that the replacement of patronym by matronym will realize (as if by retroactive reflection) his illusory unilinear descent, his desire to exclude the father, to be created by mother alone.

Lucien's situation in language is as imaginary as his situation *en famille:* his use of language, unmediated by the father's name, based on an illusory rapport of identity between sign and referent, corresponds to his familial role, unmediated by the father's presence, based on the illusion of identity to his mother. Ironically, Lucien's first name is a well-chosen signifier. As the near homophony Lucien/illusion suggests, Lucien's fundamental illusion concerns his own name and his own self. When he learns that the promised restoration of his mother's name to him is a hoax, that his imaginary self (his self-image, his aristocratic pretentions), is irreconcilable with his real self, he renounces life, renounces the self, rather than repudiating the image. Insulted by Michel Chrestien, Lucien challenges him to a duel. Of Lucien's comportment during this duel scene (which prefigures his attempted suicide on the banks of the Charente), we are told: "Pour Lucien, la vie était devenue un mauvais rêve; il lui était indifférent de vivre ou de mourir. Le courage particulier au suicide lui servit donc à paraître en grand costume de bravoure aux yeux des spectateurs" (*I.P.*, p. 540; Life had become a bad dream for Lucien; he didn't care if he lived or died. And so the courage proper to suicide allowed him to make a great show of bravery before the spectators' eyes). The suicidal attitude referred to here is of course a continuation of Lucien's everyday perspective, for the suppression of self by self (characteristic of Lucien's self-aggrandizement as well as of his suicidal stance) implies disunity, belies identity.

As the novel exposes the myth of language as transparent—the fundamental untruth of the sign—it begins to reveal the correlative incommensurability of disparate codes, a motif that is in ascendance in *Splendeurs et misères*. Codes of beauty and codes of dress turn out to be arbitrary, needful of translation from one context to the next: "Transportée à Paris, une femme qui passe pour jolie en province n'obtient pas la moindre attention, car elle n'est belle que par l'application du proverbe: *Dans le royaume des aveugles, les borgnes sont rois*" (*I.P.*, pp. 265–66; Once she has moved to Paris, a woman who passes for pretty in the provinces no longer receives the least bit of attention, for she is beautiful only in the sense of the proverb: In the kingdom of the blind, the one-eyed reign). The problem of conflicting codes ultimately refers to the incommunicability of different languages, and metaphors of language are called upon at times to evoke the semiotic problematic. When Lucien, freshly arrived in Paris from the provinces, spends an evening at the Opéra, we learn that "chacun regardait le pauvre inconnu avec une si cruelle indifférence, il était si bien là *comme un étranger qui ne savait pas la langue*" (*I.P.*, p. 278 [emphasis added]; everyone looked at the poor stranger with cruel indifference, for there he was just *like a foreigner who doesn't understand the language*).

Splendeurs et misères des courtisanes is marked by a proliferation of such mutually impenetrable codes, which could be read as the narrative focus of this novel. The narrator consistently plays the role of an interpreter mediating between various languages or idiolects that would be incomprehensible without his translation. Thus the following intercession between Jacques Collin and the reader:

Il faut faire observer ici que Jacques Collin parlait le français comme une vache espagnole, en baragouinant de manière à rendre ses réponses presque inintelligibles et à s'en faire demander la répétition. Les germanismes de M. de Nucingen ont déjà trop émaillé cette Scène pour y mettre d'autres phrases soulignées difficiles à lire. [*S.M.*, p. 746]

[Here one must imagine Jacques Collin speaking French like a Spanish cow, mumbling so as to render his answers unintelligible, so that he had to be asked to repeat what he had said. M. de Nucingen's Germanisms have been too liberally sprinkled in this Scene to add anything else difficult to read.]

While in the preceding instance the narrator acts as translator, on other occasions the text serves to record his service as simultaneous interpreter. One such occasion is Collin's conversation with Théodore Calvi, which transpires in Italian so as to be unintelligible to the attendant prison guards: "*Io sono Gaba-Morto! Parla nostro italiano,* dit vivement Jacques Collin. *Vengo ti salvar* (je suis Trompe-la-Mort, parlons italien, je viens te sauver)" (*S.M.,* p. 859; I am Trompe-la-Mort, let's speak Italian. . . . I have come to save you). Such parenthetical translations also accompany the prison argot that peppers the final quarter of the novel, so heavily sprinkled at times as to give the text the aspect of a vocabulary manual rather than a linear narrative. The narrative in fact comes to a halt at one point so that the narrator may deliver a somewhat startling dissertation on the glories of argot through the ages (*S.M.,* pp. 828–31).

As the text comes to focus more and more on language, apparently having recognized that "le langage ne peut imiter parfaitement que du langage"[35] (the only thing language can imitate perfectly is language), everything becomes a text. Mme. de Nucingen criticizes the inappropriateness of her husband's foppery, asking him: "Suis-je femme à faire de pareilles fautes d'orthographe dans une toilette?" (*S.M.,* p. 552; Am I the kind of woman who makes such spelling mistakes in her dress?). The inscrutable Corentin appears to Nucingen like "une inscription à laquelle il manque au moins les trois quarts des lettres" (*S.M.,* p. 550; like an inscription missing at least three-quarters of its letters). Jacques Collin, incarcerated, extricates a scrap of paper from the space between his head and wig, disengages a pin-thin pencil from a strand of hair, and prepares to write a message— "dans le langage convenu entre Asie et lui, l'argot de l'argot" (*S.M.,* p. 732; in the language agreed upon between Asie and himself, the slang of slangs). If all is transformed into text, or textual surface, the writing is in every case indecipherable. The secret passwords, the aliases assumed by the convicts and their mistresses, are, like the various foreign and invented languages represented, forged to dissimulate. So, too, Jacques Collin's back, branded with the initials of his convict status at the time of his first incarceration and subsequently mutilated by him to destroy the identifying letters, is unreadable, an obliterated text.

The representation of language becomes an end in itself: an end, that is, a barrier to reading. Deprived of a transparent meaning and bereft of a transcendent signified, language is opacity, disguise, occultation, and illegibility. The text renounces an external referent, represents itself. Representation becomes a game, language a plaything, as a convict's back becomes a defaced manuscript and scraps of paper anticipating messages hide under wigs. Language becomes excessive, overdetermined, contingent.

Code layered upon code clutters the text with a semantic babble that strives to rebuild or replace fallen hierarchies, to fill the void left in the wake of collapsed difference. And as the text puts its own status as representation into question, it is illuminated by a radically different aesthetic which emerges from the representational shadows where it had been lurking all along.

IV

Le réalisme (bien mal nommé, en tout cas souvent mal interprété) consiste, non à copier le réel, mais à copier une copie (peinte) du réel: ce fameux réel, comme sous l'effet d'une peur qui interdirait de le toucher directement, est *remis plus loin,* différé.

ROLAND BARTHES, *S/Z*

All is true, proclaims the narrator by way of preface to *Le Père Goriot.* Often detached from the text as a putative realist manifesto, these words (culled from Shakespeare's *Henry VIII*) imply a quite different aesthetic when replaced in context. The full sentence reads: "*All is true,* il est si véritable, que chacun peut en reconnaître les éléments chez soi, dans son coeur peut-être" (*P.G.,* p. 50; it is so true that each individual can find the basic elements [of this drama] within himself, perhaps in his heart).

Truth is withdrawn from the external domain, internalized as the heart's province, a virtual state to be placed in contradistinction to an essential reality. Writing becomes less a matter of reflecting the real than one of creating or realizing the virtual, the unreal, giving external form to the heart's shapeless desires. The voice which purportedly delivers a message of mimetic intent, affirming realism, resemblance, and reflection, is definitively betrayed by its "accent" (the italicized English), for it speaks a language of alterity and fiction. Borrowed from a foreign tongue and cited from another text, another genre, the words *all is true* most immediately refer to the Shakespearean drama in which they originally appear, and suggest that art, not life, is at the origin of representation.

Balzac's text is studded with such equivocal messages, emphatic statements of reality's primacy which are subverted in (and by) the process of stating. Thus, for example, the following statement in description of Asie's jealous contemplation of Esther and Lucien:

Le génie italien peut inventer de raconter Othello, le génie anglais peut le mettre en scène; mais la nature seule a le droit d'être dans un seul regard plus magnifique et plus complète que l'Angleterre et l'Italie dans l'expression de la jalousie. [*S.M.,* p. 484]

[The Italian genius may invent the tale of Othello, the English genius may put it on the stage, but nature alone has the right to express jealousy more magnificently and more completely than England and Italy in a single glance.]

While ostensibly proclaiming the primacy of nature, the discourse is mediated by Shakespeare and his Italian source; art is the referent upon which the illusion is modeled. The same process is responsible for constant allusions, in *Splendeurs et misères* as in other texts, to models drawn from literature and the visual arts, such as *Paul et Virginie* (*S.M.,* p. 486), *Les Mille et une nuits* (*S.M.,* p. 491), "le conte arabe" (*S.M.,* p. 503), the works of Titian, Leonardo, and Raphael (*S.M.,* p. 494).

At times the references are sustained, becoming subtexts which play a formative role within the novel and act as useful hermeneutic tools for the reader. *Romeo and Juliet* is referred to at several points: Esther's pet greyhounds, a gift from Nucingen upon whom she tests the poison intended for her suicide, are named for the protagonists of the tragedy, and later, Esther's suicide note to Lucien "augmenta l'intensité de son désir de mourir, en lui remettant en mémoire le dénouement de Roméo rejoignant Juliette" (*S.M.*, p. 787; increased the intensity of his desire to die by reminding him of Romeo uniting with Juliet). It is unclear, however, whether Juliet is ultimately played by Esther or by Herrera, for although the explicit references indicate Esther, the dramatic pattern, by analogy to its Shakespearean predecessor, points to Herrera. Lucien's determination to die is initially triggered by his belief that Herrera's end is at hand; he (like Romeo) dies because Juliet-Herrera is, in his eyes, already dead. Furthermore, anticipating his arrest after Esther's suicide, Herrera, like Juliet, asks Asie for a drug which will give the appearance of death throes without actually incurring death.[36] A bit later, the resuscitated Herrera discovers Lucien's death, and his grieving vigil beside the corpse, in the solitary prison cell, recalls Juliet's awakening to Romeo's death in the church vault. Herrera's figurative death follows, a variation on Juliet's end, for the dagger is replaced by Lucien's letter, which is, for Herrera, "une coupe de poison" (*S.M.*, p. 819). After this Herrera dies, to be reincarnated as Chief of the Secret Police.[37] He tells the authorities "Jacques Collin est en ce moment enterré . . . avec Lucien" (*S.M.*, p. 923; Jacques Collin now lies buried . . . with Lucien).

If *Splendeurs et misères* speaks on one level in displaced echoes of Shakespeare's drama, it also carries undertones of the Pygmalion myth. In this novel, as in *Illusions perdues,* Herrera, like the misogynist Pygmalion, replaces woman by art, creating art object in place of love object, only to fall in love with his creation. The metaphors used by Herrera to describe his project are often borrowed from the sculptor's vocabulary, as when he declares to Lucien: "Je veux aimer ma créature, la *façonner,* la *pétrir* à mon usage" (*I.P.,* p. 708; [emphasis added] I want to love my creature, *mold* him, *shape* him). The Pygmalion subtext is itself mediated by the text of *Sarrasine,* Balzac's own version of the myth, which emphasizes art's origin in an illusory or non-existent reality.

Thus we find ourselves once again on the periphery of *Splendeurs et misères*, referred away from the moment in this novel to which we have attributed representation's demise. And we are reminded of the truism that nothing is ever invented by a novelist; that what surfaces at a given time can always be traced to a subjacent priority.[38] Lucien's death is both cause and symbol, symbolic cause or thematization of the concomitant split between life and art. On a purely structural level (which cannot, of course, account for the irreducible haze of meaning which gives the novel its terrible beauty) *Splendeurs et misères* is a rewrite of *Sarrasine*, certainly on a more grandiose scale, more populated, set in a more amply furnished political and social domain, but nevertheless concerned with the same artistic dilemma, which inevitably leads to a similar disillusioned conclusion.

In this same sense, each of Balzac's texts rewrites all the others, wrestles with an unchanging and unsolvable problem which can only be approached from different perspectives, dramatized in varying terms, enunciated by different narrators. *Le Père Goriot*, before Lucien, bears witness to the incipient collapse of difference, and with it, narratability; *El Verdugo* deals with the destruction and attempted reconstruction of hierarchies of order and paradigms of difference; *Une Passion*, with sexual confusion which reaches beyond the confines of the story, threatening the narrator-character with castration, and the narrator-storyteller with speechlessness. *Massimilla Doni*, on the other hand, tells of successful representation, but simultaneously admits to a resultant sacrifice of the ideal, that is, a reduction of the representational source.[39]

All of these texts participate in a dual dialectic whose poles are logorrhea and silence, on the one hand and promiscuity and castration on the other, for the aesthetic problematic is consistently inscribed within the sexual metaphor. The terms proper to each of the two systems are often interchanged, a sexual cause leading to a narrative effect, a narrative problem sexually manifested, so that it is difficult to establish whether sexuality is the vehicle for an artistic tenor, or vice versa. This confusion is exemplified by Louis Lambert's impeded castration, for although his virility remains intact, a substitutive linguistic impotence is incurred. Because Balzac's narrative cosmos is regulated by a dynamic system based on a constant—and limited—energy supply, any expenditure (sexual or verbal) results in a loss (a physical or spiritual reduction), a foreshadowing of death. But the conservative alternative (the renunciation of excess or expenditure) is already a kind of death, a self-imposed castration or aphasia, a death in life. Thus Louis ironically inflicts upon himself what he sought to forestall, for within Balzac's system, any victory is Pyrrhic. Vision or form must be sacrificed, and, in the broader context, the choices are life or art, reality or representation.[40]

Apprehensive of competing with reality, of constructing a mirror whose supplementarity can only result in loss, Balzac's narrators persistently attempt to isolate art from life, to abolish external referentiality. Metaphors of theater and role-playing dominate *Splendeurs et misères* from the opening scene, where Lucien and Esther, disguised in dominoes at a masked ball, "appartenaient à la Fantaisie, qui est au-dessus de l'Art comme la cause est au-dessus de l'effet" (*S.M.*, p. 445; belonged to the realm of Fantasy, which stands above Art as cause is above effect). Art's referent is fantasy, or illusion; mimesis becomes an internal aesthetic as art imitates art and fictional characters wander from narrative to narrative. As Lucien loses his illusions he learns that writing is no derivative of life, but rather an alternative to it. Lousteau offers these enlightening words:

Pour faire de belles oeuvres, mon pauvre enfant, vous puiserez à pleines plumées d'encre dans votre coeur la tendresse, la sève, l'énergie, et vous l'étalerez en passions, en sentiments, en phrases! Oui, vous écrirez au lieu d'agir. [*I.P.*, p. 347]

[In order to write fine works, my boy, you will draw quillfuls of tenderness, sap, and energy from your heart, which you will display in the form of passion, feeling, and phrases. Yes, you'll write instead of acting.]

Journalism's status as representation is even more specious. The official report of Lucien's death attributes it to an aneurism, whence the narrator's wry comment: "Ainsi, comme on le voit, les plus grands événements de la vie sont traduits par de petits faits-Paris plus ou moins vrais. Il en est ainsi de beaucoup de choses beaucoup plus augustes que celles-ci" (S.M., p. 798; Thus, as is obvious, the greatest events of life are translated into little Paris news items bearing some semblance of truth. The same is true of many things much loftier than these).

Even when writing is most obviously sublimation it replaces and denies the reality it displaces. While Herrera abhors Esther for her passion, he can tolerate Clotilde's desire for Lucien because it remains epistolary, a thing of words: "Elle se dédommage de ses privations par l'écriture, cette fille: ça me va!" (S.M., p. 501; This girl compensates for all her privations by writing; that suits me!) It is precisely because Herrera has this ability to regard form as a separate entity, devoid of significant content, that he emerges eternally triumphant. His series of "incarnations" is merely formal; sterile, self-created identities sired by no man and inspired by no reality, they are roles rather than embodiments, figures in an empty game of exchange. As he blithely turns from outlaw into figure of justice, he explains: "Les états qu'on fait dans le monde ne sont que des apparences; la réalité, c'est l'idée!" (S.M., p. 912; The roles we take in the world are only appearances; reality is the idea!)

The idea is not nullified for Herrera, merely detached from any representation (and consequently, consigned to remain forever amorphous, if rather high-sounding, for the reader), just as appearance is freed from responsibility to any referent. As a result an unfounded proliferation of forms, an unmotivated series of substitutions, whereby Herrera/Collin/Vautrin/Trompe-la-Mort emerges as master of the underworld and/or police chief. His qualifications for this post are rather exceptional: "J'ai toutes les qualités voulues pour l'emploi. . . . On m'a fait suivre mes classes jusqu'en rhétorique," he assures his prospective employers (S.M., p. 925; I have all the requisite qualities for the job. . . . They made me stay in school up to the *classe de rhétorique*). Master of substitutions, he has dominated difference and in a sense passed beyond rhetoric. Thence arises his certainty of reigning always over the society based on sexual difference, duped by linguistic difference, by representation, by letters:

Les fantaisies d'une femme réagissent sur tout l'Etat! Oh! combien de force acquiert un homme quand il s'est soustrait, comme moi, à cette tyrannie d'enfant. ... Procureur général, ministre, les voilà tous aveuglés, tordant tout pour des lettres de duchesses ou de petites filles. ... Je régnerai toujours sur ce monde, qui, depuis vingt-cinq ans, m'obéit." [S.M., p. 934]

[A woman's caprices affect an entire State! Oh! How much force a man gains when, like me, he eludes that childish tyranny. ... Attorney-general, minister, there they all are, blinded, twisting everything for the letters of duchesses or little girls. ... I will always reign over this world, which, for twenty-five years, has obeyed me.]

Balzac, a would-be Proteus fashioned in Herrera's image, likewise masked himself in multiple incarnations, avoiding any consistent self-projection, denying the very notion (and the threat) of self-representation. He was, however, less successful than his sosie at keeping life and art distinct, for if life is necessarily transfigured in becoming art, the reverse process is considerably more problematic. The legends are legion: Balzac on his deathbed, calling for Bianchon, real-life rooms furnished after descriptions in La Comédie humaine, mythomaniacal business ventures resembling novelistic plots, epistolary infatuations indicative of the invasion of letters in life, a life lived very much in the manner of a literary enterprise. Like Borges's Tlön, the invented world infiltrated the real, surpassing life, threatening its creator.

In the beginning, when Balzac embarked upon the creation of an imaginary world, he peopled it, expanded it, internally reinforced it. As time went on, he made it more intricate, convoluted, and organized, so that, like Tlön, it was a labyrinth, but "a labyrinth devised by men, a labyrinth destined to be deciphered by men."[41] And when he saw what he had made, he grew afraid. Like a god fearful of what he had wrought, he began to undo his creation. He invalidated the matter of which he had formed it: "Eh! comment pourrions-nous reproduire par des gloses les vives et mystérieuses agitations de l'âme, quand les paroles nous manquent pour peindre les mystères visibles de la beauté?"[42] (How can we gloss the intense, secret movements of the soul, when we lack words to paint the visible mysteries of beauty?) He persistently curtailed the ordering power of language, as if to preserve the vision inchoate: "Les sensations que ... causèrent les différents morceaux exécutés par la religieuse sont du petit nombre de choses dont l'expression est interdite à la parole, et la rend impuissante"[43] (The sensations . . . produced by the various pieces played by the nun are among the few things whose verbal expression is forbidden, and which render language impotent). And he further debilitated writing through metaphors of pruning and castration, as if to maintain a space between art and life where meaning might reside: "La hardiesse du vrai s'élève à des combinaisons interdites à l'art, tant elles sont invraisemblables ou peu décentes, à moins que l'écrivain ne les adoucisse, ne les émonde, ne les châtre" (S.M., p. 873; The boldness of truth rises to combinations which are forbidden to art, because they are improbable or indecent, unless the writer modifies them, prunes them, castrates them).

Thus Balzac created, in *La Comédie humaine,* a strange hymn to language, in language, whose primal and final objective is silence; a hymn to writing, that terrible power which consigns all it touches to language, to form, to substance. It is no wonder that at times the words of invocation have the resonance of an exorcist's chant.

Every fragment of this verbal edifice bears the imprint of the words found by Benassis on the door of his monastery cell: "Fuge, late, tace."[44] The cry to flee, hide, and be silent, to preserve the ineffable, plaintively resounds through every novel, every story, every essay written by Balzac. But it is not unaccompanied. The call to silence is always doubled by a whispered fear that nothing but language separates the ineffable from the unmeaning, the absolute from the void; that the silence can never be filled to saturation, but must be sought, designated, and emphatically, incessantly spoken.

Afterword

"Ci-gît monsieur Goriot, père de la comtesse de Restaud et de la baronne de Nucingen, enterré aux frais de deux étudiants."

BALZAC, *Le Père Goriot*

 T is time now to lay the Balzacian father to rest. To do so means returning to *Le Père Goriot* and miming Balzac's emblematic interment of paternity at the end of that novel: in the guise of closure, to open another text.

At the center of a series of embeddings that takes us from the nineteenth-century novel and its fictions of the father, to the realist novel, to the Balzacian novel, ever inward toward the heart of the traditional novel, literary history enshrines *Le Père Goriot*.[1] It teaches that if we are to understand anything at all about the centrality of the paternal metaphor in nineteenth-century fiction, we must begin by reading Goriot's story. But the lesson of Balzac is perturbing. For to begin with Goriot is to begin at a gravesite; it is to bury the father and to discover his death as generative principle. To begin with Goriot is to read the inscription on the father's tombstone and to discern its double message: annunciation as well as obituary, Goriot's epitaph is the incipit of the traditional novel.

If, as Proust observed, "un livre est un grand cimetière où sur la plupart des tombes on ne peut lire les noms effacés"[2] (a book is a great cemetery where, on most of the tombstones, the effaced names cannot be read), it is equally true that a cemetery is a collection of texts which record the traces of the lives they eradicate. Goriot's epitaph is, then, a summary of his own novel, but it is more. It is a metaphor for the nineteenth-century novel,

that other text inscribed in memory of a dead father. The nineteenth-century novel *is* that gravestone text, that monument to
paternity whose precondition is the father's death.

When we say that the traditional novel was a response to
paternity's demise, we are of course alluding to the death of a
certain father figure. More precisely, we mean the death of the
father *as* figure, that is, as metaphoric embodiment of cosmic
order and immanent meaning. A glance at the imagery of paternity, continuity, and fixity proper to the traditions of the ancien
régime gives some indication of the sense of displacement (or, to
borrow Lukács's metaphor, "transcendental homelessness"[3])
suffered by a culture newly bereaved of the paternal figure:

Comme L'Eternel attacha de sa main toute-puissante, au pied même de
son Trône, le premier anneau de la grande chaîne, qui lie tous les êtres
créés par lui depuis ces milliers de globes qui roulent sur nos têtes, jusqu'à ce tertre mobile, sur lequel nous vivons, la paternité des Rois re-
montoit jusqu'à celle de Dieu même. Pour tâcher de faire oublier cette
descendance sacrée . . . on a disputé à Dieu l'encens de la Terre, aux
Rois les tributs de leurs Sujets, aux Pères les respects de leurs Enfans.[4]

[Just as the Eternal attaches with his all-powerful hand, to the foot itself
of his Throne, the first link in the great chain which ties all beings created by him, from the thousands of spheres which rotate over our heads
to the moving mounds of earth on which we live, so too the paternity
of Kings ascends to that of God himself. In order to make people forget
this sacred lineage . . . the radicals disputed God's right to the incense
of the Earth, Kings' rights to the tributes of their subjects, and Fathers'
rights to the respect of their Children.]

When Balzac, some forty years after the Revolution, had
Goriot proclaim: "La société, le monde roulent sur la paternité,
tout croule si les enfants n'aiment pas leurs pères" (*P.G.*, p. 275;
Society, the whole world, is centered on paternity; everything
must collapse if children don't love their fathers) he was nostalgically invoking this outmoded hierarchic model, this great chain
which linked mortal beings to the Divine through the mediation
of kings.[5] One might say that all of Balzac's writing is an attempt
to repair the severed links of the great chain, to reinstate the
"sacred lineage" that, as Lynn Hunt has astutely remarked,

served as the "master fiction" or "cultural frame" within which social and political (and, let us add, narrative) authority had traditionally defined itself.[6]

Balzac's efforts to rewrite the worn-out master fiction do not succeed; his fictions of the father are condemned endlessly to mime, within their bounds, a pattern of authority that is no longer available without. Precisely because the external model is gone, the father figure and the patriarchal family configuration cannot sustain the burden of signification Balzac imposes upon them. Because the chain of authority is undone, the father can be no more than a severed link, deprived of his sacred lineage and hence divested of his transcendent power. Paternal authority, detached from the great chain, is a form which has lost its meaning: form and transcendence are forevermore split. One can choose paternity, incarnation, representation, and language, or one can opt for celibacy, the spirit, the ineffable, and silence. The choice, of course, exacts a sacrifice, and Balzac's use of paternity as a figure of textual generation is consequently fraught with ambivalence.

Balzac's failure to write a latterday master fiction is not worth lamenting. If he (or anyone else) had revived the father in his integrity, that is, as earthly representative of the sacred, then the novel, in all likelihood, would have disappeared. For the traditional novel fills the space between the ancien régime construct of paternity as a "master fiction" and the modernist deconstruction of paternity as a "legal fiction" (as Joyce was to put it);[7] caught between a nostalgic desire for paternal models and a dawning consciousness that these are superannuated forms, the nineteenth-century novel, as it suppresses and recalls the father at will, is simply *fiction*. We might well invoke the Freudian concept of disavowal as the central mechanism by which the nineteenth-century novel operates[8]: its instinctive awareness of the father's demise is the very reason that, refusing to admit the void, it fills its pages with paternal reincarnations. By denying the father's absence, the novel surreptitiously acknowledges it.

If the nineteenth-century novel was the father's death knell, what took his place? Where was the new master fiction? While it is tempting to answer that disorder became the new order, lawlessness (in and of the novel form) the new law, and that the conscious loss of the old master fiction became the new one, we need to remember that this is a twentieth-century argument which more properly describes the twentieth-century novel.

In the nineteenth century it is the novel as quest that takes the place of—but cannot replace—the father. In futile search of an obliterated master fiction, nineteenth-century plots play out endless fictions of mastery: representations of detectives, the police, the law, trials, and incarcerations are so many avatars of the father. When one considers the great courtroom scenes (and the array of often questionable judicial decisions) which haunt the nineteenth-century novel, from *Le Rouge et le noir* to *Illusions perdues* to *Great Expectations* to *The Brothers Karamazov*, one can only infer that what is on trial in these fictions is patriarchy itself.

Nineteenth-century revivals of the father's law are not, however, limited to thematic stagings of it. The realist aesthetic, with its emphasis on mimesis and its reliance on observation, omniscience, documentation, and control, may well be a nostalgic paternalistic fantasy, the broadest manifestation of the attempt to recuperate, in the novel, the authority and power of a bygone age. Both Aristotle (in the *Poetics*) and Freud (in *Beyond the Pleasure Principle*) trace mimesis, or representation, back to children's attempts to control their environment through imitative play. As Christopher Prendergast has pointed out, this early pattern suggests that the roots of mimesis are to be found in a "profound psychic connection between the principle of mimesis and . . . the desire for mastery."[9]

Certainly this correlation between representation and the will to power is borne out by the language in which the realists describe their project. From Balzac's oft-repeated metaphor of observation as penetration to Flaubert's well-known recommendation that "l'auteur, dans son oeuvre, doit être comme Dieu dans l'univers, présent partout et visible nulle part" (the author, in his work, must be like God in the universe, present everywhere and visible nowhere), to Zola's decree that "l'oeuvre d'art . . . doit embrasser l'horizon entier"[10] (the work of art . . . must embrace the entire horizon), the expression of realist techniques evokes an all-encompassing vision which, as D. A. Miller has argued, is in fact an "infallible super-vision," a penetrating stare which places the world under surveillance.[11]

When realism, however, reaches it authoritarian peak in the form of Zolien naturalism, its ruling principles of mimetic vigilance and control are, curiously, challenged from within. Zola's monumental *Rougon-Macquart* cycle begins by casting the doctor/author/scientist, Pascal Rougon, in the role of narrator qua observer, but it ends by displacing Pascal and reattributing the narration to his chimerical niece and lover, Clotilde. Pascal, as self-appointed family historian, is implicitly responsible, initially, for that family history called the *Rougon-Macquart,* but the project is aborted when he dies. His history, had it been written, would no doubt have been a documentary. In its virtual state, it consists of a family tree, assorted records, and multiple files which detail the lives of every past, present, and foreseeable future member of the extended Rougon-Macquart family: in short, the records which provide the foundation for the novels we are reading. These records are burned after Pascal's death, but Clotilde, sole witness to the documents, remembers their contents, and, we must infer, goes on to reconstruct the history, recasting it in novel form.

Clotilde's appropriation of the project and of the narrator's role is the culmination of a narrative struggle which dominates the last novel of the cycle, *Le Docteur Pascal,* and dramatically represents Zola's own aesthetic conflict. The battle is played out in a series of skirmishes over the illustrations Clotilde provides for her uncle's treatises on botanical heredity. She usually complies with the realist aesthetic which Pascal demands of her work, applying herself with "une minutie, une exactitude de dessin et de couleur extraordinaire" (a precision, an extraordinary exactness of design and color); however, "C'était ... parfois, chez elle, des sautes brusques, un besoin de s'échapper en fantaisies folles, au milieu de la plus précise des reproductions"[12] (At times she was given to sudden mood changes, a need to escape into wild fantasy, in the midst of the most precise reproductions).

Together Pascal and Clotilde personify Zola's warring tendencies toward realism on the one hand and myth on the other.

The dominant tone of the text is containing, controlling, and closural. At one exemplary point, Pascal, confronted by Clotilde's most recent botanical fantasy, asks the housekeeper to sew up her head, "qui a des fuites"[13] (which has some leaks). Nevertheless, the leaks in Clotilde's head are part of an insistent, if suppressed, female-associated system of myth, fantasy, and extravagance, which, throughout the cycle threatens to burst, drip, flow, or gush through its containing (realist) cover. One easily imagines Zola, like Flaubert, secretly confessing his submerged projection: "Clotilde Rougon, c'est moi."

As we move from early realism and Balzac to late realism and Zola, it is as if the father's ghost (in the form of mimesis and figures of mastery) had to become a stronger and stronger presence in proportion to a growing consciousness of the father's death (since the impact of recognition had to be met with an equivalent force of denial). But at the same time, it is as if this consciousness crossed a certain critical threshold, in Zola, with the result that the paternal metaphor of textual generation was seriously weakened and could not stand alone. We have then in Zola, a metaphorical shift from male potency toward female fecundity and a correlative shift from narrative dissemination toward narrative flow. Zola, in spite of himself, seems to have written a "man-womanly" text, anticipating Virginia Woolf's hypothesis of "two sexes in the mind corresponding to two sexes in the body [which may fuse so that] the mind is fully fertilised and uses all its faculties."[14]

My passage from Balzac to Zola suggests the rough course of a trajectory which could be followed in order to extend the context of the present study. This larger study might adopt as its framing question Roland Barthes's query: "S'il n'y a plus de Père, à quoi bon raconter des histoires?"[15] The question, as Barthes posed it in 1973, is of course anachronistic, and needs to be projected backward into the nineteenth century. Once we do this, however, we find that the question is already its own answer. This answer is implied by a good many nineteenth-century novels, but it is most eloquently (if elliptically) expressed by Dostoevsky's well-known aphorism: "Of course, God is only a hypothesis, but . . . I admit that He is needed . . . for the order of the universe and all that ... and that if there was no God He would have to be invented." [16] As many other novels of the period make clear, it is precisely because there is no more father that one must tell stories.

The history of the father figure in the novel remains to be written, but when it is it will be neither a chronicle of paternity nor a record of paternal absence. It will be instead, as Dostoevsky suggested, the story of the multiple reinventions of the father.

Notes

INTRODUCTION

1 Honoré de Balzac, *Avant-propos de La Comédie humaine*, ed. Pierre-Georges Castex, I (Paris: Bibliothèque de la Pléiade, 1976–81), pp. 12–13.

2 Balzac, *L'Elixir de longue vie*, in *La Comédie humaine* XI, p. 474.

3 Patricia Drechsel Tobin, *Time and the Novel: The Genealogical Imperative* (Princeton: Princeton University Press, 1978), p. 37; Edward W. Said, *Beginnings: Intention and Method* (New York: Basic, 1975), p. 66; Roland Barthes, *Le Plaisir du texte* (Paris: Seuil, 1973), p. 75.

4 Tobin, *Time and the Novel*, p. 29.

5 For a study of *La Nouvelle Héloise* as an eighteenth-century precursor of nineteenth-century narrative subversions of the father, see Tony Tanner's excellent chapter on that novel, "Rousseau's *La Nouvelle Héloise*: Le Bosquet profané," in *Adultery in the Novel: Contract and Transgression* (Baltimore: Johns Hopkins University Press, 1979).

6 For a thorough discussion of the relationship between public, private, and religious patriarchal orders before and after the French Revolution, see Jacques Donzelot, *La Police des Familles* (Paris: Minuit, 1977), and Jean-Louis Flandrin, *Familles* (Paris: Hachette, 1976).

[187]

7   Although paternity has been called "the dominant metaphor of the *Comédie Humaine*" by Peter Brooks, and "le thème le plus profond" (the deepest theme [in the Balzacian corpus]) by Gaëtan Picon, its place in Balzac's work curiously has not been studied at length. (References are from Brooks, *The Melodramatic Imagination* [New Haven: Yale University Press, 1976], p. 120; Picon, *Balzac par lui-même* [Paris: Seuil, 1956], p. 114.) But see, in addition to the above, Christopher Prendergast's provocative if brief discussion in the last chapter of *Balzac: Fiction and Melodrama* (London: Edward Arnold, 1978). Prendergast links Balzac's paternal obsessions to representational issues, via impulses toward authority and mastery common to both; this is similar to my own understanding of the problem. See, too, Samuel Weber's *Unwrapping Balzac: A Reading of* La Peau de chagrin (Toronto: University of Toronto Press, 1979), which is often insightful on the father question in *La Peau de chagrin*. Finally, see Lucienne Frappier-Mazur's magisterial study, *L'Expression métaphorique dans* La Comédie humaine (Paris: Klincksieck, 1976), especially chapter 4, "Le Patriarcat," and chapter 5, "Le Corps humain."

8   The two approaches are well summarized by the titles of two books: the historical by St.-Paulien's *Napoléon Balzac et l'Empire de* La Comédie humaine (Paris: Albin Michel, 1979), and the psycho-mythical by André Maurois's biography, *Prométhée ou la vie de Balzac* (Paris: Hachette, 1965).

9   Barthes, *Le Plaisir du texte*, p. 20.

10 Gérard Genette, "Vraisemblance et motivation," in *Figures II* (Paris: Seuil, 1969), p. 79; p. 85.

11 Balzac, *Avant-propos*, p. 10.

12 Balzac, *Le Père Goriot*, in *La Comédie humaine* III, p. 50.

13 Sigmund Freud, "Family Romances," in *The Standard Edition of the Complete Psychological Works of Sigmund Freud*, ed. James Strachey, IX (London: Hogarth Press, 1953–74). See, too, Marthe Robert's interesting discussion of the novel as an elaborated "family romance" in *Roman des origines et origines du roman* (Paris: Grasset, 1972).

14 For a more comprehensive treatment of nineteenth-century science and the revolution in time, see two excellent studies which are the major sources for my summary: Stephen Toulmin and June Goodfield, *The Discovery of Time* (New York: Harper & Row, 1965; reprint, Chicago: University of Chicago Press, 1982); and Daniel J. Boorstin, *The Discoverers* (New York: Random House, 1983; see especially parts 12 and 14).

15 George Steiner, *The Death of Tragedy* (New York: Knopf, 1961; reprinted, New York: Oxford University Press, 1980), p. 320.

16 Frank Kermode, *The Sense of an Ending* (New York: Oxford University Press, 1966; reprint 1975), p. 56.

17 Peter Brooks, "Fictions of the Wolfman: Freud and Narrative Understanding," in *Reading for the Plot* (New York: Knopf, 1984), p. 270. On the connection between the fading of Christianity and the rise of narrative, see also Kermode, *The Sense of an Ending;* Steiner, *Death of Tragedy;* Georg Lukács, *The Theory of the Novel,* tr. Anna Bostock (Cambridge: MIT Press, 1971).

18 Susan Sontag, *Illness as Metaphor* (New York: Farrar, Straus and Giroux, 1977), p. 55.

19 Henry James, "The Lesson of Balzac," in *The Future of the Novel* (New York: Vintage Books, 1956), pp. 123–24.

CHAPTER ONE: THE NARRATOR AS STORY SELLER

1 Balzac, *Louis Lambert,* in *La Comédie humaine* XI, p. 591.

2 With apologies to Gérard Genette, *Mimologiques: Voyages en Cratylie* (Paris: Seuil, 1976).

3 A notable exception to the otherwise general critical dismissal of the first part of *El Verdugo* can be found in Pierre Citron's helpful introduction to the text in *La Comédie humaine* X, pp. 1123–31. Citron points out the incestuous element of the Clara-Juanito couple and indicates that it is analogous to the equally impossible Clara-Victor couple; he also sheds light on the parricidal aspect of the text.

4 Diana Festa McCormick, *Les Nouvelles de Balzac* (Paris: Nizet, 1973), p. 105; emphasis added.

5 Ibid, 110–11: "Clara, la seule qui se soit pendant un moment détachée de l'union familiale pour affirmer son individualité, rentre vite dans le cadre des Léganès auquel sa fierté et son devoir la lient" (Clara, the only one to detach herself momentarily from the family unit to affirm her individuality, quickly reenters the Léganès clan, to which she is bound by her pride and her duty).

6 Wayne Conner, "The Genesis of Balzac's *El Verdugo,*" *Leuvense bijdragen: Tijdschrift voor moderne filologie,* 46 (1956–57): 135–39.

7 Balzac, *Pensées, sujets, fragmens,* ed. Jacques Crépet (Paris: A. Blaizot, 1910), pp. 94–95.

8 "Introduction par Félix Davin aux *Etudes Philosophiques,*" in *La Comédie humaine* X, p. 1213; emphasis added.

9   Balzac, *El Verdugo,* in *La Comédie humaine* X, p. 1133. Subsequent references to this work are given parenthetically in the text.

10   Balzac, *Facino Cane,* in *La Comédie humaine* VI, p. 1020; emphasis added. Subsequent references to *Facino Cane* are given parenthetically in the text.

11   As in *Adieu,* where Shoshana Felman has noted a similar specular relationship between Stéphanie and Philippe, and a similar specular destiny which informs my reading: "En tuant Stéphanie dans l'illusion même de la 'sauver,' c'est aussi bien sa propre image que Philippe frappe dans le miroir" (When he kills Stéphanie in the very illusion of 'saving' her, Philippe is also striking his own mirror-image) ("Les Femmes et la folie: Histoire littéraire et idéologique," in *La Folie et la chose littéraire* [Paris: Seuil, 1978], p. 152).

12   See also Barthes's comment on the moon in *Sarrasine:* "La lune est le *rien* de la lumière, la chaleur réduite à son manque: elle éclaire par pur reflet, sans être elle-même origine; elle devient ainsi l'emblème lumineux du castrat" (The moon is the *nothingness* of light, warmth reduced to its lack: it illuminates by mere reflection, without itself being an origin; it thus becomes the luminous emblem of the castrato; S/Z [Paris: Seuil, 1970], p. 31).

13   McCormick states that contrasting emotions are aroused in the reader "par un drame qui le fascine et le révolte à la fois" (p. 110) (by a drama that simultaneously fascinates and revolts). Pierre Gascar believes that Balzac's scenes of violence imply "moins un fresque héroïque que le plus sombre des tableaux dénonciateurs" (less a heroic fresco than the darkest accusatory tableau), yet several pages later he maintains that the execution confers upon Juanito a "suprême noblesse" (supreme nobility) (preface to Balzac, *Le Colonel Chabert* suivi de *El Verdugo, Adieu,* et de *Le Requisitionnaire,* ed. Patrick Berthier [Paris: Gallimard, 1974], pp. 9, 20). Henri Evans comments that Balzac "avait ici à prouver que l'homme est un monstre superbe" (here needed to show that man is a superb monster) (preface to *El Verdugo,* in *L'Oeuvre de Balzac,* ed. Albert Béguin and Jean Ducourneau, XII [Paris: Club Français du Livre, 1966], p. 12.

14   We should situate this particular contradiction within a series of paradoxical and obscured elements that characterize this text: the discordance between Clara's name and the dark fate she bodes; the curious choice of the name Victor for a character who is first militarily disgraced and later romantically deprived; the awarding of a "title of nobility" (El Verdugo) which bears all the marks of a stigma; two scenes of festivity (a ball in the first place, a banquet

in the second) superimposed on the two most somber spots of the text (the Spanish insurrection and the final massacre). In each case, the paradox marks a crucial knot of the intrigue. I shall have more to say about these contradictions later.

15 Freud's description of the mechanism of reversal in dreams is instructive: "The way in which dreams treat the category of contraries and contradictories is highly remarkable. It is simply disregarded. "No" seems not to exist so far as dreams are concerned. They show a particular preference for combining contraries into a unity or for representing them as one and the same thing. Dreams feel themselves at liberty, moreover, to represent any element by its wishful contrary; so that there is no way of deciding at a first glance whether any element that admits of a contrary is present in the dream-thoughts as a positive or as a negative." *The Interpretation of Dreams,* in *The Standard Edition,* IV, p. 318.

16 Balzac, *Béatrix,* in *La Comédie humaine* II, p. 810; emphasis added.

17 Ibid., 814.

18 In *El Verdugo,* the mother is occulted, replaced by the sister in the representation of an incestuous relationship. We can see the traces of this substitution in the two ocular details mentioned above, which evoke Juanito's rather intimate rapport with mother as with sister, and tend toward assimilating the two women. It is interesting that Juanito murders his entire family *except for his mother:* "La marquise comprit que le courage de Juanito était épuisé, elle s'élança d'un bond par-dessus la balustrade, et alla se fendre la tête sur les rochers" (p. 1142) (The marquise realized that Juanito's courage was exhausted; she instantly threw herself over the balustrade, and split her head on the rocks below). The fate Calyste planned for Béatrix—because he could not have her—was an identical death on the rocks above the sea. The significant difference is that Calyste pushed Béatrix; the intentional element is suppressed in *El Verdugo.* It is also worth noting that in some versions of the Oedipus story (notably, Corneille's) the Sphinx, like the marquise, leaps to her death on the rocks below.

19 As we know nothing of Victor's mother or sister, we cannot speculate on the path of this projection. We do, however, know of Balzac's unending yearning for the mother by whom he felt continually rejected, and we can surmise that he played out this desire through the succession of lovers who bore his mother's name (which was his sister's as well). We know of his aristocratic infatuation, his quest for women of higher and higher social standing,

and his token self-ennoblement (the addition of the *particule* to his very *roturier* patronym). We can thus speculate that he lived a family romance not unlike the one he writes by interposing Victor Marchand as day-dreamer.

20 The erotic significance of the letter in Balzac's text is extratextually confirmed by Stefan Zweig's account of his many and prolific epistolary romances: "Madame de Castries was not the only woman whose acquaintance he owed to the postman. There was a series of affectionate women friends . . . who eventually followed up their letters with personal visits, and one of them . . . had a child by him. . . . Balzac read these epistles from his feminine admirers with particular care. They strengthened him in his feeling that he could mean a great deal to a woman, and whenever the tone of a letter or any special phrase awakened his curiosity he replied at considerable length. When a communication of this sort reached him it was as though a delicate and alluring fragrance suddenly pervaded his isolated, closely curtained chamber." Stefan Zweig, *Balzac,* trans. William and Dorothy Rose (New York: Viking Press, 1946), p. 184.

21 A biographical anecdote casts an interesting light on the relationship between Balzac's story and Victor's. In 1846, Mme. Hanska was expecting a child fathered by Balzac. Before the child's birth, Balzac, convinced that he would have a son, had already chosen his name: Victor-Honoré. The child, stillborn, was a girl. Whereupon Balzac wrote the following to Mme. Hanska: "I was so anxious to have a Victor Honoré. A Victor would not have abandoned his mother" (cited by Zweig, *Balzac,* p. 362).

22 McCormick, *Nouvelles de Balzac,* maintains that "le cadre dynastique . . . a rendu toute individualité des Léganès opaque et presque invisible" (p. 111) (the dynastic order . . . has dimmed and almost effaced the individuality of the Léganès). Gascar, preface to *Le Colonel Chabert,* remarks that "la narration . . . réduit la dimension intérieure des personnages, et . . . l'intensité dramatique impose leur schématisation, en fait des marionettes raidies par les préjugés espagnols de caste et de grandeur" (p. 16) (the narration . . . reduces the inner dimension of the characters, and . . . dramatic intensity requires their schematization, turns them into puppets made rigid by Spanish traditions of caste and nobility.)

23 The terminology is Genette's. See "Proust et le langage indirect," in *Figures II* (Paris: Seuil, 1969), p. 248.

24 Michel Foucault, "Le 'Non' du père," *Critique,* 18, no. 178

(March 1962), pp. 205–06. The translation is taken from "The Father's 'No,'" in Foucault, *Language, Counter-Memory, Practice: Selected Essays and Interviews,* ed. Donald F. Bouchard and Sherry Simon (Ithaca: Cornell University Press, 1977), p. 82.

25 As John T. Irwin has pointed out, fatherhood involves "not just generation but acknowledgment as well." *Doubling and Incest/ Repetition and Revenge: A Speculative Reading of Faulkner* (Baltimore: Johns Hopkins University Press, 1975), p. 133.

26 I am referring to Freud's account, in his discussion of repetition as mastery, of a game he observed being played by a child of one and a half. See *Beyond the Pleasure Principle,* in *The Standard Edition,* XVIII, pp. 14–17.

27 Cited by Zweig, *Balzac,* p. 91.

CHAPTER TWO: THRICE-TOLD TALE

1 See Patrick Berthier, "Histoire du texte," *Une Passion dans le désert* by Balzac, in *La Comédie humaine* VIII, pp. 1839–40. Subsequent references to *Une Passion* are given parenthetically in the text.

2 Félicien Marceau, *Balzac et son monde* (Paris: Gallimard, 1955), p. 10.

3 Léon-François Hoffmann, "Eros camouflé: En marge d'*Une Passion dans le désert,*" *Hebrew University Studies in Literature* 5, no. 1 (Spring 1977): 19–36.

4 Ibid., 23.

5 Ibid., 32.

6 Ibid., 36.

7 The locution "faiblement sans doute" signals a curious mélange of narrative voices, for certainly the soldier should know whether he received a bite or a nip. The anonymously voiced qualifier "sans doute" depersonalizes and neutralizes the sexual pleasure alluded to.

8 Pierre Fontanier, *Les Figures du discours,* introduction by Gérard Genette (Paris: Flammarion, 1968), p. 135; emphasis added.

9 See Léon-François Hoffmann's more detailed argument for a permuted relationship betwen Mignonne and "la fille aux yeux d'or" in "Mignonne et Paquita," *L'Année Balzacienne,* 1964, pp. 181–86.

10 Quoted by Hoffmann, "Mignonne et Paquita," p. 185.

11   Balzac, *La Fille aux yeux d'or,* in *La Comédie humaine* V, p. 1089.
     Subsequent references appear in the text.
12   Paquita of course problematizes all sex roles in this novel, for the
     Marquise is as virile as Henri is effeminate.
13   Balzac, *Sarrasine,* in *La Comédie humaine* VI, p. 1074.
14   Barthes, *S/Z.* See especially pp. 204–08.
15   More specifically, semantic emptiness results from a destruction of
     the concept of binary opposition, or difference (of which sexual
     difference is the model), which permits the production of meaning
     through substitution.
16   Balzac, *Voyage de Paris à Java,* in *Oeuvres complètes de M. de
     Balzac,* ed. Jean A. Ducourneau, XXV (Paris: Les Bibliophiles de
     l'Originale, 1973). This text, first published in November 1832 in
     the *Revue de Paris,* is not included in *La Comèdie humaine.* Sub-
     sequent references appear in the text.
17   Pierre Citron links this text to a series including *La Fille aux yeux
     d'or, Sarrasine, Une Passion dans le désert;* his grouping is made
     on the basis of their expression of a common Oriental myth. While
     my association of texts is similar, it is motivated instead by their
     adherence to a common erotic myth which I believe is the signified
     referred to by the Oriental signifier. See Pierre Citron, "Le Rêve
     asiatique de Balzac," *L'Année Balzacienne,* 1968.
18   Raphael de Valentin has a similar fantasy: "En présence de mes
     romanesques fantaisies, qu'était Pauline? Pouvait-elle me vendre
     des nuits qui coûtent la vie, un amour qui tue et met en jeu toutes
     les facultés humaines?" (In the presence of my fantasies, what was
     Pauline? Could she sell me nights whose price is life, a love that
     kills and calls into play all human faculties? [Balzac, *La Peau de
     chagrin,* in *La Comédie humaine* X, p. 143]).
19   "Il songea involontairement à sa première maîtresse, qu'il avait
     surnommée 'Mignonne' par antiphrase, parce qu'elle était d'une si
     atroce jalousie, que pendant tout le temps que dura leur passion, il
     eut à craindre le couteau dont elle l'avait toujours menacé" (He
     involuntarily recalled his first mistress, whom he had ironically
     nicknamed "Mignonne" because she was so atrociously jealous
     that for every minute of their passion he lived in fear of the knife
     with which she had always threatened him [*Une Passion,* p.
     1228.])
20   Paquita Valdès, too, is compared to a gazelle. See *La Fille,* p. 1096.
21   Freud, "Fetishism," in *The Standard Edition,* XXI, p. 156. See also
     p. 157: "Affection and hostility in the treatment of the fetish—
     which run parallel with the disavowal and the acknowledgment of

castration—are mixed in unequal proportions in different cases, so that the one or the other is more clearly recognizable."

22   The following examples, drawn from less concentrated contexts, are indicative of a general phenomenon.

a. (The following is a description of the courtesan Aquilina, whose name is significantly derived from the Latin word for a bird of prey, *aquila*, "eagle.") "L'oeil, *armé* de longs cils, *lançait* des flammes hardies, étincelles d'amour! ... *Elle paraissait leste, souple, et sa vigueur supposait l'agilité d'une panthère, comme la mâle élégance de ses formes en promettait les voluptés dévorantes.* ... *Peut-être eût-elle ravi des gens blasés, mais un jeune homme l'eût redoutée.* C'était une statue colossale tombée du haut de quelque temple grec, sublime à distance, mais grossière à voir de près. ... *espèce d'arabesque admirable où la joie hurle, où l'amour a je ne sais quoi de sauvage,* où la magie de la grâce et le feu du bonheur succèdent aux sanglants tumultes de la colère; *monstre qui sait mordre et caresser, rire comme un démon, pleurer comme les anges, improviser dans une seule étreinte toutes les séductions de la femme,* excepté les soupirs de la mélancolie et les enchanteresses modesties d'une vierge; *puis en un moment rugir, se déchirer les flancs, briser sa passion, son amant; enfin se déchirer elle-même* comme fait un peuple insurgé" (Her eyes, *armed* with long lashes, darted hardy flames, sparks of love! ... *She seemed lithe, nimble, and her vigor suggested a panther's agility, just as the virile elegance of her shape promised consuming sensuality.* ... *Perhaps men who were blasé would have found her ravishing, but a young man would have feared her.* She was a colossal statue fallen from a Greek temple, sublime at a distance, but coarse if seen from up close. ... *a kind of awesome arabesque where joy screams, where love has a wild quality,* where a magical grace and fiery happiness succeed the bloody turmoil of anger; *a monster who knows how to bite and to caress, who laughs like a demon, cries like angels, and can improvise, in a single embrace, all of woman's seductions,* except melancholy's sighs and the charming modesty of a virgin; *then in an instant, roar, tear her own flanks, destroy her passion, her lover; then tear herself asunder,* like a nation in revolt [*La Peau de chagrin,* p. 112]).

b. "Oui ... vous voulez que cette madame Marneffe abandonne la proie qu'elle a dans la gueule! Et comment feriez-vous lâcher à un tigre son morceau de boeuf? Est-ce en lui passant la main sur le dos et lui disant: minet! ... minet! ..." (Yes ... you want this Madame Marneffe to abandon the prey she has in her mouth?

How would you make a tiger give up his piece of beef? By stroking his back and saying: "here, kitty ... here kitty?" [*La Cousine Bette*, in *La Comédie humaine* VII, p. 388]).

c. "Les naturalistes nous ont dépeint les moeurs de beaucoup d'animaux féroces; mais ils ont oublié la mère et la fille en quête d'un mari. C'est des hyènes qui, selon le Psalmiste, cherchent une proie à dévorer, et qui joignent au naturel de la bête l'intelligence de l'homme et le génie de la femme." (Naturalists have described to us the habits of many wild animals; but they have forgotten the mother and daughter in search of a husband. They are hyenas who, according to the Psalmist, seek a prey to devour, and who add to the nature of the beast the intelligence of man and the ingenuity of woman [*Le Contrat de mariage*, in *La Comédie humaine* III, p. 592]).

23   Bladelike images regularly characterize Balzac's representations of the femme fatale. The duchesse de Langeais is felt by her lover to be "froide et tranchante autant que l'acier" (as cold and cutting as steel [*La Duchesse de Langeais*, in *La Comédie humaine* V, p. 985]). The ruthless sharpness which is attributed to the courtesan Aquilina can be glimpsed in her explanation of a former lover's fate: "La guillotine a été ma rivale" (The guillotine was my rival; *La Peau de chagrin*, p. 113).

24   Freud, "The 'Uncanny,'" in *The Standard Edition*, XVII. See especially pp. 220–26.

25   Ibid., p. 241.

26   Barthes's comment on "la solidarité des formes narratives, des structures familiales et des interdictions de nudité, toutes rassemblées, chez nous, dans le mythe de Noé recouvert par ses fils" (the solidarity of narrative forms, familial structures, and interdictions of nudity which all coincide, in our culture, in the myth of Noah covered up by his sons) is extremely relevant to this tableau (*Le Plaisir du texte*, p. 20).

27   See Pierre Citron, introduction to *La Peau de chagrin*, p. 21 (emphasis added). Balzac's father died in June, 1829; three tales of parricide swiftly followed his death: *El Verdugo* in October 1829, *L'Elixir de longue vie* in October 1830, and *Une Passion* in December 1830.

28   The possessive adjectives of course denote the third member, the soldier.

29   Balzac, *L'Enfant maudit*, in *La Comédie humaine* X, p. 913. Subsequent references appear in the text.

30   Balzac, *Le Lys dans la vallée*, in *La Comédie humaine* IX, p. 1159.

31 We are aware, of course, that Balzac never forgave his own mother for farming him out to a wet-nurse and thereby renouncing her maternal role. This grievance is aired ad infinitum in the pages of the *Comédie humaine*. The following is a typical cry: "En attachant les enfants au sein de leurs mères, Jean-Jacques rendait déjà un immense service à la vertu" (By placing children at their mothers' breasts, Jean-Jacques was already rendering a great service to virtue; *La Physiologie du mariage*, in *La Comédie humaine* XI, p. 1007).

32 A more detailed study of the "sons and lovers" theme in Balzac would explore the obviously pertinent denouement of *La Peau de chagrin*, in which the dying Raphael leaps up and bites Pauline's breast.

33 The metaphoric network we have gradually disengaged establishes a pattern of great internal consistency within the text, for every element of the network touches all the others. A two-dimensional diagram, while not entirely representative, at least evokes the pattern of interconnections:

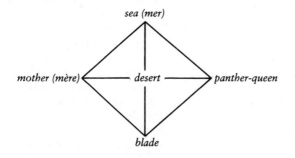

34 As Claude Lévi-Strauss remarks in the course of his structural analysis of the Oedipus myth (which is based on the juxtaposition of all available variants of the myth): "Il n'existe pas de version 'vraie' dont toutes les autres seraient des copies ou des échos déformés. Toutes les versions appartiennent au mythe" ("La Structure des mythes," in *Anthropologie structurale* [Paris: Plon, 1958], p. 242; There is no "true" version of which all others are copies or deformed echoes. All versions are part of the myth).

35 An interesting study could be made of the numerous avatars of the sphinx in the Balzacian corpus. Such a study might begin with the following citations: (a) Henri to Paquita, in *La Fille aux yeux d'or:* "Tu es . . . une charade vivante dont le mot me semble bien difficile

à trouver" (p. 1090) (You are ... a living charade whose key seems difficult indeed to find); (b) Sarrasine to Zambinella (the castrato) in *Sarrasine:* "J'aurai toujours dans le souvenir une harpie céleste qui viendra enfoncer ses griffes dans tous mes sentiments d'homme, et qui signera toutes les autres femmes d'un cachet d'imperfection. Monstre! toi qui ne peux donner la vie à rien, tu m'as dépeuplé la terre de toutes les femmes" (p. 1074; My memory will always contain a celestial harpy who will sink her claws into all my manly sentiments, and who will mark all other women with a stamp of imperfection. Monster! You, who can give life to nothing, have emptied the earth of all women). These three "sphinxes" (the panther Mignonne, Paquita Valdès, and the castrato la Zambinella) share a common feature: they are all "women" whose femininity becomes problematic. An analysis of the sphinx motif might associate these beings of uncertain sex with the queue de poisson and queue de crocodile metaphors mentioned earlier, which seem to be appended to women as sexual question marks, signs of sexual ambiguity.

36 Freud, *Civilization and Its Discontents,* in *The Standard Edition* XXI, p. 104.

37 The embedded text symbolically represents a coming together of different narrative levels, for the narrator's manuscript is based on the soldier's tale and refers, by its supplementary title, to the finished literary product, the text which reaches the external reader. The symbolic convergence becomes a perceptible reality at the end of the narrative, when we witness the collapse of narrative levels, a "fading of voices" (in Barthes's terms) in which the soldier's words emerge in the middle of the narrator's interrupted text, against the backdrop of the external narration—the report of a dialogue between the lady and the narrator—which is the matrix from which the other two levels issue.

38 Ernest Jones, *Hamlet and Oedipus* (New York: Norton, 1949; reprint, New York: Norton Library, 1976), p. 89, note 3.

39 This is similar to what happens in the *Sarrasine* frame. See Barthes's discussion in *S/Z.*

40 In the same vein, it is interesting that Balzac never wrote the two sequels to *Une Passion* which were to constitute, together with this story, the trilogy *Les Français en Egypte.*

41 Saussurian linguistics teaches that the production of meaning in language is dependent upon paradigmatic opposition. The concept of binary opposition alone allows chains of signifiers to be substituted for each other; thus the destruction of opposition or differ-

ence subverts the signifying process. See Saussure, *Cours de linguistique générale*, ed. Tullio de Mauro (Paris: Payot, 1972).

42 Michel Foucault, "Le 'Non' du père," 205.

43 Ibid.; emphasis added.

CHAPTER THREE: MIRRORS AND FATHERHOOD

1 Jorge Luis Borges, "Tlön, Uqbar, Orbus Tertius," in *Labyrinths*, ed. Donald A. Yates and James E. Irby (New York: New Directions, 1964), p. 15. Subsequent references to this story will be given parenthetically in the text.

2 Richard Burgin, *Conversations with Jorge Luis Borges* (New York: Avon, 1969), p. 94.

3 Balzac, *Le Lys dans la vallée*, in *La Comédie humaine IX*, p. 915; emphasis added.

4 Balzac, *La Peau de chagrin*, in *La Comédie humaine X*, p. 173. Subsequent references to this novel are given parenthetically in the text.

5 Balzac, *Illusions perdues*, in *La Comédie humaine V*, p. 184. Subsequent references to this novel are given parenthetically in the text, preceded by the abbreviation *I.P.*.

6 Balzac, *Le Père Goriot*, in *La Comédie humaine III*, p. 268. Subsequent references to this novel will be given parenthetically in the text, preceded by the abbreviation *P.G.*.

7 See *I.P.*, p. 346*n*1.

8 Balzac, *Splendeurs et misères des courtisanes*, in *La Comédie humaine VI*, p. 574. Subsequent references to this novel are given parenthetically in the text, preceded by the abbreviation *S.M.*

9 Another example is the honey which Rastignac's probing look seems to pump from the Parisian hive (*P.G.*, p. 290).

10 Balzac's consistent reworking of the real is aptly summarized by Gaëtan Picon: "Il substitute au monde donné un autre monde qui lui emprunte ses éléments, mais qui les organise différemment selon les lois d'une mythologie personnelle" (He replaces the real world with another world which borrows its elements, but organizes them differently according to the laws of a personal mythology; preface to *Balzac lu et relu*, by Albert Béguin [Paris: Seuil, 1965], pp. 9–10).

11 He does, however, apply the same investigatory methods to Vautrin as to Goriot. At one point he rebuffs Vautrin's questions by telling him: "Je ne dois compte de mes affaires à personne, attendu que je ne cherche pas à deviner celles que les autres font la nuit" (I

owe no one an account of my affairs, given that I don't seek to find out what others are doing in the night), referring, despite his denial, to the night he spied a light in Vautrin's room and listened in on the breathing of two men and the clink of gold. Whereupon Vautrin keenly reproves him: "Mon petit, quand on ne veut pas être dupe des marionettes, il faut entrer tout à fait dans la baraque, et ne pas se contenter de regarder par les trous de la tapisserie" (*P.G.*, p. 119; my boy, if you don't intend to be fooled by the puppets, you must go all the way into the tent, and not satisfy yourself with looking through peepholes).

12 The word *ainsi* refers to the fact that Rastignac's head is at this moment in Victorine's lap; thus the look Victorine anticipates is ambiguous. While she assumes it will be a sexually piercing stare directed toward herself, we as readers know better, and interpret it either as a sexually penetrating gaze at Rastignac, or a jealous stare focused on Victorine.

13 Likewise, when Lucien de Rubempré abandons himself to Vautrin/Herrera, he becomes a passive instrument. And in *Splendeurs et misères,* which is the record of this puppeteer-puppet relationship, Lucien gives up writing.

14 Jean-Paul Sartre, *Baudelaire* (Paris: Gallimard, 1963), p. 134.

15 Of all Balzac's characters, it is Gobseck who most successfully attains the ideal of integrity and the illusion of mastery, because his sterility and avoidance of carnal investment guarantee his power.

16 The curiously versatile nature of the money metaphor cannot be overlooked. While it is most often a phallic equivalent, some of its usages (notably, the sisters' gift and the mother-milking metaphor cited earlier in this chapter) clearly associate it with female sexuality. The lack of symbolic differentiation is striking, and suggests a lack of sexual distinction as well. This symbolic merging of the sexes must be categorized with a very pervasive phenomenon of effaced antitheses (particularly, sexual fusion, as epitomized by the figure of the hermaphrodite, the panther, and the soldier-panther chiasmus) which I have noted before and will have occasion to return to.

17 External evidence (*Le Député d'Arcis*) informs us that Rastignac later marries Delphine's daughter.

18 Barthes, *S/Z,* pp. 85–86.

19 One thinks of Baudelaire's harvesting skeletons, an image of death itself begetting life. See "Le Squelette laboureur" in *Les Fleurs du mal.*

20 Balzac, *Le Chef-d'oeuvre inconnu,* in *La Comédie humaine* X, p. 436.

CHAPTER FOUR: MADMEN AND VISIONS, SAGES AND CODES

1 Balzac, *Facino Cane,* in *La Comédie humaine* VI, p. 1019; emphasis added.

2 Balzac, *Théorie de la démarche,* in *La Comédie humaine* XII, p. 266. Subsequent references to this essay are given parenthetically in the text, preceded by the abbreviation *T.D.*

3 Balzac, *Massimilla Doni,* in *La Comédie humaine* X, p. 549. Subsequent references to *Massimilla Doni* are given parenthetically in the text.

4 We again find the metaphor of the abyss in *Théorie de la démarche;* here it directly refers to the formulation of an idea: "Je laissai là cette grande idée, comme un homme effrayé d'apercevoir un gouffre. . . . Néanmoins, je fus si curieusement affriandé par la vue de cet abîme, que, de temps en temps, je venais goûter toutes les joies de la peur, en la contemplant au bord, et m'y tenant ferme à quelques idées bien plantées, bien feuillues" (p. 272; I abandoned this great idea, like a man frightened by the sight of a chasm. . . . Nevertheless, I found the view of this abyss so strangely alluring, that from time to time I came and tasted all the joys of fear, which I contemplated from the edges, holding on to a few sturdy, leafy ideas).

5 Balzac provides the key to the allegory in a letter to Mme. Hanska: "Dans cinq ans, *Massimilla Doni* sera comprise comme une belle explication des plus intimes procédés de l'art. Aux yeux des lecteurs du premier jour, ce sera ce que ça est en apparence, un amoureux qui ne peut posséder la femme qu'il adore parce qu'il la désire trop et qui possède une misérable fille. Faites-les donc conclure de là à l'enfantement des oeuvres d'art!" 22 janvier 1838, *Lettres à Madame Hanska,* ed. Roger Pierrot (Paris: Les Bibliophiles de l'Originale, 1967, 1:580; In five years, *Massimilla Doni* will be understood as a fine illustration of the most intimate workings of art. In the eyes of its first readers, it will be only what it appears to be: a lover who can not possess the woman he adores because he desires her too much, and who possesses instead an easy woman. Expect them to understand that in terms of engendering works of art!).

6 Balzac, *Louis Lambert,* in *La Comédie humaine* XI, p. 594.

7   Ibid., p. 680.

8   David summarizes their separate destinies: "Au boeuf l'agriculture patiente, à l'oiseau la vie insouciante, se disait l'imprimeur. Je serai le boeuf, Lucien sera l'aigle" (*I.P.*, p. 147; "The ox is made for laborious farming, the bird for a care-free life," the printer told himself. "I will be the ox, and Lucien the eagle").

9   "Chaque mot, chaque geste, a . . . des dessous dont Balzac n'avertit pas le lecteur et qui sont d'une profondeur admirable." Proust, *Contre Sainte-Beuve,* ed. Pierre Clarac (Paris: Bibliothèque de la Pléiade, 1971), p. 273; Each word, each gesture, has hidden recesses of awesome depth that Balzac does not indicate to the reader).

10 Lucien's "madness" is implied on several occasions and even clinically labeled. His friend Michel Chrestien implores: "Sois le Tasse sans sa folie" (*I.P.*, p. 325; Be Tasso without his madness). When Lucien determines to end his life, we are told that he has fallen into a meditation which "arrive à la manie" (approaches a mania) and that, "selon quelques grands médecins *aliénistes,* le suicide, chez certaines organisations, est la terminaison d'une aliénation mentale" (*S.M.*, p. 787; according to some great *specialists in mental illness,* suicide, for certain constitutions, is the culminating point of mental illness); furthermore, a hallucinatory state ascribed to monomania is attributed to him and described in considerable detail (*S.M.*, pp. 793–94).

11 For a detailed development of the tension between life and death instincts, see Freud, *Beyond the Pleasure Principle,* in *The Standard Edition,* XVIII.

12 Lucien has "les hanches conformées comme celles d'une femme" (a woman's hips); "l'air d'une jeune fille" (the appearance of a young girl); he has a "tournure molle . . . pleine de grâces féminines" (a languid . . . femininely graceful physique; *I.P.*, pp. 145, 451, 146). Such characterizations abound; these examples are merely indicative.

13 She is also a hermaphroditic figure, who, raised without a mother, received a "mâle éducation"; her tutor "communiqua sa hardiesse d'examen et sa facilité de jugement à son élève, sans songer que ces qualités si nécessaires à un homme deviennent des défauts chez une femme" (*I.P.*, p. 154; passed on to his pupil his bold spirit of enquiry and his facility for decision-making, without realizing that such qualities necessary to a man are seen as defects in a woman).

14 His friends of the Cénacle quickly realize that his bond to them is

scarred by "un effroyable égoisme" (*I.P.*, p. 325; an appalling egoism).

15 Proust, *Contre Sainte-Beuve*, p. 277.

16 Balzac's "case history" of Lucien here converges with Freud's theories about homosexual models of desire. See Freud, "On Narcissism: An Introduction," in *The Standard Edition*, XIV, and *Leonardo da Vinci and a Memory of His Childhood*, in *The Standard Edition*, XI.

17 Marguerite Drevon and Jeannine Guichardet perceptively remark: "L'Etre Séraphîta est un ange du paradis de Swedenborg, androgyne ou asexué; sans mettre en doute la portée mystique du roman, il faut avouer que la particularité du personnage principal confère une curieuse résonance aux tendres propos de Wilfred et de Minna" ("Fameux Sexorama," *L'Année Balzacienne*, 1972, p. 258; The creature Séraphîta is an angel out of Swedenborg's paradise, androgynous or asexual; without challenging the novel's mystical tenor, one must admit that the main character's essential feature confers a curious resonance upon Wilfred and Minna's tender exchanges).

18 Plato's text reads: "In the first place there were three sexes, not as with us, two, male and female; the third partook of the nature of both the others and has vanished, though its name survives. The hermaphrodite was a distinct sex in form as well as in name, but now the name alone remains" (*The Symposium*, trans. Walter Hamilton [Harmondsworth: Penguin, 1951], p. 59.)

19 *La Fille aux yeux d'or*, p. 1109.

20 Martin Kanes, "Balzac and the Problem of Expression," *Symposium* 23, no. 3–4 (Fall–Winter 1969), p. 291.

21 In his introduction to *Illusions perdues,* Roland Chollet suggests that the same episode is "transposé sous deux éclairages tout à fait opposés. . . . L'ombre est allée au pacte d'Herrera avec Lucien. . . . Tandis que la lumière se concentrait dans l'ardente et pure amitié d'adolescence qui lie David et Lucien" (*I.P.*, p. 28; transposed in two contrasting lights. . . . a shadow is cast on Herrera's pact with Lucien. . . . while the pure, ardent bonds of adolescent friendship between David and Lucien are cast in light). Although in another light, David would more appropriately receive the shadow metaphor, since his is the occulted relationship, the chiaroscuro image aptly identifies and contrasts the two relationships.

22 The term is used by Drevon and Guichardet, "Fameux Sexorama", p. 264.

23   Additionally, see *I.P.*, p. 345, where literary reputation is compared to a prostitute, and p. 393, where Lucien assures Coralie: "Vous aurez la virginité de ma plume" (You will have the virginity of my pen).

24   Although he quickly learns to play by the rules of the game, Lucien does not realize, until it is too late, that journalism (and by extension, language) is precisely a game, divorced from reality and deprived of any intrinsic truth value. When we turn to a more detailed analysis of Lucien's naive belief in the linguistic sign, it will become apparent that his credulity, on the level of *lexis,* or language, precludes any conviction on the level of *logos,* or rational process.

25   *La Peau de chagrin* is the most direct narrative application of this theory; *Louis Lambert* and *Gobseck* are also illustrative.

26   Eventually, Lucien will have affairs with two *mondaines,* Mme. de Sérizy and Mme. de Maufrigneuse. They are, however, married, thus unattainable in terms of legitimacy, family, and so forth. And despite the best-laid plans of Carlos Herrera, Lucien never does marry Clotilde, representative of "la noblesse du nom, la race, les honneurs, le rang, la science du monde" (*S.M.*, p. 518)—values proper to the savant but not to the fou.

27   The common belief that prostitutes are sterile persisted through much of the nineteenth century, and has been attributed to "a desire to consider the prostitute an 'unnatural' being" (Charles Bernheimer, personal letter). See, too, Alexandre Parent-Duchâtelet, *De la prostitution dans la ville de Paris* (Paris: J. B. Ballière, 1836), 1:230ff. My thanks to Charles Bernheimer for this reference.

28   Also, "Allez, confessez-vous hardiment, ce sera absolument comme si vous parliez à vous-même," says Herrera (*I.P.*, p. 694; Be bold, confess; it will be exactly as if you were talking to yourself).

29   That a Spanish nobleman, a M. de Hérédia (whose name bears an evident phonetic resemblance to that of Lucien's protector) was imputedly among Balzac's mother's lovers, leads to some interesting speculations. Given that Balzac, like Lucien, forever sought to reappropriate his mother, the juxtaposition of the two couples (Hérédia-Mme. Balzac and Herrera-Mme. Chardon) enlightens both stories, clarifying the motivation for Lucien's identity with Herrera. For information on Hérédia and his transpositions in the Balzacian text, see Pierre Citron, Introduction (*S.M.*, pp. 407–08) and "Sur deux zones obscures de la psychologie de Balzac," *L'Année Balzacienne,* 1967.

30 The entire text of the letter as Lucien wrote it reappears as Herrera reads it. Admittedly there are several minor stylistic differences between the two texts, which the critical enterprise might render significant; given Balzac's penchant for revision and the relative triviality of the changes, I prefer to attribute them to an oversight on the part of Balzac or his printer. The skeptical reader might wish to compare the two letters, which appear on pp. 789–90 and 819–20 of *S.M.*, respectively.

31 In the interests of brevity, the entire string of inversion metaphors will not be reproduced. Among them, however, are the following: "Jamais tigre trouvant ses petits enlevés n'a frappé les jungles de l'Inde d'un cri aussi épouvantable que le fut celui de Jacques Collin" (*S.M.*, p. 816; Never did a tiger, finding her young gone, rend the jungles of India with a cry as terrible as that of Jacques Collin); "Ah! jamais une bonne mère n'a tendrement aimé son fils unique comme j'aimais cet ange. . . . Enfin, Lucien était une femme manquée" (*S.M.*, p. 898; Ah! never did a good mother tenderly love her only son as I loved that angel. . . . In short, Lucien was a *femme manquée*); "On est venu m'arracher ce corps que je baisais comme un insensé, comme une mère, comme la Vierge a dû baiser Jésus au tombeau" (*S.M.*, p. 899; They came to tear away from me the body I was kissing like someone bereft of his senses, like a mother, like the Virgin must have kissed Jesus at the tomb).

32 Structurally, the scene is remarkably similar to the opening scene of *Sarrasine*, in which, according to Barthes's analysis, the narrator's body acts as a similar bridge, or "transgression of antithesis." See *S/Z*, pp. 33–35.

33 The portrayal of Vautrin as father/creator has been well studied by Robert T. Denommé in an article comparing Vautrin and Daedalus: "Création et paternité: Le Personnage de Vautrin dans *La Comédie humaine*," *Stanford French Review* (Winter 1981): 313–26.

34 One might argue that the illusion being exposed here belongs as much to nineteenth-century French society as to Lucien, for society generally was willing to motivate the aristocratic name.

35 Genette, "Frontières du récit," in *Figures II*, p. 55.

36 "'Donne-moi quelque chose qui me rende bien malade, sans me tuer, dit-il à Asie, car il faut que je sois à l'agonie pour pouvoir ne rien répondre aux *curieux*.'" (*S.M.*, p. 694; "Give me something that will make me very sick without killing me," he said to Asie "for I must be in agony to avoid inquisitive people.").

37 "Changer, n'est-ce pas mourir?" asks the narrator. The last part of *Splendeurs et misères* is significantly entitled "La Dernière Incarnation de Vautrin."

38 Such an intuitive or subconscious knowledge of what one later learns is axiomatic to Oedipus's inquiry into his origins, during which he desperately tries to ignore what he already too well "knows"; Pascal's Jesus speaks the same truth when he teaches: "Console-toi, tu ne me chercherais pas, si tu ne m'avais trouvé" (*Pensées* [Paris: Garnier Frères, 1964], p. 212; Be consoled, you would not be looking for me if you had not already found me).

39 *Adieu* tells a similar story; there, the flawless reproduction of a traumatic scene from the past cures madness but results in death.

40 We have observed that this is often thematized as a struggle between father and son. Otto Rank's study of the double provides an interesting anthropological analogy: "Savages who believe that the soul of the father or grandfather is reborn in the child fear . . . too great a resemblance of the child to his parents. Should a child strikingly resemble its father, the latter must soon die, since the child has adopted his image or silhouette. The same holds for the name, which the primitive views as an essential part of the personality" (Otto Rank, *The Double* [Chapel Hill: University of North Carolina Press, 1971], p. 53).

41 Borges, "Tlön," pp. 17–18.

42 Balzac, *La Peau de Chagrin*, in *La Comédie humaine* X, p. 154.

43 Balzac, *La Duchesse de Langeais*, in *La Comédie humaine* V, p. 909.

44 Balzac, *Le Médecin de campagne*, in *La Comédie humaine* IX, p. 573.

AFTERWORD

1 The examples of such a multilevel canonization are legion; a small sampling follows. Harry Levin asserts that "it is Balzac who occupies the central position in any considered account of realism, who claims and earns and duly receives the title of novelist before all others" (*The Gates of Horn* [New York and Oxford; Oxford University Press, 1966], p. 151). In her introduction to the novel, Rose Fortassier declares: "Du vivant de Balzac comme plus tard, *Le Père Goriot* a été tenu pour le fleuron de la couronne. C'est avec cet ouvrage que le romancier devient le maître incontesté du réalisme" (*P.G.*, p. 3; In Balzac's lifetime, as later, *Le Père Goriot* was regarded as the finest jewel in the crown. This is the work by which

Balzac becomes the uncontested master of realism). And a quotation from Albert Thibaudet on the back cover of a paperback edition of *Le Père Goriot* has this novel (as representative of the Balzacian oeuvre) testify to the presence of (God) the Father:

"Quand j'ai été père, dit Goriot, j'ai compris Dieu." Voilà un mot extraordinaire qui nous met aux sources de la création balzacienne. La présence de Dieu, le consentement à Dieu sont aussi évidents, aussi nécessaires, aussi absolus dans l'oeuvre de Balzac, pleine comme un jour de la création, que l'absence, l'inexistence de Dieu dans l'oeuvre de Proust, procès-verbal d'un monde qui se détruit. [*Le Père Goriot*, ed. Pierre Citron (Paris: Garnier-Flammarion, 1966)]

["When I became a father," said Goriot, "I understood God." This is an extraordinary statement that takes us to the very sources of Balzacian creation. The presence of God and the affirmation of God, are as evident, as necessary, as absolute in Balzac's works, which are as full as one of the days of creation, as the absence, the inexistence of God, in Proust's works, which bear witness to a world in the process of destroying itself.]

2 Marcel Proust, *A la Recherche du temps perdu*, III (Paris: Bibliothèque de la Pléiade, 1954), p. 903. This passage was brought to my attention by Naomi Schor, who referred to it in "Mythe des origines, origine des mythes: *La Fortune des Rougon*," *Les Cahiers Naturalistes* 52 (1978): 130.

3 Georg Lukács, *The Theory of the Novel* (Berlin: Cassirer, 1920; reprint Cambridge: MIT Press, 1971).

4 Quoted from the conservative *Gazette de Paris*, 6 January 1792. This was brought to my attention by Lynn Hunt in *Politics, Culture, and Class in the French Revolution* (Berkeley, Los Angeles, and London: University of California Press, 1984), pp. 87–88. The English translation is essentially Hunt's, but I have modified it.

5 See Dostoevsky's similar cry: "But if parricide is a prejudice, and if every child is to ask his father why he is to love him, what will become of us? What will become of the foundations of society? What will become of the family?" (*The Brothers Karamazov*, trans. Constance Garnett [New York: Random House, 1950], p. 909).

6 Hunt, *Politics, Culture, and Class*, pp. 87–88. "Master fiction" and "cultural frame" are terms borrowed from Clifford Geertz, "Centers, Kings, and Charisma: Reflections on the Symbolics of Power," in Joseph Ben-David and Terry Nichols Clark, eds., *Culture and Its Creators: Essays in Honor of Edward Shils* (Chicago, 1977), pp. 150–71.

7   James Joyce, *Ulysses* (New York: Modern Library, 1961), p. 207.

8   For a detailed explanation of disavowal, see Freud, *An Outline for Psychoanalysis*, in *The Standard Edition*, XXIII.

9   Christopher Prendergast, *Balzac: Fiction and Melodrama*, pp. 181–82.

10   Flaubert's comment comes from a letter to Louise Colet (9 December, 1852), which can be found in *Extraits de la correspondance ou Préface à la vie d'écrivain*, ed. Geneviève Bollème (Paris: Seuil, 1963), p. 95. Zola's declaration is from a letter to A. Valabrègue (18 August, 1864), in *Correspondance, Oeuvres complètes*, ed. Maurice Le Blond, XLVIII(Paris: François Bernouard, 1928), p. 256.

11   D. A. Miller, "The Novel and the Police," *Glyph* 8 (1981): 141. My own argument is indebted to Miller's brilliant analysis of the novel as representation and embodiment of modern policing power.

12   Emile Zola, *Le Docteur Pascal*, in *Les Rougon-Macquart* V, ed. Henri Mitterand (Paris: Bibliothèque de la Pléiade, 1967), p. 920.

13   Ibid., p. 921. For a more detailed analysis of narrative voice in *Le Docteur Pascal*, see Janet L. Beizer, "Remembering and Repeating the *Rougon-Macquart:* Clotilde's Story," *L'Esprit Créateur*, Winter 1986.

14   Virginia Woolf, *A Room of One's Own* (San Diego, New York, and London: Harcourt Brace Jovanovich, 1929, reprint, 1957), p. 102.

15   Barthes, *Le Plaisir du texte*, p. 75.

16   Dostoevsky, *The Brothers Karamazov*, p. 671.

Index

Androgyne, 203n17; Plato's myth of, 151, 156, 203n18
Aristotle, *Poetics*, 183

Balzac, Honoré de: epistolary romances, 192n20; and family romance, 191n19; as father, 192n21; father's death, 41, 86; and M. de Hérédia, 204n29; and Napoleon, 45; and patronym, 41; as realist, 11, 106; stylistic evolution of, 106–09; threat of fiction for, 107, 178; as visionary, 11, 106
—works: *Adieu*, 206n39; *Avant-propos de la Comédie Humaine*, 1–2; *Béatrix*, 15, 31; *Le Chef-d'oeuvre inconnu*, 201n20; *Les Chouans*, 50; *Le Contrat de mariage*, 195–96n22; *La Cousine Bette*, 195–96n22; *Le Député d'Arcis*, 200n17; *La Duchesse de Langeais*, 196n23; *L'Elixir de longue vie*, 2, 29; *L'Enfant maudit*, 87–88, 89, 115; *Facino Cane*, 23–26, 35–36, 114, 140; *La Fille aux yeux d'or*, 64–67, 155–56, 194n20; *Le Fou et le savant*, parable of, 140–41, 146, 148, 149; *Gobseck*, 200n15, 204n25; *Illusions perdues*, 11, 111, 113, 118, 140–79, 183; *Lettres à Mme Han-*

ska, 72, 109, 201n5; *Louis Lambert*, 15–16, 143–44, 175–76, 204n25; *Le Lys dans la vallée*, 88–89, 107–08; *Massimilla Doni*, 142–43, 175; *Le Médecin de campagne*, 179; *Une Passion dans le désert*, 11, 48–99, 106–19 passim, 123, 155, 156, 159, 165, 175; *La Peau de chagrin*, 109–11, 194n18, 195n22, 196n23, 197n32, 204n25; *Pensées, sujets, fragmens*, 189n7; *Le Père Goriot*, 11, 103–39, 150, 153, 172–73, 175, 180, 181, 199n9; *La Physiologie du mariage*, 197n31; *Sarrasine*, 67–68, 71, 77, 155, 174, 175, 198n39; *Scènes de la vie militaire*, 50; *Séraphîta*, 156; *Splendeurs et misères des courtisanes*, 11, 113–19 passim, 126, 128, 140–79, 200n13; *Théorie de la démarche*, 140–42, 149, 201n4; *El Verdugo*, 11, 15–47, 106, 108, 112, 113, 119, 155, 175; *Voyage de Paris à Java*, 69–71
Barthes, Roland, 1–8 passim, 68, 185, 190n12, 196n26, 198n39
Baudelaire, Charles, 127, 200n19
Beizer, Janet L., 208n13
Bernheimer, Charles, 204n27
Berthier, Patrick, 58, 193n1
Bisexuality, 67, 157

Boorstin, Daniel J., 188n14
Borges, Jorge Luis, 105; "Tlön, Uqbar, Orbis Tertius," 103–06, 178
Brooks, Peter, 10, 149, 188n7
Burgin, Richard, 199n2

Castration: anxiety, 158; and aphasia, 144, 175–76; and blindness, 25–26; contagion of, 68, 97; and fetishization, 71; maiming metaphors, 90, 92; moon as emblem of, 190n12; and myth of Cronos, 126; and narrative, 35–38, 97; paternal interdiction as, 92; and phallic woman, 76–77, 78; and Sapphism, 67
Child, quest for, 121, 126
Childhood sexual theories, 68, 77
Christianity: as ordering force, 1–2, 4, 6, 8, 9, 181
Citron, Pierre, 189n3, 194n17, 204n29
Closure, 98
Combined parent-figure, 77, 79, 92, 94, 160, 161–62
Conner, Wayne, 19
Corneille, Pierre, Oedipe, 30
Cronos, myth of, 126

Darwin, Charles, 8, 9
Davin, Félix, 17, 20
Denommé, Robert T., 205n33
Deus abdicatus, 137
Diana and Actaeon, myth of, 28
Dickens, Charles: Great Expectations, 11, 183
Difference: abolition of, 98, 163–66, 194n15, 200n16, 205n32; collapsed, 172; and identity, 156, 157; paradigms of, 175, 198n41. See also Indifferentiation, sexual
Donzelot, Jacques, 187n6
Dostoevsky, Fyodor, 185–86; The Brothers Karamazov, 11, 183, 207n5
Dream-work: as model for writing, 29
Drevon, Marguerite, 203n17, 203n22

Encyclopédie, 19
Eros: and Thanatos, 148–49, 163; as transgression, 20, 25–37 passim,

98; and vision, 21–28 passim, 32, 33, 35, 112, 124–25, 191n18
Evans, Henry, 190n13

Fading of voices, 36, 37, 97, 198n37
Family: disrupted paradigms of, 155; as ordering force, 1–2; overdetermined relations, 132, 133, 135–38; plots of, 2, 3, 10, 129–32
Family romance, 34, 90, 98, 108, 119, 120, 121, 150; Freud's essay on, 7
Father: crime against, 130–32; death of, 11, 40, 41, 139, 180; law of, 8, 41, 42, 43, 44; as metaphor, 180–81; name of, 42; nominating function of, 42, 98; "no" of, 42, 132; principle, 3, 4, 8; quest for, 6–7, 10, 121, 126, 128–29, 135, 183; repudiation of, 7, 32, 150, 162–63; and stories, 185–86; and tree metaphor, 84–85, 86, 92
Felman, Shoshana, 190n11
Femininity: allegory of, 73; and cutting images, 75–76, 89–90; and devouring images, 76–77
Fetishism: and denial, 77; and Foedora, 110; and queue de poisson, 66–67, 71, 197–98n35
Flandrin, Jean-Louis, 187n6
Flaubert, Gustave, 183, 185; La Légende de Saint Julien l'hospitalier, 11
Fontanier, Pierre, 193n8
Fortassier, Rose, 206n1
Fort/da, 44
Foucault, Michel, 42, 199n42, 199n43
Framed narrative, 24–26, 50–51, 52–53, 57–58, 92–97, 107; and narrative "framing," 57, 95
Frappier-Mazur, Lucienne, 188n7
Freud, Sigmund, 8, 10; disavowal, 182; game of fort/da, 44; reversal in dreams, 191n15
—works: Beyond the Pleasure Principle, 183, 193n26, 202n11; Civilization and Its Discontents, 198n36; "Family Romances," 7–8; "Fetishism," 194n21; The Interpretation of Dreams, 191n15; Leonardo da Vinci and a Memory of

His Childhood, 203n16; *On Narcissism,* 203n16; *An Outline for Psychoanalysis,* 208n8; "The 'Uncanny,'" 82

Gascar, Pierre, 190n13, 192n22
Gazette de Paris, 207n4
Geertz, Clifford, 207n6
Generation: of Balzac's realist works, 12, 108–09; metaphor of, 11; of novel, 181–82
Generational triad, 43
Genette, Gérard, 6, 189n2, 192n23, 205n35
Goodfield, June, 188n14
Great chain, 181–82
Guichardet, Jeannine, 203n17, 203n22

Hamlet, 95
Hermaphroditism, 67, 109, 114, 123, 146, 155–65 passim, 200n16, 202n13, 203n18; and journalism, 158
Hoffmann, Léon-François, 52–54, 193n9
Homer: *The Odyssey,* 48–49
Homosexuality, 123–24, 135, 146, 152–57 passim, 162, 163, 203n16; and textual obliteration, 146–48; and underwater realm, 160–61
Hunt, Lynn, 181, 207n4

Incest, 32, 133, 135, 151, 152, 155, 156, 163. *See also* Oedipus (myth and complex)
Indifferentiation, sexual, 27, 98, 109, 114, 138, 200n16; inversion metaphors, 164, 205n31; paradigms disrupted, 153, 155; physical traits, 73–74; and prostitutes, 159. *See also* Difference
Irwin, John T., 193n25

James, Henry, 11
Jones, Ernest, 95
Journalism: and hermaphroditism, 158–59; and scandal of language, 166–68; and representation, 176–77
Joyce, James, 182

Kanes, Martin, 156
Kermode, Frank, 9, 189n17

Lacan, Jacques, 42
Levin, Harry, 206n1
Lévi-Strauss, Claude, 197n34
Lukács, Georg, 181, 189n17

Marceau, Félicien, 52
Martin, Henry, 53
Master fiction, 182, 183
Matricide, 37, 92, 191n18
Maurois, André, 188n8
McCormick, Diana Festa, 19, 190n13, 192n22
Les Mille et une nuits, 173
Miller, D. A., 184, 208n11
Mimesis, 185; and Balzac's language, 6; and desire for mastery, 183; as internal aesthetic, 176; as intertextuality, 173–75; and narrative illusion, 103–06; and nineteenth-century fiction, 3. *See also* Representation
Monarchy, as ordering force, 1–2, 4, 6, 8, 181
Money, as sexual metaphor, 130–32, 157, 200n16
Mother: and aquatic metaphors, 86–88; child of, 150, 169; and milk metaphors, 89, 115, 152; name of, 150, 158, 168–69; and panther-queen, 86

Naming, 11; and Cratylism, 17, 34, 38, 39, 45–46, 149–50; empty signifier, 46; father's name, 42; and father's role, 42, 98; and God, 97–98; and homophony, 29–30, 169; misnomers, 28, 144; mother's name, 150, 158, 168–69; onomastic fallacy, 22; signature in text, 38–39. *See also* Patronym
Napoleon, 5, 45, 61, 62
Narcissism, 151, 152, 153, 159–63 passim
Nineteenth century: narrative, 3, 10–11, 180–86; historicizing imagination of, 8–11; and Oedipus myth, 10; and sources of authority, 11, 46–47, 182
Noah, 85

Oedipus (myth and complex), 30, 90–95 passim, 108, 133; accepts Law, 37; Corneille's *Oedipe*, 30; and Freud's "Family Romances," 7; and generational triad, 43; and nineteenth century, 10; and riddle of sexuality, 122–23; and self-knowledge, 206*n*38; Sophocles' *Oedipus the King*, 90; two crimes of, 33
Othello, 173

Palinode, 168
Parent-Duchâtelet, Alexandre, 204*n*27
Parricide, 2, 5, 6, 11, 16, 18, 19, 20, 41–42; and acknowledgment of fatherhood, 43; and catastrophe of signifier, 41–43; as filial obedience, 29–30; manifest and latent, 32, 33, 34; and rejection of patronym, 163
Pascal, Blaise, 206*n*38
Paternity: and incarnation, 182, 201; as "legal fiction," 182; and literary creation, 5, 125, 165, 185; as "master fiction," 182, 183; patterns of, 5
Patriarchy: fantasy of, 125, 128; institutions of, 2, 4–5, 6, 8, 181–82, 187*n*6; on trial, 183
Patronym, 18; as empty signifier, 46; and father's law, 32–33, 41–45 passim; as legacy, 40, 41, 149–50; rejected, 163, 169; replaced by matronym, 169; and use of language, 169. *See also* Naming
Paul et Virginie, 173
Père-Lachaise cemetery, 139
Picon, Gaëtan, 188*n*7, 199*n*10
Poe, Edgar Allan: "The Purloined Letter," 72
Prendergast, Christopher, 183, 188*n*7
Prometheus, 5, 6, 85, 103, 105
Prostitutes: and sterility, 159, 204*n*27
Proust, Marcel, 147, 153, 180
Pygmalion, myth of, 174

Rabelais, François: *Quart Livre*, 15, 17
Rank, Otto: *The Double*, 206*n*40
Realism: from Balzac to Zola, 185; as

copy of copy, 172–76; as paternalistic fantasy, 183
Religion. *See* Christianity
Representation, 11, 97; crisis of, 98, 99, 139, 156, 172; dependent on difference, 165; and generational conflict, 206*n*40; and incarnation, 141–44, 145, 146, 158–59; of language, 171–72; and procreation, 127, 139; refusal of, 177–79; and sacrifice of ideal, 142, 143, 175–79; and will to power, 183. *See also* Mimesis
Reticence, 60–61
Revolution, French, 181; and leveling of hierarchies, 5, 8
Revolution, scientific, 8, 9
Robbe-Grillet, Alain, 4
Robert, Marthe, 188*n*13
Romeo and Juliet, 174
Rousseau, Jean-Jacques, 197*n*31

Said, Edward, 3, 4
St.-Paulien (Maurice Ivan Sicard), 188*n*8
Sartre, Jean-Paul: *Baudelaire*, 127
Saussure, Ferdinand de, 198*n*41
Schor, Naomi, 207*n*2
Semantic babble ("babil sémantique"), 136, 172
Shakespeare, William: *Henry VIII*, 172–73
Signifier: catastrophe of, 42, 43, 135–39; empty, 46, 138; and signified, 143, 145; transparent, 169, 205*n*34
Silence: call to, 179
Society: as ocean, 113–15, 118; as woman, 111–15, 118
Sontag, Susan, 10
Sophocles: *Oedipus the King*, 29
Sphinx, 112, 123, 131, 191*n*18; avatars of, 197*n*35; and hermaphrodite, 123; and panther, 90–92
Steiner, George, 9, 189*n*17
Stendhal (Henri Beyle): *Le Rouge et le noir*, 11, 183

Tanner, Tony, 187*n*5
Thibaudet, Albert, 206–07*n*1

Time: authority of, 9, 10; discovery of, 8, 9
Tobin, Patricia, 3, 4
Tolstoy, Leo: *Anna Karenina*, 11
Toulmin, Stephen, 188n14
Traditional narrative. *See* Nineteenth century, narrative
Twentieth century: narrative, 3–4, 183

Uncanny, 82

Weber, Samuel, 188n7
Wilde, Oscar: *The Picture of Dorian Gray*, 161
Woman: and aquatic metaphors, 22, 113–15, 118; as beast, 53, 58–65 passim, 69–76 passim, 83, 109, 155, 195–96n22; as metaphor, 63–67 passim, 72, 91, 141, 185; and mud metaphor, 115–17, 120; as society, 111–15, 118
Woolf, Virginia: "man-womanly" text, 185
Writing: and eros, 26, 35–36, 95, 96–97, 113–14, 157; paradigms of, 144–45, 146, 149; as sublimation, 177; and transgression, 107–08

Zeus, myth of, 126
Zola, Emile, 183; *Le Docteur Pascal*, 184–85; *Les Rougon-Macquart*, 11, 184
Zweig, Stefan, 192n20, 193n27